THE UNDERGRADUATE'S GUIDE TO STUDYING LANGUAGES

Linda Hantrais

Centre for Information on Language Teaching and Research

The views and opinions expressed in this publication are the author's and do not necessarily represent those of CILT.

First published 1989

Copyright © Centre for Information on Language Teaching and Research

ISBN 0 948003 97 9

Set by Laserprinter, Department of Modern Languages, Aston University, Aston Triangle, Birmingham B4 7ET

Printed in Great Britain by C.M.D. Limited

Published by Centre for Information on Language Teaching and Research, Regent's College, Inner Circle, Regent's Park, London, NW1 4NS

All rights reserved. No part of this publication may be reproduced, stored in a retrieval system or transmitted in any form or by any means, mechanical, photocopying, recording, or otherwise, without the prior permission of the Copyright owner.

CONTENTS

Preface   vii

How to read this book   ix

1 AN INTRODUCTION TO STUDYING FOR A DEGREE IN LANGUAGES   1
    Structure and content of language degree programmes   2
       Degree structure   3
       Choice of language   7
       Disciplinary studies   11
       Implications of the choice of degree programme   16
    Language learning objectives   17
       Change in language learning objectives   17
       Objectives of contemporary language programmes   18
    Approaches to the study of languages to degree level   20
       The weighting of language on degree courses   20
       The communicative approach   23
       Language learning methodology   25

2 STUDY METHODS AND RESOURCES   28
    General study habits   29
       Justifying effective academic study   29
       Finding the best place to study   30
       Managing study time   32
    Accessing language learning resources   40
       Libraries   41
       Language resource centres   47
       Computers and language learning   47
    Preparing for assessment and examinations   50
       Patterns of examination and assessment   51
       Planning for continuous assessment and revising for examinations   56
    Difficulties with study methods   61
       Personal tutors or advisors   62
       Advice on departmental matters   63
       Counselling services   63
       Learning from difficulties   63

3 STUDY SKILLS   65
    Reading   66
       Reading techniques   67

       Improving your reading skills   69
    Note-taking   71
       Content and organisation   71
       The form of notes   73
       Taking notes on lectures   77
    Abstracting and analysis.   79
       Abstracting and summary writing   80
       Text analysis and commentary   81
    Academic essay writing   89
       The purpose of academic essay writing   91
       Stages in essay writing   91
       Referencing and presenting source materials   98
       Evaluation of essay writing   100
    Group interaction   101
       Characteristics of oral interaction   102
       Understanding para-language   104
       Learning from oral interaction   106

4 TASK-BASED LANGUAGE EXERCISES   109
    Text manipulation in intra-language transfer   112
       Formal correspondence   113
       Official documents   119
       Reports   122
    Self-presentation in the written and spoken channels   125
       The curriculum vitae   125
       Job interviews   130
    Oral presentation and interactive communication   131
       Interviewing   132
       Telephoning   136
    Translating   137
       Objectives of translation   139
       Stages in translation   140
       Problems of translation   141
       Learning from translation   143
    Interpreting   143
       Interpreting objectives   144
       The qualities and skills of the interpreter   145
       Liaison interpreting   146

5 THE PERIOD OF RESIDENCE ABROAD   152
    Types of placement   154
       Higher education courses   155
       Assistantships   161
       Work placements   163

Administrative procedures	165
Local Education Authority grants for residence abroad	165
Applications for placements	166
Official documents	171
Insurance	173
Taxation	176
Banking	177
Finding accommodation	177
Coping with administrative procedures	178
Researching and writing a dissertation, project or work report	180
The purpose of the project	180
Choosing a topic	181
Researching the topic	182
Drafting the project	186
Presentation of the project	187
The work report	188
Gaining maximum benefit from the placement	188
Social interaction	189
Improving linguistic skills	191
Adopting a positive frame of mind	192

6 LANGUAGES AND CAREERS 194

The labour market for linguists	195
The growing need for language graduates	195
Languages as a bonus	197
Degree subjects and career prospects	198
Developing and consolidating skills by further training	199
Patterns of employment for graduates	201
Careers using languages	204
Working as a professional linguist	204
Language teaching	209
Using languages as a secondary skill	210
Language skills and real life tasks	214
Communicative skills	214
Oral and aural skills	215
Reading and writing skills	216
Relevance of undergraduate training	218
Planning and pursuing a career with languages	218
Career planning	218
Factors affecting career choice and development	220
Changing direction	223

Deploying intellectual training, analytical and
   communicative skills   225
  *Personal qualities and skills acquired from a
   language degree*   225
  *Personal qualities and general skills sought by
   employers*   226
  Adapting to the world of work   227

Suggestions for further reading   230

Index   241

PREFACE

Amongst the growing body of information available to help students in universities, polytechnics and other institutions of higher education to learn how to study for their degree subject, there is no single publication aimed specifically at language undergraduates. Yet language programmes and language teaching methodology in the higher education sector have undergone substantial shifts of emphasis in recent years, and it is increasingly difficult for potential students to know how to choose a course. Once they have made their choice, it is not always easy for them to find out what to expect from a particular programme of study: A book which brings together information about the many aims, structures and components of language degree programmes and the variety of approaches to language learning they adopt and then guides students through the stages in their career as undergraduates should therefore make a timely and useful contribution to the study skills literature.

In the past a language degree was thought to be a suitable course in higher education for the sixth former who enjoyed the subject, performed well in it and intended to pursue a career in teaching. Today this will be the main source of motivation for a much smaller proportion of the students reading for a degree in languages. The ability to communicate easily in one's own language and in a foreign tongue, coupled with a liking for travel abroad, may still explain the initial choice of a language as a sixth form subject. But discriminating students generally decide on their preference from amongst the plethora of language degree programmes in higher education on the basis of knowledge about their own intellectual potential and the career ultimately to be pursued, which nowadays is less often in teaching. The course will generally be selected on the grounds that it is considered to offer the best means of achieving longer term goals. In the field of languages, the majority of degree applicants are now looking for programmes of study which will help them to reach a high level of proficiency in their chosen language, or languages, in combination with a number of practical skills, leading on, they hope, to a wide range of employment opportunities.

The higher education sector has also changed its attitude. This is, partly, a reaction to the perceived shift in the aspirations of students. It is also due to the recognition of the need for greater accountability towards society at large, and more especially towards the labour market.

However, courses which may answer some of the needs of employers by offering intensive language training and tuition in a limited number of specific tasks, such as drafting a business letter, do not have the intellectual content necessary to qualify as degree subjects. There are many other less expensive ways, in terms of both time and money, of acquiring these language skills. Although any academic programme will provide some instruction in skills, it must also be mind-stretching and help the student to learn how to identify, analyse and synthesise complex issues, clarify and solve problems. This involves knowing how to find and use appropriate materials, to work co-operatively with others and to communicate effectively both orally and in writing. These are the aims attributed to all higher education courses, but they are particularly appropriate for language students, who will become qualified communicators.

The purpose of this book is to suggest ways of making the learning process as effective and systematic as possible. Many of the study skills needed by language undergraduates, particularly where area studies are a core course component, are the same as those required of other humanities and social science subjects. The intellectual demands made of language students are also similar, as are many of the main study activities (attending lectures and seminars, preparing for assessed work and examinations), involving the use of secondary materials, developing note-taking techniques, planning, researching and writing essays, reports and projects. They differ from other humanities and social science studies in that the language degree contains a major additional dimension: mastery of a foreign language as an essential key to the understanding of another society and its culture. Studying materials in another language requires a more specialist knowledge and different technical skills, many of which will not have been learnt at school.

The experience gained from observing several generations of undergraduates going through the learning process and from following their progress subsequently in their careers has prompted me to want to make available to other undergraduates some of the information and ideas about language degree work which have proved to be useful to previous students. Since my own experience has been directly acquired in only a small number of higher education institutions and particularly in one language, I am grateful to colleagues at Aston University and elsewhere, in particular Dennis Ager, Geoffrey and Cathy Hare, Peter Myers and Chris Upward, for their constructive comments on the draft chapters, and to Mechthild Bröhl, Edguardo Aguirre-Ruiz and Paul Juckes for their help in preparing the examples in German and Spanish. I am also indebted to former language undergraduates for the feedback received from them and to Claire Turner for providing valuable assistance with the typesetting.

HOW TO READ THIS BOOK

The chapters in this book are arranged in a roughly chronological sequence which reflects the path of the undergraduate through a degree course. If you are just beginning your study for a degree, you will probably want to focus on the earlier chapters in the book for the moment, but you may find it useful to skim through the later chapters so that you have an idea of what to expect as your course progresses and you start to think about your career plans. If you have already completed part of your course, you should need to do no more than scan Chapters 1, 2 and 3 and parts of Chapter 4 to familiarise yourself with their contents and to check that you have covered the ground, before concentrating on other sections of Chapter 4 and the whole of Chapters 5 and 6, as appropriate.

By offering an **Introduction to studying for a degree in languages**, the first chapter is intended to set your undergraduate study for a language degree within its wider context. It should give you a clear idea of the components of your course, its structure and the way it is taught, the implications in terms of your personal motivation and goals and what is expected of you by the institution.

The purpose of Chapter 2 on **Study methods and resources** is to introduce you to the general study habits which you should want to improve or develop. Guidance is given on how to organise your work sensibly and effectively, on where to look for materials and information and how to prepare yourself for the process of examination and assessment which will be with you throughout most of your time as an undergraduate.

Chapter 3 takes you through the basic **Study skills** which you, like other undergraduates in the social sciences and humanities, will need to master or perfect. It covers the different reading and note-taking techniques, skills in extracting and summarising information, analysis and commentary on written and spoken texts, essay writing and small group work. Many of the skills involved will not be taught formally, so the onus may be on you to work at them by yourself in order to make your study more effective.

Since it is always more difficult to acquire and practise the basic skills when you are working in a foreign language, advice is offered about aspects of your study which will need special attention. For example, you may want to know how to set about improving your reading speed and learning to read extensively and intensively in another language; you will need to develop your sensitivity to different language varieties and to ensure you check effectively any essays written in a foreign language for accuracy and style; you should be looking for ways of gaining maximum benefit from opportunities to practise your oral and aural skills.

The basic study skills are presented as a preparation for their application to specific **Task-based language exercises** which are the focus of Chapter 4. Following on from comments in the first chapter about the communicative approach to language learning and from the guidelines in Chapter 3 for analysing language in relation to the communicative process, the exercises selected have in common their relevance to real life situations in which you may find yourself, either while living abroad as a student or in professional life.

Some of the exercises included are taught routinely on most language programmes, for example translation. For others, although there may be no formal tuition or assessment, you will probably need to know how to deal with particular situations when you are preparing to spend a prolonged period of residence abroad or when you are researching a work report or collecting information, using interviews, to write a project. Exercises such as self-presentation in a *curriculum vitae* or job interview may help you when you are thinking about your career, particularly if you are planning to work abroad. Translation and interpreting, interviewing and telephoning are all tasks which you may be expected to perform professionally.

The guidelines presented in this chapter make reference to task-based language exercises conducted in French, German and Spanish, which are the subjects studied by most undergraduates reading for a degree in languages. Applications to real life situations which you may encounter in France, Germany or Spain are then produced in Chapter 5.

You may also want to refer back to the relevant sections in the previous chapter when you are working on language exercises: the points made in Chapter 3 about text analysis, for example, may be useful when you are preparing a translation, and the suggestions about note-taking should help with interpreting.

The experience of living and studying abroad, while not reserved for language students, is a normal part of most language courses. Although much of the advice about general study skills applies to all undergraduates in the social sciences and humanities, the contents of Chapter 5 on **The period of residence abroad**, like many of the exercises in Chapter 4, do not appear in the study skills literature for non-language subjects. You will probably want to begin to read the chapter when you are planning to go abroad in order to find out more about the various types of placement and what they involve. The notes on administrative procedures in France, the Federal Republic of Germany and Spain and the guidance on how to make the most of the placement should prove useful both before you go and while you are abroad. If you have to carry out research for a project, you should read the relevant section in conjunction with the material about essay writing in Chapter 3 and telephoning and interviewing in Chapter 4.

The final chapter on **Languages and careers** could be read when you are embarking on your degree course and it may also help you to decide how to spend your period of residence abroad. It should be particularly useful when you are giving serious consideration to planning your career. If you are intending to work abroad, you should find it helpful to refer back to the annotations and examples in Chapters 3 and 4 which suggest how you can present yourself in a *curriculum vitae* in French, German or Spanish and how to prepare for an interview in the relevant country. If you expect to be using your languages in your career, you should be interested to read about the skills required and the real life tasks which graduates are asked to perform as well as finding out more about employers' views of linguists and the qualities they are looking for in graduates.

When you have been through the section in the third chapter about different types of reading, you will be aware that this book is intended to be read in a number of ways. You will probably need to skim and scan the chapters to see what will be of most relevance and interest to you personally at a particular point in your career as an undergraduate. You could make a mental note of sections to which you may want to return at a later stage for more detailed study. You will probably want to read some sections intensively as you practise the skills and exercises described or prepare for the period of residence abroad.

The layout of the chapters is intended to help you to use the book as a reference tool. Each chapter is introduced by a brief outline of the contents and some suggestions about how to use the material. The main points are summarised both within sections and at the end of chapters, and cross-references are made to other parts of the book which you should find relevant. The **Contents** page gives you a clear overview of the book, and the **Index** should help you to find any references you need quickly. The **Suggestions for further reading** at the end of the book provide annotated bibliographies for each of the topics examined.

1 AN INTRODUCTION TO STUDYING FOR A DEGREE IN LANGUAGES

Having accepted a place on a language degree course, you will want to know what to expect and how to prepare yourself mentally for several years of study in a new environment. This chapter should help you find out more about what your particular course will involve and how it relates to the broader framework of studying for a degree in languages. The topics covered are:

1. Different types of language degrees, ranging through single, double, combined or joint honours to joint study programmes and courses with a modular structure.

2. The choices between different languages and their implications both in the short and the longer term.

3. The content and scope of disciplinary studies in literature, linguistics and society, taught either as an integral part of a language programme or in combination with a language.

4. Personal and institutional learning objectives of language programmes in higher education.

5. Approaches to language learning, including the relative importance of the language compared with other subjects, the integration or separation of language and contextual studies, the concept of communicative competence and language learning methodology, with reference to written as well as oral and aural skills.

Information received secondhand and the experience of others are never quite the same as finding out for yourself. Although you most probably gave considerable thought to selecting your degree course by reading the relevant literature in undergraduate prospectuses, visiting institutions and consulting with teachers, careers advisors and former students, it is not easy to know how you are going to react to a particular situation and whether the course you have chosen will live up to expectations. You may have been influenced in your original decision by non-academic factors, such as the geographical location of an institution, the proximity or otherwise of your home town, the opportunity to be in accommodation on campus or by what seemed, on the visiting day, to be a friendly atmosphere.

A small proportion of undergraduates discover they have made the wrong decision: the course does not turn out to be what they expected, it is too demanding or not demanding enough, or they feel they cannot cope with academic life in a particular institution. Others may be disappointed not to have been offered a place at the institution of their first choice. In these cases it is sometimes possible to transfer to another course or institution. The vast majority of students do, however, persevere and settle down more or less quickly within the first term. The process of adapting to academic life is generally made easier if you have a clear idea of the way the course is structured, what the learning objectives are and how you can hope to achieve them.

This chapter is primarily informative and provides a basis for the material and concepts presented in the rest of the book. Its purpose is to explain the most common features of language degree programmes in British higher education, so that you can understand what the system is designed to do and what it expects of you as an undergraduate. You should find it useful at least to skim through all the sections, and you may want to refer back to some parts later as you progress through your course.

STRUCTURE AND CONTENT OF LANGUAGE DEGREE PROGRAMMES

Language degree programmes are available in most universities, polytechnics and colleges of higher education in the United Kingdom, giving a choice of over eighty possible institutions, several of which offer more than one course. Languages are still amongst the most popular subjects studied in higher education, and there are currently over 20,000 language students in universities and almost 9,000 in polytechnics and colleges.

An important trend in higher education since the early 1970s has been the shift away from single honours degrees in language and literature towards the study of two languages to degree level and, increasingly, towards a language in combination with the study of the foreign society or a non-language subject. The terms 'modern languages' and French, German, Spanish or Russian 'studies', used to describe courses or departments, are an indication of the way in which languages are broadening their base.

In the late 1960s the majority of language students would have been reading for single honours degrees with literature as the main component. Less than a third of the language undergraduates in higher education today are following a single honours degree programme; a third are studying two languages, and the remainder a language together with a non-language subject.

This trend has been accompanied by an increasing interest in the wider applications of language learning. In the past language study implied mastering the structures and vocabulary needed to read and manipulate written language over a narrow range of exercises, intended primarily to enhance the understanding of literary texts. More emphasis is now being placed on foreign language usage over a much larger number of situations in both the written and the spoken medium. The move away from single honours and literature reflects the concern amongst undergraduates with the relevance of degree studies to professional life.

With these changing patterns over the past ten to twenty years in the structure and content of language degrees, the distinction between the ways in which languages are studied in the different types of institution in higher education has tended to become less marked. Many university courses have shifted away from their traditional orientation. Single honours in a language and literature is, nonetheless, still more commonly offered in universities, whereas language study as part of a multidisciplinary degree is more likely to occur in polytechnics and colleges.

Degree structure

Because there are so many possible permutations within the British system, it is important to understand what you have committed yourself to do. In this section the characteristics of different types of degree structure are examined, as well as their implications in terms of the weighting of the language component and the level of attainment in the language.

Generally your studies will last for four years (or five in Scotland), and you will be required, or advised, to spend up to a year of residence abroad. As far as the organisation of courses is concerned, in most institutions residence abroad is arranged in the third year. In some cases, particularly for students of two languages, the period abroad may be split between two consecutive years. Normally, you would expect to spend the whole of your first and final year at your home institution, although there are other variations in the pattern for students on joint study programmes.

As an undergraduate studying languages, you will be enrolled on one of several types of programme: single, double, combined or joint honours, a joint study programme or a modular degree. The importance of the language(s) component in a degree can vary substantially from one course to another: it may be the main subject for a single honours degree; it may be one of many subjects on a multidisciplinary degree; or it may be studied at a subsidiary level. Whatever the nature of the programme, you will probably have the opportunity to choose some optional courses. These different possibilities are summarised in the following chart and are then described in more detail below:

DEGREE STRUCTURE

Single honours	1 main language, often + 1 subsidiary (language or another subject)
Double honours	2 main subjects (languages or language related)
Combined honours	2 main subjects (1 language and a non-related subject)
Joint honours	Integrated study of 2 or more subjects
Joint study	International programmes taught jointly by 2 or more institutions
Modular	Language as one of a series of modules
Options	In-depth specialist study of a language or non-language topic

SINGLE HONOURS

If you are studying for a single honours degree in French or German—referred to as 'majoring' in a language—you will generally also be taking a subsidiary or minor subject, probably for two years. This may involve sharing your time equally between the two subjects in the first two years and then concentrating your effort on one subject during the period of residence abroad and in the final year. The subsidiary subject will probably count towards your degree result, and you will be expected to pass it before you can proceed into the final year. Often a subsidiary will be another language, possibly one that you have studied *ab initio*, but it could be a closely allied subject, such as linguistics, or a less clearly related subject, for example drama, American studies or computing science. The advantages of the single honours degree is that students are given maximum exposure to one subject and can focus on a narrower area of knowledge and expertise than if they are spreading their effort over subjects involving different disciplinary approaches.

DOUBLE HONOURS

Double honours will, in theory, require you to allocate the same amount of time to two subjects, generally within the same discipline. Again they could be two languages, which may or may not be taught by the same department or school. In order to achieve a good degree result, you will need to reach the same level of proficiency in both. Ideally you should spend a prolonged period of residence abroad in each country. Many students find that one language is stronger than the other and that it is difficult to maintain a balance. The advantages of taking two languages to degree level are, however, considerable, particularly for anybody wanting to pursue a career as a linguist, and there is evidence to suggest that two languages studied at the same time are mutually reinforcing.

COMBINED HONOURS

Combined honours courses offer the possibility of taking two subjects from different disciplines to degree level. While you will have to face the same problems of maintaining a balance between the two areas, especially when the disciplines involve very different teaching methods (for example because of the emphasis on laboratory experiments in the sciences), there are important advantages in career terms. Graduates from courses which cross the binary divide between the arts and the sciences possess a rare combination of skills which are attractive to employers.

JOINT HONOURS

Joint honours courses, as compared with double or combined honours, imply that there is some integration between the two subjects. Probably the most common joint honours are in international business and languages or European studies. There are also a number of degrees which integrate subjects such as politics, international relations, economics, history, law, accountancy or computing with a language. The amount of integration may not be very great, as it is not easy to recruit academic staff with the relevant qualifications and expertise or to coordinate teaching across departments. It is not uncommon in a multidisciplinary course for the language to be considered as a minor or secondary subject rather than half the degree, as for double or combined honours. Graduates from joint courses have the advantage of the combined honours students in that they learn different methodological techniques and are able to approach problems from several conceptual angles and apply their disciplinary knowledge to the relevant language area. Where there is full integration, they may have the added advantage of being conversant with other disciplines in and through their foreign language.

JOINT STUDY PROGRAMMES

A few institutions—more often polytechnics or colleges than universities—have arrangements with partner institutions abroad, whereby students spend part of their course in Britain and the rest in France, Germany or Spain, following agreed programmes which lead to the joint award of diplomas from the different institutions involved. Such programmes are becoming more widespread due to support from ERASMUS (European Action Scheme for the Mobility of University Students). Under these arrangements students are taught together in multinational groups from two or more countries. A high level of fluency in the foreign language(s) is assumed from the beginning of the course and is normally a prerequisite for entry, since classes are taught by and for native speakers. Most joint study programmes have a European business focus, but they also provide opportunities for studying a variety of non-language subjects such as law or politics. They offer the advantage over other types of courses that graduates are able to function in a foreign language in the relevant contexts. Language is, however, considered as an instrument rather than an object of study.

MODULAR DEGREES

The modular degree programmes, which have been introduced in a number of institutions, offer students the opportunity to make an *à la carte* selection from a wide menu of courses. By choosing a series of related modules, it is possible to reach a high level of proficiency in a language, while also encompassing a number of other subjects. This degree pattern therefore has the advantage of maximum flexibility, and students sometimes find that they decide to continue with a subject which was not initially their first choice. If you are following a modular course, you need to pay careful attention to ensuring you acquire the right prerequisites, otherwise you may be excluded from a higher level module. In some institutions only the first year of a combined honours course may be modularised, and the number of subjects is narrowed down in subsequent years. This arrangement provides an opportunity to discover new disciplines and to keep options open in the early stages of a degree programme. It is a structure which will be particularly well suited for future developments in studying for a degree whereby credits for completed modules will be transferable from one institution to another.

OPTIONAL SUBJECTS

While not being modular, most language degrees offer optional courses which provide the opportunity to extend horizons or to look in more depth at a topic of particular interest. Options may be taught within the language department or by other departments, and sometimes by staff from a different faculty or institution. They range from the analysis of language for specific purposes, computing and linguistics, the study of political parties, trade unions and international marketing to special study of a literary figure, period or genre, the cinema or media and fine arts.

IMPLICATIONS OF DEGREE STRUCTURE

In summary, the structure of your degree programme will determine:

- The amount of time spent studying the language.
- The range of subjects which can be studied in conjunction with the language.
- The level of proficiency which can be achieved in the language.
- The career openings which are immediately available on graduation.

Choice of language

When you applied for a particular course, you may have been attracted by the possibility of continuing with a language or languages which you had studied at school, or you may have wanted to begin a new language. An additional attraction of some courses may be the opportunity to start another language as an option, as part of a general studies programme or through an assisted self-tutoring system. The purpose of a degree course should not be to teach you what you could learn by following evening classes for tourists or by attending summer schools abroad for foreigners. However, by acquiring a rudimentary knowledge of a new language, you may be motivated to study it in more depth.

If you begin a language from scratch and it is going to count towards a degree classification, your aim should be to reach a high level of proficiency in the spoken and written channels, while also being knowledgeable about the cultural environment within which the language is used. Learning a new language to this standard in a relatively short time requires a strong commitment and considerable effort. These and many other factors need to be taken into account when you are considering your choice of languages in relation to the goals you hope to achieve.

The language(s) you study in higher education may be determined for you by previous experience and by limits on the available options: for example it is rare, if not impossible, to study French *ab initio* in higher education, and students without an 'A' or 'AS' level in French will be debarred from many courses. On the other hand, a Spanish 'A' level may not be a prerequisite for an honours degree course in that language, particularly if it is taken as a subsidiary subject. Only a few institutions offer the opportunity to study 'hard' languages, such as Arabic, Chinese, Japanese or Russian at undergraduate level. These languages can generally be started without any prior knowledge and will require accelerated and intensive preliminary study in order to reach a standard which can provide the foundation for degree level proficiency.

Where you are able to exercise choice, you will want to take into account factors such as the rarity value on the labour market of the course you followed and the qualification you obtain. Gender bias and the expectations and motivation associated with learning a common or a rare language may also influence your decision.

RARITY VALUE OF LANGUAGES

French is by far the most common language in higher education with almost 20,000 undergraduates studying it, followed by German with half that number, by Spanish with just over 5,000, Italian with about 2,250 and Russian with just over 2,000. Arabic, Chinese and Japanese account for only a few hundred students between them. Since about a third of language undergraduates are studying more than one language, the total for the number of students for each language is greater than for the total number of students of languages mentioned at the beginning of this chapter.

The dominance of French reflects the situation in secondary schools, where it is almost always the first foreign language offered. This pattern has most probably been reinforced in recent years as attempts have been made to rationalise language teaching in higher education by eliminating courses which attract only a small number of students.

The present distribution of language 'choices' bears no relationship to the real need or demand for different languages in foreign trade or international relations and even less to the number of speakers of each of the languages in the world.

Advantages of studying one of the less commonly taught languages are that there are fewer people to compete with on the labour market and, while you are in higher education, class size is smaller and tuition is more individualised. By the same token, as French, German and Spanish are the main languages taught to degree level, graduates wanting to use them professionally will face stiffer competition for jobs.

GENDER AND LANGUAGE CHOICE

Gender bias is another characteristic of language learners in British higher education, which is not without relevance to language choice since some programmes seem to recruit almost exclusively from one sex. About three times as many women as men are studying languages in Britain. Women would appear to be particularly attracted to Spanish, whereas they are almost equalled by men in the study of Arabic and Japanese. The sex ratio is slightly more balanced for combined subject degrees, but language study would still seem to be very much the prerogative of women. To a large extent this is due to the gender stereotyping which still takes place in schools, whereby girls are more frequently directed towards the arts, humanities or social sciences and boys towards mathematics and the sciences.

Gender bias is reinforced through the career openings which have traditionally been available for linguists: until quite recently the main employment for graduate linguists in the most common languages was the teaching profession, which has consequently become highly feminised. The current shift away from teaching towards employment in business has meant that many female language graduates wanting to use their languages in their career enter employment as bi- or trilingual secretaries or personal assistants, which are also seen today as typically female positions.

Courses where a language can be combined with business would seem to be attracting more male students to language study, with the object of entering international marketing or sales. As international dealings require a much wider range of languages, this trend may help to reduce not only the predominance of women but also that of French, and it should extend the career opportunities for language graduates of both sexes.

EXPECTATIONS ASSOCIATED WITH CHOICE OF LANGUAGES

When considering the implications of studying a particular language, you may want to bear in mind the institutional expectations associated with different languages as well as your own motivation.

Although there is no concrete evidence to prove the claim, it is often assumed that undergraduates studying French should achieve a higher standard at the end of their course than students of less common languages. Having generally spent more years in contact with the language, the expectation is that French students should be more proficient after three or four further years of study than somebody who has started a language *ab initio* or without an 'A' level. Since French students do not need to devote so much time to learning basic structures or acquiring new vocabulary and idiomatic expressions, they should be able to read more widely in the language, understand the spoken word more readily and manipulate both written and spoken language in a far more sophisticated way than those who begin learning a new language.

The challenge of bringing a new language up to a high level is, however, a good incentive for study, particularly if you are learning more than one language and therefore have a visible target and standard of comparison. Many students feel they are becoming stale in a language they have been using for a number of years and that it is not easy to record progress when they have already achieved quite an advanced level. On the other hand, students who begin a hard language, like Japanese, sometimes find they are out of the habit of rote learning which is essential if they are to master the complexities of the writing systems. They can also feel frustrated at not being able to express themselves fluently at an early stage in the learning process. Where a hard language is started from scratch and studied as a subsidary subject for the first two years of a degree course, it may be difficult to devote enough time to it without sacrificing the main degree subject.

ADVANTAGES AND DISADVANTAGES OF LANGUAGE CHOICES

The advantages and disadvantages of studying a new language or of continuing with one in which you have a thorough grounding can be summarised as follows:

- *Advantages of a new language*
  A new language, particularly a hard language, offers a challenge and a means of widening experience, it has novelty value, smaller classes are likely, progress is visible and fast, at least initially, and there is less competition on the labour market.

- *Disadvantages of a new language*
  The disavantages are that a lot of time has to be devoted to learning basic information, and the amount of ground to cover is extensive, with the likelihood that the level of proficiency will not be so high as that achieved for a language studied over a longer period.
- *Advantages of continuing with a language*
  The advantages of continuing with a language which has already been studied for several years are that students should have a good foundation and can build on knowledge and pursue their study in greater depth.
- *Disadvantages of continuing with a language*
  The disadvantages are that progress is much less obvious than with a new language, a higher level of attainment is expected, and there is likely to be more competition on the labour market.

Disciplinary studies

Another choice which you had to make in selecting your course was between the more traditional programmes where literature or linguistics is the major disciplinary component and those, broadly described as non-literary or based on societal or area studies, where the foreign society is studied in respect of its institutions, culture and language. The traditional attitude towards languages has meant that disciplinary studies have come to be seen as the main intellectual substance of a language degree. Whether they are the main, an equal or a subsidiary component, they can be considered to add other approaches and skills to language study, while generally offering the opportunity to investigate topics in greater depth.

In many courses the disciplinary component is taught separately from the study of the language, while elsewhere it may be completely integrated. Whether or not disciplinary studies are integrated with the language, undergraduate prospectuses and degree course guides usually describe them under separate headings.

You are probably already familiar with the outline syllabuses for your particular course, but you may also be interested to learn what other students will be doing who are enrolled on different programmes, sometimes in the same department or institution, and who may be following common language classes.

LANGUAGE AND LITERATURE

Course content
Programmes for literary studies generally aim to give an overview of most periods of the relevant country's literature, covering poetry, drama and prose writing, while also offering an opportunity for specialist options. The overview may be structured thematically, for example by concentrating on the nineteenth century novel, the theatre of the absurd and other major literary movements, or it may focus on significant works from each period, possibly going back to the Middle Ages. Emphasis in many courses is increasingly on the more recent periods to the exclusion of Medieval and Renaissance literature, but generally an attempt is made to ensure that students have an opportunity to cover what are considered as the high points of each country's literary heritage.

Variants on the traditional literature course are the introduction of cinematographic texts and the study of art and culture in a wider sense. Another alternative is the study of philosophical writers in different countries or during a particular period.

Teaching methods
Literature courses are most often centred on the lecture, with seminar or tutorial support, where students present papers for comment and discussion. In most cases emphasis is placed on style and message, but some courses will require students to situate literary works in relation to a broader social context. Close textual study and the development of critical skills are usually combined with at least an introduction to literary theory.

The main skills involved are those concerned with reading analytically and making a critical appraisal of a text or group of texts in an essay or commentary. Some translation work may also be related to the text under study. Close analysis of a literary work in the foreign language will require a high degree of language proficiency, and detailed examination of texts can enhance linguistic appreciation and knowledge.

Value of literary studies
Where there has been a shift away from the study of language and literature as the main degree subjects, literature may still have a place in any understanding of the cultural heritage of another society. It is argued that the thought processes of other nations cannot be understood without an awareness and appreciation of their literary works. Part of learning about different language varieties is knowing how to read and interpret aesthetic writing. Just as literature courses often justify the inclusion of civilisation teaching on the grounds that

some knowledge of historical events, institutions and social structure is necessary to understand the context within which a literary author was writing, an appreciation of contemporary events can be illuminated for students of linguistics or society by reading their portrayal in creative writing.

LANGUAGE AND LINGUISTICS

Course content
Linguistics can be defined as the scientific study of the structure and functions of language. It is normally divided into the study of semantics, syntax and phonetics. Semantics is concerned with describing the meaning of words within a language and generally covers the lexical system or vocabulary. Syntax involves the relationship between words as used in sentences. The sound systems of a language are analysed in phonetics and phonology. Some courses focus on the morphology of the language or, in other terms, its forms and their historical development. The relationship between language and the context in which it is used is known as pragmatics, looking, for example, at the effect a speaker is trying to achieve.

A linguistics course would normally include theoretical and descriptive linguistics and might offer specialist options in psycholinguistics, sociolinguistics, applied linguistics, computational linguistics, experimental phonetics and historical linguistics.

With the increasing emphasis on language and the context in which it is used and on communicative approaches to language learning, more courses are stressing sociolinguistics and applied linguistics. Sociolinguistics is particularly relevant for students who are interested in communicating in a foreign language, since it involves looking at the relationship between language and society, through the study of the characteristics of different language varieties, their functions and their speakers, as well as the way the three interact. For example, students may be looking at the speech of different social or regional groups or at gender and age differences in language usage.

Combined subjects
Linguistics may be offered as a degree course in combination with a foreign language or with a non-language subject such as psychology. Some psychologists see linguistics as a branch of their own discipline. In a number of institutions computational linguistics has been introduced as an important component of linguistics programmes. Students who combine computing and a language often find that the two subjects are complementary and mutually reinforcing. For some

students, however, the fact that techniques and terminology are derived from the sciences may present difficulties.

Teaching methods
Linguistics programmes will normally cover general linguistic theories as well as the descriptive linguistic analysis of a particular language. Students are expected to become conversant with theories and concepts through lectures and reading. They are required to write essays and often to carry out practical projects, involving some experimental work.

Value of linguistic studies
Even if linguistics is not one of your degree subjects, as a student of languages, you will want to be familiar with linguistic terminology and the concepts concerned with the analysis of language, since you will be interested in examining how and why it functions in different contexts. An introductory linguistics course may be compulsory, and you may have the opportunity to take options in subjects such as sociolinguistics or computational linguistics.

LANGUAGE AND SOCIETY

The development of area studies courses
In considering degree structure and the relative weighting of language on different types of courses, reference was made earlier in this chapter to the fact that most language programmes include some study of foreign societies, their institutions, structures and cultures, either in addition to literature and linguistics or as an alternative. The place of these background studies and their scope were shown to vary considerably from one course to another.

As recently as the 1960s, while conceding that language is not produced in a vacuum, commentators argued that the main point of looking at a country's history and geography, or its institutions and structures and fine arts, was to gain a better understanding of the literature. Study of civilisation was seen very much as a background for reading, since most authors showed some awareness of life around them. Students venturing abroad were warned to avoid entering into arguments with the natives about contemporary events and issues, because they would be at a disadvantage.

Today the pendulum has swung very much in the opposite direction, to the extent that the study of literature is seen on a number of courses as only one amongst many aspects of a language degree programme, rather than its central focus. In some cases, the study of literature or linguistics has been replaced by what was initially described as civilisation and is now more commonly referred to as area studies. Sometimes the term societal studies is also used, or reference may be to the foreign society's economic, political and social institutions and structures or to contemporary affairs. Area studies is a very broad concept ranging across the social science disciplines but generally concentrating on sociology, politics and economics and bringing into play the approaches and teaching methods they adopt. It has also become an umbrella term for a multifaceted approach to learning about language in context.

Some academics argue that language degree courses which focus on the study of law, economics or politics cannot provide the same intellectual stimulation found in the study of literature. Where reference to another society's institutions and structures is limited to a factual and descriptive overview of historical events or an encyclopedic knowledge of its geography, this claim may be justified, but it could also be levelled against literature survey courses. The counter-argument is that interdisciplinary or multidisciplinary courses require an equally scholarly, rigorous and critical approach for the study of subjects such as economics, political science or sociology. In addition, by being exposed to very different learning methodologies, students can develop a much deeper appreciation of all their degree subjects.

Approaches to area studies
In some institutions, particularly for European studies, courses in politics, economics and other subjects are taught separately by specialists from a different department and in English. A course on contemporary French politics or the German economy may be taught simultaneously to students of political science or economics, in which case it will be subject to the same teaching methods and require the same skills as any other social science discipline, namely reading, essay writing and group discussion. While this has the advantage for language students that they are acquiring the skills of other disciplines, it does mean that the onus is on them to make the linkages between the subject and its analysis in a foreign language. In some cases, although language students are encouraged to read the relevant materials in the foreign language, they are expected to write assignments in English, if the course is taught by non-linguists.

Course content
Whether they are taught by other departments in English or, in the foreign language, by linguists with appropriate knowledge and training in the relevant subject, area studies programmes usually begin with a historical overview of social, economic and political institutions and structures and culminate in the final year with an

analysis of contemporary events. In some cases the focus is on a selective study of particular aspects of social life, often approached thematically. Most programmes cover socio-cultural, political and economic systems, giving varied attention to theoretical and practical aspects.

There is normally a mix between the broad brush approach and the opportunity for in-depth study of a specialist option, for example on educational or electoral systems. The range of options available generally depends upon the expertise of the staff in post. Even in cases where the main focus of the course is on business studies, international marketing, law or other specialist areas, students have the opportunity to follow courses which help them to become familiar with the broader social, political and economic scene as the environment in which business or the legal system operates.

Teaching methods
The main teaching method is likely to be the lecture with supporting seminars for the discussion of particular themes, often with native speakers. Essays, reports and projects are all commonly used as teaching tools, and students are expected to learn to identify relevant information, to constitute dossiers of materials, to confront views and to argue a case both orally and in writing. The linguistic analysis of texts may be incidental or it may be a central part of the activity, depending upon the aims of the course and who is responsible for the teaching.

Implications of the choice of degree programme

Although formal procedures have to be observed for approving degrees, there is room for considerable flexibility in the way in which they can be structured. Individual variations from one institution to another are characteristic of the British system. While a degree is an officially recognised qualification, irrespective of the institution from which it is obtained, there is not, as for example in France, a national diploma which is of the same market value for all degrees wherever they are awarded.

Equivalent standards are maintained throughout the country in Britain by various means, including external course reviews and the appointment of external examiners. This does not mean there is uniformity of teaching methods, nor that degrees from different institutions are considered to have the same status in the eyes of the outside world. You may have discovered this fact for yourself when you were investigating the opportunities available to study the subjects of interest to you. When you ranked your preferences in a particular order, you were no doubt influenced by the reputation of different institutions and courses.

Prospective employers may not know about the variations in emphasis between institutions. Nor will they necessarily be aware of the changes which have and are taking place in the study of languages in higher education. When you are entering professional life, you will need to be able to explain the characteristic features of the degree programme you followed and to sell your particular brand of skills and qualifications.

You may also need to offer an explanation for the fact that, even though you consider yourself to be a student of the arts or humanities, the degree awarded at the end of the course may be a BSc, rather than a BA, as is the case in some of the technological universities. The actual designation of the degree is probably less important in an employer's eyes than the class of degree obtained. You cannot do much to change the title of a degree, but it is important to choose subjects and programmes where you are motivated to do well. It is therefore useful to take into account the benefits to be derived, both in intellectual and professional terms, from studying a particular combination of languages, subjects and options throughout your period as an undergraduate.

LANGUAGE LEARNING OBJECTIVES

When you were choosing your course, you probably asked a number of key questions at interviews and on open days about the objectives and goals of different courses. Will graduates from the course be fluent in the written and spoken language? What range of topics will they have covered? What practical skills will they have learnt? How does this information match what is needed for a career? In this section, some answers are suggested to these questions.

Change in language learning objectives

In the past the aims of language degree courses were described as learning to read a language with full appreciation of style and content and being able to write it correctly using as wide a range as possible of expression and tone. In the case of students of linguistics, the objective was to investigate language for its own scientific and human interest. No reference was made to being able to master the spoken language, except incidentally in recommending visits abroad, preferably to stay in a family. Students were advised to read widely, including the foreign press, but with the warning that the modernisms found in journalese should not enter their own writing.

Stress was laid on rote learning of grammar and vocabulary. Language learning was not intended to be relevant to real life tasks and situations which the graduate might later encounter. The assumption was that those who entered teaching—at that time the main career outlet for language graduates—would learn any practical applications they would need by following postgraduate teacher training courses.

Although the emphasis still varies from one institution to another and from one sector of higher education to another, and despite many cases of entrenched resistance, the general objectives of language degree courses in higher education today are shifting towards proficiency of language use in both its oral and written forms. Emphasis is placed increasingly on the applications of language studies to real life situations and on the analysis of the characteristic features of language within its many contexts.

The distinction which is often made between the graduate and the non-graduate is that the graduate knows why he or she does something, whereas the non-graduate is only interested in what to do and how to do it. Applied to languages at degree level in the present-day context, this means students should be able to do much more than use the language mechanistically.

Objectives of contemporary language programmes

The aims of language learning programmes orientated towards performance can be broadly summarised as follows:

- By the end of the degree course students might be expected to achieve a near-native level of proficiency and articulacy in the target language, implying that they should be able to interact with educated native speakers of that language in a defined range of situations both orally and in writing.
- They should be able to use the language at a level of accuracy and appropriateness which will enable native speakers to accept them as partners and on equal terms with other native speakers of a similar standing.

These aims are intellectually demanding and challenging, and it is unlikely that the standard of proficiency expected of the language graduate will be reached, unless serious study is devoted to the language itself and the many contexts in which it is used.

APPROPRIATENESS AND PURPOSEFULNESS

According to the conception of language study which has been developing in recent years, the learner needs to be able to deploy systematic and formal knowledge of the relationship between grammar, vocabulary and meaning (and sound in the spoken language) in order to use language appropriately and purposefully in a given situation.

Appropriateness implies that the user knows how to adapt language in accordance with the norms and expectations of speakers in a particular context: an exchange of views in a board meeting, for example, requires very different language from a conversation amongst a group of students.

Purposefulness refers to using language in order to produce a result: for example as applied to instructions for operating a piece of equipment, in telephone negotiations or in a political speech exhorting voters to support a particular candidate or party. It follows that, if language use is to be appropriate and with a recognisable purpose in a range of situations, the learner must be able to identify and reproduce or imitate the characteristics of different language varieties, their functions and also the characteristics of their speakers.

KNOWLEDGE OF LANGUAGE VARIETIES

The term 'varieties' is used in a general sense to describe manifestations of language, including different languages, dialects and registers or styles, defined in relation to their social context. For the language learner this means being able to use linguistic and paralinguistic strategies, such as non-verbal forms of communication, including gestures or tone of voice, which are known to be effective in performing particular tasks in a number of well-defined contexts.

Being able to recognise and adopt behaviour which is appropriate to a wide range of situations or contexts in a foreign society requires much more than a nodding acquaintance with the country's institutions or main literary figures, or even a more specialised knowledge of some of them. The language degree course should provide the opportunity to get beneath the skin of the other society and understand how and why it functions as it does.

If you are following a course which subscribes to these objectives, during your studies as an undergraduate you should be building up the necessary knowledge and expertise which will enable you to master a repertoire of language varieties appropriate to different social roles and situations. Your object will be to achieve sufficient competence so that you can switch from one situation to another as the need arises.

ACQUISITION OF SKILLS

Most undergraduates studying languages today expect to master both academic and professional or technical skills—receptive, productive, analytical and social—which will help to prepare them for their potential career. Typically these skills would include:

- Intellectual training in analysis, logical argument and independent thinking.
- An awareness of contemporary issues and ideas.
- The ability to perform both academic and real life tasks in situations, ranging from contact with administration and the employment context to social interaction with friends or colleagues.

APPROACHES TO THE STUDY OF LANGUAGES TO DEGREE LEVEL

In order to know how you are going to achieve the goals associated with your course, you should be considering another set of questions. You will want to find out how the language learning process is organised, by asking how much weight is given in the teaching and assessment to the different components of the degree, whether the language is taught separately from contextual studies, what language exercises you will be practising and what teaching methods are used.

Practices vary from one institution to another in the methodology adopted for language learning. In considering some of the different approaches reference will be made in this section to the relative importance of language and other subjects in teaching and assessment, the integration or separation between language and contextual studies, the implications of communicative approaches to language learning and the main language learning methodologies.

The weighting of language on degree courses

The survey of the structure of degree courses in languages at the beginning of this chapter gave some indication of the many ways in which languages are taught in combination with other subjects, often belonging to different disciplines. Close scrutiny of course descriptions and assessment packages suggests that four patterns can be identified in the study of languages for a degree, including three which are common and one which is less widespread:

1. As in many of the language and literature courses, language study may be seen merely as a tool for the analysis of literary texts. Alternatively, it may serve as an exemplar of usage for students of linguistics or, where it is a subsidiary to another discipline, it may be learnt in order to understand primary source materials.

2. There may be no link between the language and the other degree subject(s).

3. The language may be taught as an integral and integrating component in the study of one or more disciplines, as for joint degrees, although the other disciplines may also be subsumed within language studies.

4. A less common pattern is for competence in using the language to be seen as the primary objective of study and for other materials to be subordinated to it. In the small number of undergraduate courses where performance at particular language tasks is paramount, as for degrees which train translators, the study of subject matter may be wide-ranging but strictly subordinated to proficiency in the task.

There are infinite variations within this model, but it may help you to understand the place of language study within your own degree if the two contrasting patterns are considered, namely where language is a tool and where it is an integrating force.

LANGUAGE AS A TOOL

Traditionally when languages were taught in higher education, they had the instrumental function of servicing the study of literature or another subject. Not very long ago, it was considered essential for students of chemistry, for example, to be able to read the relevant scientific literature in German. In both cases the foreign language was learnt in order to read materials which were needed for the study of another discipline.

As with the traditional literature degree or German for chemists, in some institutions where languages are taught in combination with subjects from other disciplines, they are still considered to have a secondary or service role. This may be the function attributed to languages in relation to business studies. Knowledge of the foreign language and the speech community associated with it may be limited to the vocabulary and concepts which are needed for a narrowly defined area of study. Language learning in this case means primarily the study of linguistic forms and structures, with less emphasis on meaning. Knowledge of context may be restricted to being able to comment intelligently on cultural allusions.

Where language is considered as the object of study, for example in linguistics, again the primary aim is not to be proficient in language performance. Linguistic applications to a specific language will be for illustration rather than to improve practical expertise. A fascination with language can result in a high level of competence, but generally as a by-product.

In many language courses, particularly the more traditional programmes based on literature or linguistics, not only is language subordinated to the other subject, but a clear distinction is also made between the two areas. The two dimensions may be taught by different people, sometimes by different departments. This is even more likely to be the case for the multidisciplinary degrees where a language is studied in combination with economics, politics, sociology, law, computing or accounting. Although the language may be seen as a tool, language exercises sometimes bear little relationship to the topics being examined elsewhere in the course, except insofar as translations for a language and literature course are likely to be of literary texts, and exercises in abstracting on the multidisciplinary courses may have a social science orientation.

In oral work, there is generally greater recognition that language cannot be taught in a vacuum and that some of the more esoteric topics do not readily lend themselves to debate: a conversation class will quickly founder if students in the group are told to discuss a topic about which they know very little or have difficulty in formulating their thoughts, even in their own language. Where language study is isolated from other degree subjects, usually an attempt is made, especially for oral work, to relate language learning to a wider societal context by introducing what is commonly referred to as civilisation teaching, background or contextual studies. Where contextual studies are treated as a minor or supporting element, they may be confined to expanding on references which occur in materials being used for language exercises, or they may involve survey courses of institutions or social structures.

INTEGRATION OF LANGUAGE AND CONTEXTUAL STUDIES

If the aim of language acquisition is to become proficient at analysing different language varieties and using a foreign language expertly in a range of situations, it follows that language cannot be studied in a vacuum and in isolation from other disciplines. However perfect the theoretical knowledge of syntax and lexis, some intellectual content is needed in order to be able to write or speak. The deeper this knowledge, the more competent language learners will be in expressing themselves authoritatively on a subject.

With this aim in mind, in some institutions the study of language and its many situations are closely integrated. All teaching may be in the foreign language, as are materials and assignments, with the result that little or no distinction is made between language and the study of its many contexts.

Taken to its logical conclusion, the integration in a degree programme of language with knowledge of the real life contexts or situations within which it is used should imply that students are able to produce language which is appropriate and also answer the questions how and why something is said or written in a particular way. When they complete the administrative formalities needed to make a social security claim, for example, they should understand how the system works, how the form will be processed and why they need to reply to every question. If they write a formal letter, they will not simply be following a prescribed model by inserting the appropriate words, they will also understand the reasons why particular verb forms, syntax or vocabulary should or should not be used and what their effect is likely to be on the reader.

The communicative approach

Courses in higher education which expose students to a wide range of situations and help them to master the linguistic and para-linguistic strategies needed to deal with various tasks effectively and appropriately can be said to have adopted the communicative approach to language learning. This approach, which is implicit in the language learning objectives described earlier in this chapter, requires knowledge of the rules of grammar in order to avoid making errors of syntax and lexis. It also involves knowing the characteristics of the many situations in which language is used and how to produce language for a purpose by being aware of its different functions and their variations from one context to another.

The communicative approach to language learning stresses the interrelatedness and interdependence of language and culture. If communication between individuals from different speech communities is to be effective, contextual knowledge is needed of the value systems and traditions, or culture, of the people whose language is being studied. Culture can be defined as the beliefs and practices governing the life of a society for which a particular language is the vehicle of expression. It is also reflected in para-language or non-verbal communication, such as gestures, pronunciation, voice dynamics, including intonation, rhythm, speed and continuity of speech. Integration of language study with in-depth analysis of institutions and structures and their linguistic and paralinguistic manifestations is therefore central in this approach to language learning.

The learner observing the communicative process can be depicted diagrammatically, as shown below. The diagram illustrates how the different components of the communicative process are linked together and how they are mutually dependent on one another. When the learner becomes an active participant, rather than simply an observer, he or she assumes the role of the sender or the receiver of the message and needs to respond to what is happening in all parts of the interaction.

THE COMMUNICATIVE PROCESS

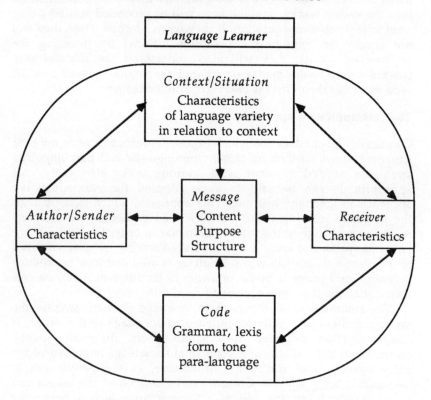

Language learning methodology

The methods which can be used to impart knowledge of language and culture are many and varied. They include:
- Presentation of concepts and information and demonstration of techniques through lectures.
- Follow-up or parallel seminar discussions and language classes.
- Work on specific assignments or language exercises, individually or in groups, in the classroom or resource centre, under direct supervision or as private study.
- Correction and analysis of exercises and feedback used to improve performance.

Surveys of language courses in higher education show that the range of language exercises intended to develop language skills is often limited to those which were used traditionally on language and literature courses: translation from and into English and the general essay. Final examinations in many institutions are still confined to these exercises, especially in the university sector, although a wider range may be introduced for course work. The language learning exercises most often added to the standard three are abstracting or summary writing, commentary, paraphrase, stylistic analysis and pastiche. Interpreting may also be introduced as a potential professional skill. These exercises are sometimes assessed in examinations at the end of the first and second year of a course and occasionally in the final year. Where there is integration between language and the study of the foreign society, its literature and culture, the academic essay, as opposed to the general essay, may be an important study method.

In an increasing number of institutions, oral and aural skills are now incorporated into the mainstream of language work. The learning of spoken language is often based on analysis of the speech act, with the object of identifying the characteristic features of different language varieties. Studies of the language skills used by graduates show that the oral and aural language tasks rate high. In professional contexts, linguists are expected to be proficient in a wide range of situations where effective and purposeful communication through spoken language is paramount.

At the home institution most situations, tasks and strategies will be simulated, but the period of residence abroad will provide the opportunity to experience the real life contexts where the strategies mastered are put to the test and the range of situations in which you are seeking to become a competent communicator can be extended.

Success in achieving your goals will depend to a great extent upon the amount of time and effort devoted to gaining maximum exposure to situations in which the language is used actively, as well as being able to analyse the tasks and strategies needed to deal with these situations. The skills involved are therefore receptive and productive as well as analytical, and it is important to take full advantage of all the resources available in higher education and to exploit as many methods and approaches as you can.

SUMMARY OF SUGGESTIONS

1. It is important to know both what to expect of your language degree programme and what is expected of you, particularly since language courses in British higher education have been undergoing substantive changes in recent years in structure, content and emphasis.

2. In the British educational system there is a considerable flexibility in the structure of degrees and in the possible combinations of components. You therefore need to find out as much as you can about the different opportunities available. The choices you make will determine the amount of time you spend studying the language, the level you can hope to achieve and your career prospects.

3. You will want to be aware of the advantages and disadvantages of the language(s) you choose to study, as far as their rarity value is concerned, and also of gender bias and the motivational factors associated with them.

4. Your language course is likely to involve disciplinary studies of literature, society or linguistics, which can be considered as a means of achieving a multidisciplinary and multiskilled approach to language learning.

5. You can expect the study of literature, society or linguistics to include both an overview, or survey approach, and in-depth study, or specialisation, in selected topics with emphasis on theory and practical applications. Teaching methods are similar for the three areas, ranging from lectures to seminar papers and

discussions, with written assignments focusing on essays, projects and the detailed critical analysis of texts.

6. As a language undergraduate, you will need to be familiar with at least some aspects of these three disciplines in order to gain a full understanding of the foreign society and its language.

7. Whatever choices you have made, you should be conversant with their merits so that you can sell your particular combination of knowledge and skills to prospective employers.

8. It is worth remembering that language learning objectives today are often very different from those in the past, where the more passive skills of reading and listening were dominant. Emphasis is now more evenly spread over receptive, productive, analytical and social skills in the oral and written medium, generally implying closer integration between language and its many contexts of usage.

9. You should try to ensure that you understand the relationship between your own goals and the different approaches to language learning adopted in your institution.

10. If your aim is to achieve a high level of communicative competence, you will need to ensure that you gain maximum exposure to a wide variety of spoken and written foreign language source materials and that you take advantage of opportunities to practise purposeful interaction in a number of situations.

2 STUDY METHODS AND RESOURCES

Whatever the subjects you have selected, the nature of the learning objectives and the approaches to language learning in the institution where you are reading for your degree, there are a number of study habits, which you will need to acquire if your work is to be effective. You will also want to know how to take full advantage of the available learning resources and how to monitor your progress. In suggesting how you might approach your undergraduate studies, in this chapter the focus is on:

1. The general study habits you will need to develop.

2. How to gain access to materials, how to keep yourself informed of developments in your field of study and how to use the whole range of language learning resources.

3. Preparing for assessment and examinations, by knowing what to expect and learning how to organise your work and your revision sensibly.

4. Ways of coping with any difficulties you are having with your studies.

Many students find the first few weeks of higher education bewildering. At school you may have been used to working in small groups, where you knew the teachers and other students and were instructed exactly how to prepare for every lesson. If there was something you did not understand, you were probably not afraid to ask. Your parents may have kept a watchful eye on your academic progress and social life. Now you may find yourself attending lectures with as many as a hundred other students, whom you do not know, and you are left to your own devices to organise yourself around a relatively small number of structured hours. You will be expected to search for reading materials for yourself and to prepare assignments with little supervision. You may have difficulty in knowing where to concentrate your effort and how to monitor your progress. Social life on campus is varied and exciting, and it may not be easy to establish a balance between the many activities competing for your time and energy. You have to accept that ultimately you alone are responsible for your success or failure and it is up to you to learn how to manage the situation.

As you will have discovered from your past experience, study is a very personal matter. There are no hard and fast rules about the best and most effective ways of approaching a programme leading to a degree. Even if you feel that you are already well organised and have thorough working habits, as you embark on three—or in many cases four—more years of study, this may be an appropriate moment to review your work pattern to see whether you can make any improvements.

There is an abundant literature on study methods, which you should be able to consult in your university, polytechnic or college library. Some of the most useful titles are quoted in the relevant section of the bibliography. Several of the books recommended include practical exercises which you can work through by yourself, but few give specific consideration to students of foreign languages.

GENERAL STUDY HABITS

Study can be defined as the process whereby a deliberate attempt is made to extend learning in a systematic way. It implies a conscious decision to organise effort with a particular purpose and sense of direction. Most of the literature on study methods suggests that, in order to be able to work out a sensible study routine, you should be asking yourself a number of basic questions about the reasons why you are studying, where, when and how you study. In this section attention is paid to the justification for learning how to study effectively and to issues of spatial organisation and time management which are central to the development of good study habits.

Justifying effective academic study

Research has shown that motivation is a key factor in the success of undergraduates. It is therefore essential to have a clear idea of what you expect to learn from being a student and to be committed to achieving the objectives you have set yourself, even though they may seem distant. It has been found that undergraduates who are well motivated more often attend classes regularly and that they follow a carefully planned schedule and work steadily towards their goals. The main reasons for wanting to learn to study effectively can be summarised as:

- Attaining academic objectives.
- Mastering specific skills.

- Furthering personal development and character building.
- Learning self-awareness and critical self-appraisal.
- Acquiring good work methods for life.
- Preparing for a satisfying career.

The primary purpose of higher education, for students, is generally considered to be the pursuit of scholarly learning and the attainment of an academic qualification. As an undergraduate enrolled for a language degree, you have committed yourself to several years of study in higher education, implying that you have thought through your reasons for wanting to read for a degree. You should be planning to make optimal use of the time not only to acquire the specialised skills you have identified but also to develop as a person. You should expect to be stretched mentally by your degree course and be prepared to devote adequate time, effort and energy to your studies in order to achieve your goals. Learning the self-discipline, reliance, awareness and intellectual maturity expected of a graduate should be major items on your agenda.

Another important ingredient for success, apart from the will to succeed, is a realistic view of your own abilities and capacity for work. As a student of the arts, humanities or social sciences, you will be called upon to make a critical analysis of other people's work. If you have not already done so, this is a good time to engage in introspection, self-awareness and appraisal in order to get to know your own strengths and your limitations.

Motivation, ability, effort and self-awareness can all be enhanced by effective study methods, which will require self-discipline and the development of personal management skills. The work habits you adopt as a student may remain with you throughout professional life, so you are making a long-term investment by ensuring that you know how to maximise your effort.

Finding the best place to study

You will want to organise yourself both spatially and temporally, so that your work pattern is as efficient as possible within the constraints imposed by the timing of lectures and supporting activities.

In the first year of study many undergraduates are accommodated either on campus or in halls of residence belonging to their institution. Whether you are in private or institutional accommodation you would normally expect your study bedroom to serve as your main workplace. It is important to have somewhere to group together your materials and to be able to work undisturbed for several hours at a time. If you have to share a room with another student, if your neighbours have different work patterns, or if you are in lodgings which are not conducive to study, you may need to find an alternative, such as a public or academic library. This may be only second best, since there are usually people moving around and other sorts of disturbance, and you cannot have your own personal permanent work station. Most libraries do have a small number of carrels for isolated private study, but they generally have to be booked in advance, and priority may be given to postgraduate students at busy times of the year.

You should know whether you work best in an environment where you are surrounded by other people who are also studying or whether you prefer to be relatively isolated. It may be worthwhile experimenting with different settings and even combining a number of work sites which change depending upon the tasks you are performing. It is in fact rare for effective work to be accomplished in an environment where there are external distractions, so you may be deluding yourself if you think you work best in the company of others or with the background noise of a radio or tape recorder.

Most study bedrooms are equipped with a large table or desk, a reasonably comfortable chair, a book case and a desk lamp. The study skills literature recommends that you should have a good light, plenty of fresh air and a comfortable temperature. Although these points may all seem obvious, in reality it is not always so easy to create an environment which is conducive to work: air conditioning and heating systems may be outside your control, as is the noise made by your neighbours or their late night visitors. If you cannot adapt to the conditions in which you find yourself or are unable to get them changed, it may be worth trying to find alternative accommodation. Occasionally it is possible to swap rooms with another student who is less easily disturbed by the factors with which you have difficulty in coping.

Some halls of residence have conventions about signs which can be used when you are not to be disturbed, and it is important for everybody that these conventions are observed and respected.

If you do have a permanent personal work space (and you should make every effort to secure one), then you can keep it equipped with the materials, such a pens, papers, files, dictionaries and essential reference tools, which you regulary use, so as not to waste valuable study time getting ready for work. It is also worth having a notice board where you pin timetables, work plans and notes to remind yourself of recalcitrant genders or grammar rules which you always get wrong. A map of the country you are learning about or a list of government ministers or dates of major literary works placed in your line of vision may help to imprint essential information on your memory.

In summary, the main criteria you should bear in mind in preparing a place to work are:

- Adequate light, ventilation and heating.
- Privacy.
- Absence of external distractions.
- Basic equipment.

Managing study time

Wherever you work you will need to learn to manage your time carefully. Because as a student you have so much unstructured time, it is all the more important to know how to plan in order to maximise its use. By planning you can organise your work into manageable units which are much less daunting. By setting yourself realistic goals and reasonably flexible schedules for achieving them, you will have the satisfaction of reaching your targets. Since success as a student depends to such a great extent on how you manage and use your time, the topic is dealt with in some detail in this section. Attention is paid to helping you to know how much time you should spend working, how to plan your annual, weekly and daily schedule, how to keep a time-budget diary and achieve a balance between your various activities and, finally, how to avoid distractions.

KNOWING HOW MUCH WORK TO DO

Before you begin organising your time, you need to know how much work you are expected to do, in the absence of any formal requirement stipulating the number of hours of private study for a given course. The normal expectation from lecturers is that, for every hour spent in the classroom, you carry out two or three hours of private study, both in preparation and in follow-up work. Most language students might expect to have about fifteen contact hours each week in lectures and classes. The emphasis placed on oral work in some courses may bring the number of scheduled hours closer to that expected in the sciences, where laboratory work is a requirement, but many of these will be the equivalent of private study time. The weekly figure may be as high as twenty-five to thirty timetabled hours. On average students are found to work for about thirty-five to forty hours a week in total, when private study is included.

Generally assignments are not set for the long summer vacations although you will probably be expected to hand in written work after the Christmas and Easter breaks and to use the time for reading and revision. You could estimate that, on an annual basis, you may be studying for approximately forty hours a week for thirty-eight weeks in the year. Obviously some students work faster than others; some read more widely than the prescribed work requires. The actual number of hours devoted to study may therefore vary substantially for undergraduates following the same course and may also fluctuate at different times of the year. The aim—and this applies especially to language learners—should be to establish a regular pattern which is likely to be much more effective than concentrated bursts in response to pressing deadlines or end-of-year examinations.

ANNUAL, WEEKLY AND DAILY PLANNING

Your planning can usefully be organised on an annual, weekly and daily basis. Your annual targets will be the examination dates and assessment deadlines you need to observe. These are normally made available at the beginning of the year.

An annual schedule for a first-year language undergraduate might look like the following (by using the reverse order, you can cut off or fold under the bottom of the schedule as you complete the work):

ANNUAL SCHEDULE

Late June	Examination results
Early June	Written examinations
Late May	Oral and aural examinations
Mid-May	Written examination revision and practice
Early May	Mock oral and aural examinations
Mid/late April	Examination revision
Early April	Submission of essays
Easter vac	Essay writing
	Examination revision
	Reading and preparation for third term
March	Reading for essays
February	Written language tests
January	Submission of essays
Christmas vac	Essay writing
	Checking through term 1 lecture notes
	Reading and preparation for second term
Early December	Oral tests
November	Reading for essays
October	Reading and note-taking practice

Your weekly and daily schedule will need to take account of the regular written or oral assignments which are commonly required of language students. However, you should not forget to allow adequate time for reading, checking through, revising and completing lecture notes and also for private study, both in your own room and a resource centre, using the range of media materials now generally available in most institutions.

Lecture timetables are often very complex, since they have to accommodate a range of options and small group work. You may find that your timetable has inconvenient gaps, when there is not long enough to go back to your room or to the campus library. This may be a good opportunity to make use of your department's resource centre. Because language courses require more face to face contact than other social science and humanities subjects, you may have fewer blocks of time to yourself than students in other disciplines. You will need to adapt your personal timetable and study practices accordingly and decide which types of activity are best suited to particular time slots or work sites.

Not only is it important to know where you work most efficiently but also when you are able to concentrate most and when your work is most productive. Efficient study means being able to maximise learning and retention for the least expenditure of time and effort. You therefore need to understand your own biological clock: some people are at their peak in the morning, whereas others claim that they only start to come alive in the evening and can then work late into the night. There is generally some room for manoeuvre, but you could try to plan the activities which need most concentration at the times when you know you are most effective. If this is late at night, you should avoid getting out of phase to the extent that you fail to attend early morning lectures.

You will also need to be aware of the length of time during which you can concentrate, and this may vary in the course of a day. Most people find that short breaks are necessary every hour or so. It is important to ensure that you have proper meals and a reasonable amount of exercise. When working out your schedule, if you are realistic, you should take account of intentional breaks as well as unplanned interruptions. If your timetable is too finely tuned and inflexible, an unexpected visit can upset your whole schedule. It may be more difficult to get back to work after strenuous physical exercise than it is after a short shopping expedition, so you will need to organise the sequence of activities with this in mind.

KEEPING A TIME-BUDGET DIARY

You may find it useful to keep a time-budget diary, for a few weeks at least, in which you note down how long you spend, in hours and minutes, on all your daily activities, including eating, sleeping, domestic chores, such as shopping and washing, and social interaction over a cup of coffee or a glass of beer. You can then calculate how long you take for each type of activity and track how the time devoted to different tasks is distributed over the week.

It is easy to overestimate the amount of time spent working, particularly if you have what can be described as a 'fractionated' pattern, switching from one task to another and making frequent lengthy interruptions. Keeping a time-budget diary can be quite a revealing exercise and may give you the incentive needed to make more effective use of your time. It will also help you to plan ahead by knowing, on the basis of experience, how much time you should allocate to a particular type of work. By comparing your time use with that of other students, you will be able to produce a rough yardstick to help you know whether you need to learn to work faster or to devote more time to particular tasks.

The following are extracts from two typical time-budget diaries kept by fictitious first-year students reading for a joint honours degree in French and German on the same course and living in accommodation on campus:

DAILY TIME-BUDGET DIARY

Student A
Tuesday

From	To	Activity
7.30		Woken by alarm
7.30	7.40	Listened to the 'revue de presse' on French radio
7.40	7.55	Washed and dressed
7.55	8.15	Ate breakfast, listening to German news
8.15	8.30	Washed up, made bed, prepared for work
8.30	9.50	Checked notes for French oral presentation
9.50	10.00	Walked from room to lecture hall
10.00	11.00	Attended French lecture
11.00	12.00	Checked back through lecture notes Checked work for German written language
12.00	13.00	Attended French oral class, made presentation

From	To	Activity
13.00	14.00	Had lunch in the refectory
14.00	15.00	Worked through German lab exercise
15.00	15.30	Scanned daily papers in departmental library
15.30	16.00	Drank coffee in students' coffee lounge
16.00	17.00	Attended German written language class
17.00	17.45	Shopped for basics and for evening meal
17.45	18.45	Prepared and ate evening meal, washed up
18.45	20.30	Worked in library preparing German written language text analysis
20.30	22.00	Watched television and had supper
22.00	22.30	Prepared files for next day, checked schedule
22.30	22.45	Got ready for bed
22.45	23.15	Went to bed and read German novel

Student D
Tuesday

From	To	Activity
8.00		Woken by alarm
8.00	8.45	Dozed
8.45	9.00	Washed and dressed
9.00	9.10	Shopped for milk and bread for breakfast
9.10	9.30	Ate breakfast and listened to Radio 1
9.30	10.00	Began exercise for German written language
10.00	10.05	Ran from room to lecture hall
10.05	11.00	Attended French lecture
11.00	12.00	Drank coffee in refectory, thought about French oral presentation
12.00	13.00	Attended French oral class, made presentation
13.00	14.30	Went to pub for beer and lunch
14.30	15.15	Worked through German lab exercise
15.15	16.00	Went to students' union Checked programme and booked squash court Chatted with friends
16.00	17.00	Attended German written language class
17.00	18.00	Played squash
18.00	19.00	Drank beer at bar
19.00	19.30	Fetched burger from take-away
19.30	20.30	Worked in room on French written language exercise
20.30	23.15	Went to cinema

| 23.15 | 23.45 | *Had supper and got ready for bed* |
| 24.00 | 24.15 | *Went to bed and listened to Radio 1* |

Student A has spent three hours in lectures and nearly twice that amount of time in private study. He or she has taken advantage of opportunities between classes to use the resources in the department, has eaten proper meals and found time to socialise and relax. Student D, on the other hand, has spent much less time on private study than at lectures (and was late for one of them). He or she has not used the gaps between classes to fit in library work or class preparation. Coffee breaks and non-work activities predominate. It is quite easy to see which of the two students has begun to adopt good study habits and to deduce the marks each of the two students is likely to obtain at the end of the year.

ACHIEVING A BALANCED SCHEDULE

From the importance given to different activities on the timetable, the amount of work set and your own ability to handle it, you should be able to estimate how much time you need to devote to each of the tasks you are expected to perform. This is not always easy to work out by yourself. Your tutor or advisor may be able to help you in deciding whether you are spending enough time on your work. Social interaction and the whole range of extra-curricular activities have traditionally been an important part of student life in Britain, but they are only secondary aims and should not be allowed to replace the primary purpose of studying for a degree. If you find that you are spending a disproportionate amount of time on social activities, you may need to revise your ways, bearing in mind that the amount of work done, which is not unrelated to its quality, is an important factor in academic success or failure for most students. Your tutor may also be able to help you to decide whether you have struck a reasonable balance between work and play.

Obviously there will be some activities which require regular reading or written assignments and where it is easy to adopt a weekly routine. For foreign language study—even more so than for other arts and humanities subjects—it is essential to adopt a regular pattern of study, devoting a short period of time every day to learning vocabulary, checking and revising grammar points and reading the foreign press or listening to the radio. Last minute cramming before a test or examination is no substitute for the gradual building process.

When you have an extended essay to write, however, you will probably find that you need to spend several days planning, organising and drafting, and you may prefer to concentrate your efforts on that to the exclusion, at least momentarily, of other work. This is where your ability to plan over a longer period is important. If you have been reading round the subject over preceding weeks and taking notes with the essay in mind, much of the preparatory work will have been done already, and the essay should not provide too much of a disruption to your normal schedule. You will, however, often have a number of pieces of work to submit at about the same time, and it is crucial to have planned your strategy several weeks ahead in order to avoid a crisis and prevent yourself from neglecting the more regularly spaced assignments. If you leave the preparation and writing of essays until the last minute, you will inevitably find that the books you need are no longer available. Few lecturers would accept bad personal planning as an excuse for late submission.

AVOIDING DISTRACTIONS

One of the main problems faced by students on a day-to-day basis is how to handle distractions. Although some interruptions may be unexpected and unwanted, there are many other well-documented forms of work avoidance strategies, which some students practise almost as a fine art. In an environment where there may be penalties for not submitting assignments by deadlines, but where the rewards for reading round the subject and looking for yet more ways of rephrasing a sentence, in the case of a language exercise, are not always immediately apparent, it may be tempting to get by with the minimum and postpone the essential until the last minute. Many students claim that they work best under pressure, but what they mean is that they find it difficult to discipline themselves and plan their time in such a way as to avert a last minute panic.

An American author, Bernstein (1978), who has explored the ways in which students avoid getting down to work has recorded a whole variety of 'fritter' devices, or strategies, used by students to cope with what is frequently an open-ended situation and to justify or excuse not doing work. He classifies fritters as 'person-based, social relations-based, valuative-based and task-based':

STUDENT FRITTERS

Person-based fritters Typical examples from the first category would be the work-avoidance strategies which are justified on grounds of biological necessity, such as the need to eat or wash or take exercise to offset fatigue.

Social relations-based fritters Under the second category are grouped strategies whereby time is spent with others *commiserating over the unreasonableness of an assignment. The advantage of these fritters is that they not only justify not working by protesting against the work itself, but they can also be vindicated on the grounds that they help develop critical faculties. Contact with other students may be used to compare progress, preferably with somebody who is less well advanced. Group work makes both these avoidance strategies possible and also creates a situation where they can receive group approval.*

Valuative-based fritters *These strategies encourage students to neglect the task in hand in favour of values—friendship, love, political interests, physical fitness—which are considered more worthy of attention. Alternative activities may be justified in this case as broadening knowledge or experience.*

Task-based fritters *The strategies in this category involve the way study time and work resources are handled. Students may set themselves particular starting times for activities, such as on the hour or at a specific point in day, and then while away time waiting for the right moment to arrive. Planning work schedules or rewriting them becomes a time-consuming task in itself, as is seeking postponement of deadlines. Preparing for work by clearing a desk top or moving between work sites is another way of putting off starting a task. Time may be frittered away by trying to get into the right mood, by waiting for inspiration or, in the case of examinations, by trying to find out what is likely to be in the paper as a substitute for learning the necessary information. Even when the task is underway, time may be further wasted by computing words produced per minute, setting subgoals or shifting from one task to another to avoid difficult stages.*

You will most probably recognise your own behaviour or that of fellow students in many of these examples. The dividing line between time-wasting and creating favourable working conditions is a narrow one: a short break for sustenance may make it easier to concentrate on the task in hand; discussing an assignment with other students may clarify your own thoughts; clearing your desk may help you to find your way through your notes. Taken to extremes, however, these procedures result in time-wasting and bad study habits, which would seem to be characteristic of student D in the example given above. The interest of the research into student fritters is that it highlights how easy it is to mismanage time and yet find justifications for putting off the task in hand.

In conclusion, some of the items often used in questionnaires to American students may help you to judge how well you are performing in organisational terms. You can try asking yourself the following questions:

1. Have you built your annual schedule around your deadlines?
2. Do you have a plan of work for each day of the week?
3. If so, do you keep to your schedule?
4. Do you have trouble settling down to work at the beginning of a study period?
5. Do you get your work in on time?

If your answers to questions 1, 2, 3 and 5 are positive and you have replied in the negative to question 4, then you are probably on the right path. If not, then you may need to rethink the way you manage your time.

ACCESSING LANGUAGE LEARNING RESOURCES

Resources can be defined as the materials which supply the information needed to help you to carry out study tasks. They include library and information services, people (librarians, lecturers, fellow students) and technology in the form of audio, video and computing equipment. The ability to access and handle information is an essential part of your undergraduate training, and the basic skills involved need to be mastered at an early stage to enable you to study effectively and systematically. It is worth spending some time finding out whom to ask, where to look and how to use the information which is likely to be relevant to your programme of study. The convergence in many libraries of media and computer services can mean that you may have ready access under a single roof to a wide range of resources which can sometimes be used interactively.

Whether your degree is based on literature or linguistics or you are studying the institutions and structures of the foreign society, there will be no single course book which provides a neat compendium of all the topics you are going to cover. You will be given reading lists and advice about what is essential or recommended, at what stage and in what order it should be consulted. For the literature, linguistics and society courses, there will probably be prescribed texts, many of which you are expected to purchase before beginning the course. You may also be instructed to buy a number of reference books. Even if you own several basic books, you will still need to make extensive use of library facilities and other learning resources. You will want to know how to search for a wide range of books and articles, read round a subject, identify and sift relevant materials. You should be familiar with key language texts and reference works, especially dictionaries and grammar books, which are standard tools for language students.

Libraries will probably be only one of a number of resources which you should have available to help you acquire linguistic proficiency. You will need to know how to gain access to other resources, such as audio and video tapes and computerised materials. There is no single multimedia course which spans all aspects of a language for the advanced learner. Even if there were, you should want to search further afield for information and for examples of authentic language.

In this section a range of language learning resources are examined, including audio-visual aids and materials for computer-assisted language learning, in order to show you the extent of the information available and to suggest how you can take full advantage of the facilities in your institution.

Libraries

Unless you live in one of the major cities in Britain, you will find that you must rely on an academic rather than a public library for most of the foreign language materials you require. Libraries vary considerably in their stock, depending upon how long particular courses have been established and on the policy for allocating funds to different subjects. To make effective use of the available facilities, you will need to find out about opening hours, the layout of the library, the cataloguing system and the borrowing arrangements.

OPENING TIMES AND LOAN SYSTEMS

The opening times of academic libraries are designed to correspond to patterns of use by students, so that they are generally closed in the evenings and at weekends during the vacations and open until late at night and over the weekend during term-time, although not all services will be available at all times of the day and week.

Most academic libraries have loan systems which are designed to take account of demand. A very short loan period may operate so that books which are heavily used can only be taken out overnight or for a twenty-four hour period, or they may be available for use only in the library during the standard working day of nine to five. There may also be a weekly or fortnightly loan period for books which are in demand and a termly loan for books which are not used so much. In the latter case books can be recalled if requested by another borrower. It is important to make sure you know how long the loan period is for a particular book, so that you avoid incurring fines. You also need to check how many books you are allowed to borrow at a time. Although these points may all seem obvious, they enter into your overall planning, since you may have to arrange your weekly schedule to take account of the fact that a book you have been waiting for is due back in a few days.

CATALOGUING SYSTEMS, LIBRARY LAYOUT AND SEARCH FACILITIES

To make the most effective use of a library it is essential to know how to use the cataloguing and classification systems and how to browse and select the most useful materials. You will need to be able to locate the catalogue, reference books, bound and unbound journals, periodicals or serials and the stacks containing the books in your subject areas. Most libraries provide users' guides and layout plans and arrange instruction for new undergraduates to familiarise them with the system and with the types of materials they will find most useful. Librarians may be prepared to deal with individual queries and point you in the direction of some of the less obvious sources of information.

You will want to familiarise yourself with the classification system used in your library and with the relevant codes for the categories you will be consulting frequently.

Different classification systems operate from one library to another. The Dewey Decimal system is the most widely used. It is based on a classification of knowledge into ten classes, encompassing nine major subject classes and one 'generalia' or 'form' class, which are coded by a minimum of three digits. If a number is longer than three digits there is a decimal point after the third to act as a separator. Classification numbers can be of any length: the longer the number, the greater the specificity of the subject. Sometimes letters are also added denoting the beginning of the author's name. An example of the Dewey Decimal System would be:

DEWEY DECIMAL CLASSIFICATION SYSTEM

371.3 MAD for the book by Harry Maddox, entitled **How to Study**, *where 371 tells you that the book is in the social science section (300), under education (370) and in the study skills literature (71), under the grouping for general books on the subject (.3), and where MAD indicates the author's name.*

The Library of Congress System, which is less common in Britain, has twenty-six main divisions, using letter codes further subdivided by other letters and numbers. The same book classified according to the Library of Congress System would be:

> *LIBRARY OF CONGRESS CLASSIFICATION SYSTEM*
>
> *LB 1049.M2, where L indicates education, LB theory and practice of education, 1049 methods of study and .M2 the author's name.*

Some libraries are fully computerised, so that you can search the library's stock by title, author or subject, scan reading lists, check your own borrowing information and even place a reservation on a particular book all from a seat in the library cataloguing area. In less technologically advanced libraries you will need to search through micro-fiches and, in some cases, through drawers of index cards.

Even if you think you have discovered the section of the library which holds all the books you may ever need, it is always worth consulting the subject catalogue, since the classification systems used do not necessarily bring together in one location all the books relevant to a particular topic, especially if you are following an interdisciplinary course. The basic steps involved in carrying out a search might be:

1. If you are looking for items on a reading list and do not have the class number, check the catalogue under the author's name or book title.

2. If you want to find books relevant to a particular topic which are not on a reading list, first identify the subject terms and class numbers from the alphabetical subject catalogue so that you can find them in the classified catalogue or on the appropriate shelf.

3. Consult any items which look useful and check their bibliographies for other references.

4. Check relevant abstracts, indexes and subject bibliographies for books and periodical articles.

5. Note down the full details of any items which you might want to pursue and, where appropriate, place orders or make copies of useful sections.

REFERENCE TOOLS

An important source of library materials for language students is the reference collection. In addition to encyclopedias, dictionaries and grammar books, you should be aware of the bibliographies and guides to the literature. For French, German and Spanish the most complete and up-to-date sources of bibliographical information are:

- *Les livres disponibles: French Books in Print*, Paris, Editions du Cercle de la Librairie.
- *Verzeichnis lieferbarer Bücher: German Books in Print*, Frankfurt am Main, Verlag der Buchhändler-Vereinigung.
- *Bibliografía española*, Madrid, Servicio Nacional de Información Bibliográfica.

The reference collection of the library will have a section on statistics, which you would do well to consult for up-to-date information, particularly if you are studying contemporary institutions and systems. For students reading French the *Institut National de la Statistique et des Études Économiques*, which is the main national data gathering organisation, regularly produces some excellent publications. For the Federal Republic of Germany, the *Statistisches Bundesamt* performs a similar function and in Spain the *Instituto Nacional de Estadística y Estudios*. Some examples of publications by these organisations are included in the bibliography to Chapter 1.

Since the purchase of dictionaries and grammar books is a long-term and expensive investment, you will want to delay doing so until you have consulted widely and sought advice from tutors, unless you were instructed to buy a particular title in the information sent out before you began your course.

Where you are given a choice, the best way to find out which grammar books and dictionaries are going to be your companions for the next few years, if not throughout your professional life, is to set yourself the task of trying out the available reference works in your library to see which ones suit you personally. Checking vocabulary or grammar may be one of the language tasks you are set in the first few weeks of your course. If not, you can devise exercises for yourself by selecting a grammar point which always gives you problems. Examples might be:

- In French, when to use *ce* or *il*, how to distinguish between *savoir* and *pouvoir*, or when *laisser* followed by an infinitive needs an agreement.

- For German, how to avoid confusion with English constructions in using different pronouns, as in *aus diesem Grunde, der Grund dafür* and *das Recht auf,* or how to use the passive correctly and avoid confusion between *werden* and *sein,* or which endings to use with adjectival nouns, as in *die Grünen*.
- In Spanish, the distinction between *ser* and *estar, tener* and *haber, saber* and *conocer,* or when to use the infinitive rather than the subjunctive.

When selecting reference books, there are several factors which you will want to take into consideration in order to gauge their user-friendliness. From the index in a grammar book, can you easily find the item you are looking for? How clear and detailed are the explanations? Are there useful and meaningful examples?

You may wonder whether it is better to purchase a grammar book which is written for English users of the foreign language or for native speakers. The answer to this question may be that you probably need a combination of the two, and it is always better to check a point in more than one grammar book. You will quickly discover that you need to consult both a bilingual and a monolingual dictionary in the foreign language. A dictionary of synonyms is also a useful standby. An English dictionary and a book of English synonyms should all be part of your standard reference tools as a linguist. You will have to decide whether the shorter versions of the bilingual works are adequate for your needs, since you may not be able to afford the larger volumes and the pocket versions will not give you enough breadth and depth. For some courses you may have to consult dictionaries of specialised terms in a particular area or glossaries of terminology.

If you have easy access to libraries and departmental resource centres and they are well stocked, you may want to rely heavily on the reference tools they provide and, in any case, you should expect to consult a range of materials before finding the most satisfactory answer to a particular linguistic query.

SERIALS

For all subjects, serials, periodicals or journals, as they are called, are generally grouped in one part of the library. It is worth your while trying to spend time regularly looking through those which are in your subject area for up-to-date articles. Many journals now include abstracts of articles which will help you to locate the most useful items in recent publications. For a survey going back over a longer period there are volumes of abstracts which are well indexed and could help you to track down relevant materials.

If your library does not subscribe to the journals referred to in the abstracts or does not have a book you need, you can find out from a special catalogue whether they are held elsewhere locally. If an item is not available in the vicinity, there is an efficient, though costly, system of interlibrary loans. You may have the possibility of requesting an online search to one of the major databases, when you are preparing work on a special project. Since this is also a very costly process, you may find that it is reserved for postgraduates and staff. If you are allowed to use interlibrary loans and online searches, you will most probably need the approval of the lecturer or tutor concerned.

Most libraries have facilities for photocopying. When you have identified a key article or section of a book that you will want to refer to frequently, it is often worth making a photocopy, although this is no substitute for learning to take effective notes, and you should be wary of infringing copyright regulations. Nor should it deter you from buying your own copy of a book which you use regularly. For any book or article you consult, you should always ensure that you keep a record of the full details of the source, including the author's names, title of the book or article, publisher, place and date of publication and relevant page numbers. It is also useful to note where you consulted the item and its class number.

OPEN ACCESS TO MATERIALS

In Britain libraries have the advantage that books are available on open access, so that, having located the area you are interested in, you can scan the shelves and identify the books which are likely to be of most use from their contents tables, indexes and dust covers. It is important to acquire the habit of browsing through the shelves to familiarise yourself with the literature in your field.

The advantage of the British system of open access can, however, become a drawback if library users do not respect the needs of others. Some students indulge in a practice known as squirrelling, whereby they hide away a book which they do not need immediately, often if they already have their full quota of loans, with the object of preventing other students from taking it out. Sometimes books are borrowed long before they will be used and sit on the shelves of a study bedroom when other undergraduates could be reading them. Unfortunately books, and particularly periodicals, regularly disappear. These practices are often a sign of poor personal organisation and planning as well as selfishness. There are controls and sanctions to prevent abuse: most libraries have electronic checking systems and impose fines for overdue books. Ultimately, however, students have to be relied upon to adopt a sensible attitude towards using library resources. Otherwise, the only answer may be to follow the continental system of barring direct access to the shelves.

Language resource centres

You may be fortunate enough to be in a department which has its own resource centre, or your institution's library may have a good collection of non-book materials for language students. Most language departments receive at least two or three magazines for each of the foreign languages they offer, and some have a much wider range of daily papers and weekly reviews as well as more specialised monthly, bi-annual or other journals, government and institutional publications, which supplement or complement the main library stock. Audio and video resources may include both specially made taped materials for your particular programme of study, commercially sold language courses, programmes received by satellite television and also facilities for making your own audio and video recordings.

As the emphasis in language degree courses has shifted towards the study of contemporary societies through their language, both oral and written, the press and other media have become major sources of up-to-date information for language study. It is essential to get into the habit of regularly reading at least one newspaper thoroughly as well as skimming others for key articles or information. You should be listening to radio programmes and watching as much televised material as is available. It is important to try to obtain a balanced view of events by reading papers with opposing political leanings and different intellectual styles. You should also try to extend your range of aural registers by listening to or watching different types of radio and television programmes.

Your resources centre will probably hold taped courses providing practice in morphological or phonetic drills, which you can use for private study, if they are not part of a prescribed course, to help you overcome particular problems you have identified.

Computers and language learning

Most language departments in higher education are equipped with some form of computers, and this is becoming an increasingly important learning resource for linguists. There are many different styles and types of machines, referred to as hardware, and also a variety of learning packages, known as software. You may already have had experience of working with computers at school, and it may simply be a question of adapting to a new type of machine or exercise.

If you are not familiar with computers, you should try to take advantage of the opportunity to learn about them and from them, as they have become an essential part of modern life.

HARDWARE

In some cases you will be working with individual personal computers; in others you will be linked by terminals to your institution's main-frame computer or to a network of micro-computers. Your terminal could also be connected to other sorts of machinery, such as computer-controlled audio cassettes, videodisks or interactive video. To take one example, a cassette recorder may be placed under the control of a computer and be able to handle a dictation exercise.

You will probably find that you are expected to use the computer on an open access or library basis on the recommendation of your lecturer. Less often it will be integrated into classes. If you are unfamiliar with the equipment, you will be given instruction in how to use it. There is generally a computer officer available to advise you or simple written instructions you can follow, and you will not normally be expected to learn to program. The machine is a tool to help you to learn, as is the tape recorder or video player.

SOFTWARE

You may already be familiar with some of the software from your experience at school. It is very costly in terms of time to produce language learning materials on computers, and the amount available is therefore limited, particularly at an advanced level. Most of the materials are useful for remedial purposes or for the improvement of particular skills. Even advanced learners can benefit from some of the structural drills. This is probably the type of exercise where the computer is at its most useful. It is a valuable learning tool for morphology and accuracy in cases where repetition can help reinforce knowledge. In many ways the computer offers you, in the written medium, some of the same learning tools as the audio or video cassette does in the spoken medium.

Courses, sequences or series of individual exercises rely on what are known as page-based systems. A page of information is presented. As demonstrated by the diagram, if you give the right response you are led on to other pages or texts. If your response is incorrect you may be given another chance, and there is the possibility of reinforcement for specific points where necessary. You are taken through what is described as a process of programmed learning, with a succession of learning steps or stages and a test at each point, and the possibility of continuing to the next stage or of branching to seek further help.

FLOW CHART OF THE STAGES IN A LANGUAGE EXERCISE

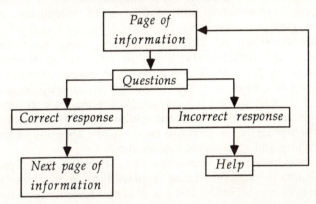

There are many variations in the types of exercises available and in their purposes. You may be asked to follow a question and answer sequence, as in the diagram, or fill in slots or gaps, the latter usually involving guesswork. Quizzes may be designed to test knowledge already possessed (grammatical, lexical and cultural) or for checking information. Other exercises require you to manipulate text, by transforming structures or building sentences. Some programs extend to translation exercises and note-taking.

Like the audio tape, the computer exercise has the advantage that you are in control and can work at your own pace by stopping or rerunning the program if you want to. Unlike the teacher, the machine has infinite patience and can wait for you to make up your mind or have another try. The computer has the added advantage over audio materials of being able to assess and react to your responses and to give you immediate comment on your performance at times when a teacher may not be available, provided that it has been programmed to answer your particular questions.

Recent developments are extending the ways in which computers can assist in language acquisition through more sophisticated learning tasks. Dictionaries and glossaries can be built up, as well as other types of database. For example a file may contain information about a town or the details you would need to enable you to compile your own bibliography. The computer can also help you to learn how to discover information by using sort and search techniques. Your bibliography can, for example, be retrieved after being sorted in alphabetical order or by subject. You can check your own work by referring to computerised dictionaries, term banks, spelling and style checkers. You may have a link to videotex systems in other countries, such as *Minitel* in France or *Bildschirmtext* in the Federal Republic of Germany. These are interactive systems whereby the viewer is connected with databases by telephone, using a modified television monitor.

Whatever stage of language learning you have reached, computers are particularly valuable as writing tools, using wordprocessing packages. The computer can assist in the structuring and writing of essays or project planning, working up from a short plan to a substantial piece of work. What makes a computer so versatile in this type of task is that it allows you to rework material, to add another reference, improve on style, pay attention to links and check spelling and agreements systematically.

You may have heard of machine-based translation. The prospects of the human translator being replaced by a machine for the translation of non-technical texts is distant. However, you may find that you can use the wordprocessing application to help you experiment with different versions of a text, and there are some packages available with translation exercises. If you are planning to become a professional translator, you will probably recognise that the personal computer is going to be an important, if not essential, tool of your trade.

PREPARING FOR ASSESSMENT AND EXAMINATIONS

However much you enjoy your course and whatever the personal benefits you feel you gain from it, the most tangible evidence of success is the degree result you achieve at the end. For some careers it is essential not just to have a degree, but to have a good class of degree. A pass, ordinary or third class may exclude you from some professions. You therefore need to ensure that you prepare yourself adequately for all the work which will count towards your final result, although you should remember that, directly or indirectly, everything you do throughout the course will contribute to your overall assessment.

You will want to know how you will be assessed, how to plan and complete assessed work and how to revise for and tackle written examination questions, what the penalties are for failure to meet course requirements and what to expect from oral examinations.

You should not, however, become so concerned with assessment and examinations that they obscure the general objectives and benefits of higher education. Approached and managed sensibly, the assessment process can be a positive learning experience, for it provides targets, a means of monitoring progress and recognising attainment and, for the institution, a way of maintaining objectively measured standards.

Patterns of examination and assessment

The first stage in preparing yourself for examinations and assessment is to find out what the pattern is in your institution and for your particular programme of study.

INSTITUTIONAL REGULATIONS

Since there is considerable variation from one institution to another, you need to check the regulations and ensure that you meet all the requirements, for example by following the right number of courses to give you the appropriate total for units of assessment.

Examinations sat at the end of the first and second year of the course may be 'qualifying', in that they allow you to proceed to the next stage of the course. If you fail to satisfy the examiners in part of the examination at the end of the year, you may be referred in one or two papers and allowed to retake them in the following September. If you fail several elements, you may be asked to repeat or resit the year, with or without attendance. You are unlikely to be given a grant to follow a course for a second time, so the consequences of failure can be serious.

In some cases, second-year examinations and some form of assessment from the period of residence abroad may count towards your final degree result, which means that you can never afford to reduce your effort and think you can have an easy year.

The method of assessing a particular course may change from one year to another, so it is always essential to check up-to-date information and to make sure you have understood what is expected. The course descriptions you receive at the beginning of the year should include details of how your work will be assessed, when the deadlines are and what form examinations will take, or this information may be posted on notice boards.

CONTINUOUS ASSESSMENT AND/OR EXAMINATIONS

Practices differ within institutions from one department to another concerning the balance between continuous assessment and papers which are written under examination conditions. Examinations may take place during the year or at the end of the year, and they may be replaced by class tests, when the institution's administration is not involved in their organisation. Some courses still rely almost solely on end-of-year examinations, and particularly on those sat at the end of the course; others combine continuous assessment and examinations in varying proportions; very few degree courses, if any, have adopted continuous assessment to the exclusion of examinations.

Examinations can take a number of forms which depart from the standard three-hour unseen paper: you may be given papers in advance of the examination; you may be allowed to take the paper away and spend several days preparing and writing up your answers; or you may have an open-book examination, where you can take your notes into the examination room. If you are given the opportunity to search for information, to prepare answers or use course notes, then the level of accuracy and depth of approach expected of you will be greater than for an answer written under time pressure without access to supporting materials. Again you need to practise accordingly.

The meaning attributed to continuous assessment is also subject to variation. It may imply that, for assessment, at different stages in the year, you are required to submit specific assignments, such as an essay or a lengthy translation, which then count towards your mark at the end of the year. In some cases the requirement may be that you complete the standard coursework assignments, although a quantitative mark is not recorded. Sometimes a grade derived from coursework will be taken into consideration by a board of examiners, if you are on a borderline or if your performance is believed to have been affected by medical or personal circumstances. At the other end of the spectrum are the courses where every piece of written work submitted is assessed quantitatively and counted towards the final mark.

Although ideally lecturers would like students to devote the same amount of care, effort and attention to all work set, whether it counts towards the final assessment or not, they are realistic enough to appreciate that students will aim to perform best at the work which they know is going to determine their final class of degree. It is in your own interest to ensure that you take account of how you will be assessed when planning your work methods. If your standard of performance is going to be judged on the basis of nine papers written under examination conditions at the end of three or four years of study, you will need to spend a great deal of time training yourself in examination techniques. Underperformance in examinations is known to be as much an indication of lack of practice and the inability to adapt skills to different circumstances as it is of inadequate knowledge of the subject and intellectual deficiency.

If, on the other hand, every language assignment you are given from the beginning of the second year is counted in conjunction with four or five examination papers based on the same exercises, you need to ensure not only that your coursework is of a consistently high standard but also that you do not neglect to learn how to work without dictionaries and other aids and within a fixed amount of time.

Where essay work is assessed outside the examination room at different points in the year, you will want to be certain that you allow adequate time for preparation and checking and that you observe instructions about length and guidelines for presentation and, especially, deadlines. In some institutions late submission is penalised by a percentage reduction, according to the amount of lateness and, if the reasons given are not considered adequate, a mark of zero may be awarded. Few students miss examinations due to poor personal organisation, but many miss deadlines for continuous assessment because they have not planned their work carefully.

MARKING PATTERNS

Marking schemes generally give roughly equal weighting to different papers, but there are many variations in practice: in some cases the oral mark may have to be in line with the average for all papers in order to justify a particular degree class; elsewhere it may be necessary to achieve a pass in written language papers to be awarded a degree; the mark for a project in the third or final year may be given extra weighting, or it may be considered as part of coursework. In order to obtain a good degree result, you will normally be expected to perform well across a wide range of papers or units of assessment, which is why, for example on combined subject degrees, it may be especially difficult to achieve a first class degree result and why you cannot neglect any part of the course by not completing assignments.

Often a particular paper will be made up from a number of different components, sometimes a combination of continuous assessment and examination. You will want to know how the different elements within a paper are weighted, how many questions you will need to answer and how long you will have to write your answers, so that you can ensure you devote an appropriate amount of time to each section. When you are preparing an assignment, it is important to observe word limits and to know how questions are likely to be phrased. The penalty for not following instructions is inevitably that you cannot achieve the marks which your effort and ability might otherwise deserve.

Examinations and work which counts towards the end-of-year result are normally marked by more than one person, and an external examiner from another institution can inspect any work which counts towards a degree result. The purpose is to ensure that common standards are observed across the country. This means that you are not dependent on only one person's opinion of your work. Nor are you competing against other students for a ranking, as there are theoretically no set limits on the number of students who can obtain a particular class of degree in any one institution. You are therefore aiming at an absolute standard, but one where your pattern of marks throughout the course is likely to offer a fair indication of your final result.

CHEATING AND PLAGIARISM

It is rare for you not to be given some test where you can rely only on your own resources. If there is a very marked discrepancy between work under examination conditions and that done with access to materials and without rigid time constraints, examiners may express doubts about your abilities. You run the risk of being suspected of not being capable of working unaided.

One of the reasons why examinations have not disappeared completely from the assessment process is that they are recognised as a fairly reliable way of measuring what students can do without assistance from others. A consequence of the need to be able to assess individual ability is that in academic life there are severe penalties for cheating. The most extreme form of punishment for cheating can be exclusion from public examinations or being sent down. Expressed more euphemistically, a student can be asked to withdraw.

One form of cheating, sometimes perpetrated unwittingly, is plagiarism, which means that an author's work is used without being attributed to its source. This can occur in examinations where a student learns a text by heart and reproduces it verbatim, although examination questions are generally designed so that they do not lend themselves to this practice. Plagiarism is more common in essays written for continuous assessment, where the dividing line between quoting, paraphrase and analysis is not always very clearly defined. Students are not expected to be an authority on a subject, but they are required to know what other people have said and to be able to analyse and evaluate the opinions expressed. There are many legitimate ways of presenting other people's ideas and arguments (see pages 98-100), which you will learn as an undergraduate.

An important learning technique for a student of language is imitation, and you may be asked to produce a pastiche or to transpose a text into a prescribed style, so that it reads like a genuine text in which the reader can identify the usual features of writing characteristic of that context. If you are asked to translate an administrative document, you will need to make the language correspond as closely as possible to the normal jargon of the appropriate register. By regularly practising the exercises during the year and carefully observing the advice given by your lecturers, you will know what is permissible and how to identify the limits between creative reproduction and plagiarism.

Boards of examiners have discretion in all matters concerning examinations and they will decide whether action should be taken in cases where students are suspected of malpractice. If you feel there are factors which may have affected your performance or which have led you to act in a particular way, it is up to you to bring them to the attention of the board by writing to its chairman. There is an appeals procedure if for any reason you think justice has not been done.

CHECKLIST OF PROCEDURES

In summary, there are a number of questions which you can try to answer in order to check whether you know and understand the arrangements for examinations and assessment:

1. According to your institution's regulations, how many units of assessment are there for your course?

2. What is the status of end-of-year examinations and what are the procedures should you fail any units?

3. Is your course evaluated on the basis of continuous assessment and/or examination?

4. What proportion of the marks are allocated to continuous assessment and to examinations and what are the different components in each paper or unit of assessment?

5. What form does continuous assessment take?

6. What is the status of coursework?

7. What form do examinations take (open-book, take-away), what is their length, how many questions do you have to answer, what type of questions are they, how are the different components weighted and are you allowed to take reference works into the examination?

8. What are the standards expected of undergraduates at a particular point in their course?

9. What are the deadlines for continuous assessment and what are the dates of examinations?

10. What are the penalties for missing deadlines?

11. What is meant by plagiarism and what are the penalties for cheating?

Planning for continuous assessment and revising for examinations

The importance of observing deadlines has been repeated on several occasions in this chapter, and you have seen that the sanctions for not doing so can be severe. You may not always be given all your essay titles at the beginning of the year, but you will know from the syllabus the topics to be covered and the questions to be discussed in seminars. By reading the supporting materials as they are prescribed, regularly attending lectures and seminars and by building up a good set of notes on each topic, you should be able to avoid a last minute panic by knowing you have covered the ground.

DEVELOPING TECHNIQUES FOR EXAMINATIONS AND ASSESSMENT

Where examinations still carry the bulk of the marks for a course, you will want to invest as much time and effort as possible in developing your examinations technique. You should plan your schedule with special care in the three or four weeks leading up to the examination period, so that you devote adequate time to preparing for each paper, bearing in mind its relative importance and the confidence you have in your knowledge of the relevant materials.

If you have developed a good note-taking technique and have organised your notes efficiently (see pages 71-9), you will be able to go back through them and highlight the main points and arguments you need to remember. Experiments on memory training demonstrate that the more you go over work during the year the easier it is to assemble knowledge for an examination. The process is one of consolidation rather than learning afresh. Revision on the evening before an examination should be aimed at reviving or reinforcing the points which are the main pegs on which you hang your knowledge. Understanding is another important component in the retention of information; it comes from thinking through concepts and ideas as you go along and when you still have a chance to check and ask questions if you are unsure.

Classes will be set aside towards the end of the year to help to guide you through your revision but, mostly, the onus is on you to ensure that you have checked the format of the examination and know what the examiners expect. You should identify the types of questions you answer best, assemble the necessary materials and go through as many practice answers as you can. Frequent testing is known to help improve performance. If you are not formally tested, you can test yourself by working through exercises from previous papers in a fixed length of time.

Many examination questions will take the form of essays, but these are likely to be different from the essays you have been writing during the year, so you will need to adopt a technique appropriate to the examination room, where time is limited and you must have information and ideas at your fingertips. There are several essential differences between the essay written in your own time and that written under examination conditions: the timed essay must be simply structured, tightly organised and selective; the extended essay must demonstrate the ability to undertake research and develop and document coherent arguments at greater length and in greater depth. In an examination where you are asked to write answers in the form of essays, it is important to remember what you have learnt about planning and structuring your work, for the way you argue your case may carry as much weight as the information you include.

Language examinations will test a number of skills which are not looked for in an essay question. The most common language exercise tested under examination conditions is the translation from and into the foreign language, generally without a dictionary. Summary and general essay writing also occur frequently on examination papers. There will normally be words in these exercises which you are uncertain of or cannot translate. Part of your examination technique is knowing how to get round the problem by using near synonyms or a periphrasis or by making an intelligent guess, based on the context and your knowledge of semantic and syntactic structures.

Many people think it is not possible to revise for a language examination. Certainly the best preparation is to have worked regularly at the exercises concerned throughout the course. The examination is designed to assess you at the culminating point of your career as an undergraduate, and the examiners presume that you have reached a peak in your knowledge and expertise. Since you are concerned with a cumulative process, but one in which hurdles are never mastered once and for all, it is very useful to go back through the work you have done, checking any commonly occurring grammatical errors and making sure you know which mistakes to look out for. You should have noted down vocabulary and useful expressions and made your own glossary of terms which you regularly referred to during the year and which you can now look back over to check for genders and spelling. In the examination itself you need to ensure that you allow adequate time for checking your work not only for accuracy but also for omissions. In a translation, if you omit a phrase or sentence, you will lose marks.

You can revise for language exercises by making a mental list of the points to look for and possible ways of interpreting them and by going back over any hints you were given during the year about idiomatic usage. If the examination is in the form of a take-away paper, if you are given the paper in advance or can take reference tools into the examination room, you are being tested not only on your ability to retain information but also on your proficiency in using previous work and accessing resources.

LANGUAGE ACCURACY IN ASSIGNMENTS

Although students in other disciplines may find that they are penalised if their work is illegible and poorly presented, generally expression and accuracy of language are not primary concerns. For linguists, fluency, clarity and precision are essential in coursework and examinations. It is not enough to know your subject and be able to handle materials and develop arguments, you also need to be able to write well in the foreign language, whether you are preparing a summary, a translation, a commentary or an essay.

In some institutions language and content are marked separately, proficiency in the language may earn you a bonus, or the lack of it result in a penalty. Elsewhere you may be told that, however good the content, you cannot score a high mark if the language is inadequate, or conversely that a good standard in the language is not enough if the ideas are poorly developed.

The communicative approach to language learning has tended to emphasise competence in performing a particular task in a given situation. The ability to convey a message may appear to be more important than being able to do so with grammatical and orthographical accuracy. You will find that examiners, and particularly external examiners, are intent on preserving linguistic standards and will not tolerate careless mistakes or work which has not been carefully checked. It is therefore in your interest to ensure that you devote attention to the presentation of your work and that you systematically eliminate any elementary errors and linguistic inadequacies. Legibility is particularly important in a language examination, as you will not be given the benefit of the doubt. When you are working under examination conditions, it is important always to leave yourself time to check back over your script (see page 68), and you should pay attention to ensuring that any work written in a foreign language does not read like a translation from English.

CHECKLIST FOR EXAMINATION PREPARATION

In developing your examination and assessment techniques, you should try to pay attention to the following points:

1. Remember that regular work during the year is the best preparation for continuous assessment and examinations.

2. Practise for examinations using timed exercises and simulated examination conditions.

3. Be aware of the distinction between work written for continuous assessment and that done under examination conditions.

4. Remember that it is possible to revise for language examinations, and make sure you know the points you will need to check.

5. Pay careful attention to linguistic accuracy and style in all your assessed work and examinations.

ORAL AND AURAL EXAMINATIONS

Oral and aural examinations take a number of forms and their weighting or importance may vary from one institution to another. You may have oral and aural examinations at the end of every year or only in finals. You may be given considerable help and guidance in preparing for the examination or you may be left to your own devices. For an oral examination, you may be judged by lecturers you do or do not know, by native speakers who have been teaching you and by an external examiner or moderator. It is important to find out how you will be examined and to think carefully how best to prepare for oral and aural assessments.

FORMS OF ORAL AND AURAL EXAMINATIONS

The oral examination can take a number of forms: you may be asked to read a short text, which you have been given time to prepare in advance, and to answer questions about its language, context and content, leading on to more general discussion; or you may be asked to make an oral presentation on a topic assigned to you some time beforehand, on a subject which you have chosen yourself or on a piece of project work. Aural examinations may consist of an exercise where you are asked to write or record a summary of a text in the same language or a second language. Where interpreting is a course component, you will probably have an oral examination to test your proficiency. This may take the form of a laboratory test or a simulated live situation.

PREPARING FOR ORAL AND AURAL EXAMINATIONS

At the end of a degree course, including a period abroad, you will be expected to know how to present information and ideas cogently and convincingly in the oral situation and how to interact at different levels of formality. Examiners will be looking for an ability to engage in discussion at quite a sophisticated level, both linguistically and in terms of the way you handle arguments and concepts.

You need to prepare yourself for what may be a fairly daunting experience. You can practise with your fellow students and with a native language speaker. You can also record yourself and listen critically to your own performance. If your institution has video recording facilities, it is useful to watch yourself so that you can try to eliminate any annoying physical mannerisms. There are many points which are worth checking: you should know what your common mistakes are; by reviewing and practising you can help to ensure that you automatically select the right gender and make the appropriate agreement; the way you conduct yourself in the oral interview and your oral delivery are also important.

Many language students, particularly on courses which stress communicative competence, perform better in oral than in written examinations. The advantages of the oral situation are that you are operating in an interactive mode, where you can respond to questioning or comments. Often you can choose a topic which interests you and generates enthusiasm. If you have a good command of the language, you should be able to field or divert awkward questions. By demonstrating that you can handle difficult points skilfully, you will have a chance to shine. Although in most parts of a language degree course it is not easy to achieve very high marks, the oral examination is one area where students are able to do extremely well by producing the right tone, stimulating discussion and debate and displaying an ability to handle material and control the situation. Conversely, neglect of the spoken language can result in a very poor overall performance.

Interpreting, like other language exercises, but perhaps even more so, is a technical skill which needs constant and regular practice in order to build up confidence and fluency. Again it is possible to achieve a high mark if your renderings are fluent, accurate and well paced.

While it is often portrayed as a major source of anxiety, an oral examination can turn out to be an opportunity to score high marks, if you prepare carefully and know what you are aiming for.

DIFFICULTIES WITH STUDY METHODS

Reference is often made in education to the learning curve: the expectation is that during your career as an undergraduate you will learn from your experience and improve your performance. Evaluating your own progress is not always easy, and it is therefore important to seek as much feedback as you can from your lecturers. Research has shown that in order to improve students need to know whether their work meets the required standard and whether they are setting themselves appropriate performance targets.

Although the end-of-year grades you are awarded during the course may simply be averages from a wide range of components, it is worth identifying your strong and your weak points by asking for a detailed breakdown of your marks. Most institutions now give students quite full accounts of their end-of-year results. Where you are required to submit work for continuous assessment during the year, you may receive detailed feedback which will help to give you some idea of how you are faring and show you how you can improve on the next assignment. When you do not understand why something is wrong or why you have not done so well as you expected, you can ask the lecturers concerned for an explanation. You should aim always to be open to criticism and try to apply the comments and advice given to you.

If you have read through the whole of this chapter attentively, you should be able to identify some of the warning signs which suggest that you need to seek help. You may have noticed that your attendance at classes is becoming erratic, that you are getting behind with assignments and cannot cope with the work load, or you may have lost a sense of direction and purpose. These signs generally mean that you need to re-examine your motivation and think about ways of improving your study methods.

If you are experiencing difficulties and are not able to analyse the reasons yourself and find solutions to them, many services are available to which you can turn. In British higher education there is a well-developed system of referral. Most departments have a number of formal and informal channels through which students can seek help with academic and personal problems. You should know what the structure of your department is and whom to consult over different types of problem.

Whatever the actual titles used to describe the positions held, the structure of an academic department or school of studies can be represented diagrammatically as follows:

STRUCTURE OF ACADEMIC DEPARTMENTS

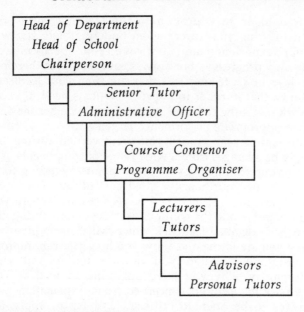

Personal tutors or advisors

Your first line of recourse will probably be a personal tutor or advisor. In most departments, when you enter the first year, you will be allocated to a member of academic staff who will retain this function throughout the programme of study. Your personal tutor may not teach you, or in some cases, where an individual academic tutoring system operates, he or she may set you regular work assignments and go over them with you individually.

Generally your tutor or advisor will have a more pastoral role. He or she will try to see you at regular intervals and be available to discuss your progress in your studies and to advise you over any personal problems. If you establish a good relationship with your tutor, you will find that you can obtain help with study methods and preparation for examinations, as well as difficulties over accommodation or with the administration and for problems of a more personal nature.

Advice on departmental matters

Your personal tutor or advisor may not be able to answer specific questions about the organisation of courses or forms of assessment. For general academic questions about a particular programme of study, there is usually a course or programme organiser or convenor. Individual lecturers and tutors will answer queries about the courses they run. If you cannot find a satisfactory solution through these channels, you may have recourse to a senior tutor, administrative officer or ultimately the head or chairperson of the department or school, who usually acts as the chairman to examinations boards.

Counselling services

Where more specialised advice is needed with learning problems or examination anxiety, a counselling service is usually available on the campus. Examination anxiety is not uncommon and can have a number of different causes: it may be due to fear of failure because of inadequate preparation, or it may be the result of setting goals too high. The solutions may be to avoid the problem by regular study throughout the year or to rethink objectives and occasionally to change courses. Counsellors are trained to identify the causes of stress and anxiety and to offer appropriate advice.

Learning from difficulties

Few, if any, students find that their three or four years as undergraduates are completely trouble-free, either because they encounter problems of a personal nature (in their relationships with other students, in managing their finances or due to ill-health) or in their academic life (achieving the standards required, meeting deadlines or coping with examination stress). Learning how to overcome difficulties and to help other students to do so is an important factor in personal development and character building. Adapting to living away from home, which is a common feature of higher education in Britain, and subsequently to living and studying abroad, as is the usual pattern for language students, is part of the process of becoming self-reliant and independent. You do, however, have the advantage of being able to resort to an extensive support network if your own resources prove to be inadequate. The way you organise yourself as an undergraduate and manage your study can enable you to establish habits and practices which may remain with you throughout your life. For these reasons it is worthwhile making sure you gain full benefit from the opportunities afforded while you are in higher education.

> **SUMMARY OF SUGGESTIONS**
>
> 1. You should make sure you know why you want to study for a degree and be aware of all the benefits to be gained as well as the effort you need to make.
>
> 2. You will want to ensure that you create optimum working conditions by having a suitable place to study and knowing how to organise your time, so that you develop a regular pattern of work.
>
> 3. You should try to eliminate time-wasting behaviour by avoiding distractions, but you should also aim to strike a healthy balance between work and play.
>
> 4. It is important to learn how to use library resources, so that you can easily find the materials you need and can fully exploit reference works, periodicals, bibliographies and statistical collections.
>
> 5. You should aim to make use of all multimedia language resources, including foreign language newsprint, video and audio cassettes, radio and television broadcasts and computers, by attending classes and setting aside time for private study.
>
> 6. You must ensure that you are familiar with the regulations for your course and that you have full details of the pattern and method of examination and assessment.
>
> 7. It is worth spending time developing your examination technique and learning how to revise effectively.
>
> 8. You should pay special attention to appropriateness and accuracy of language in all assessed work and prepare carefully for oral and aural examinations.
>
> 9. It is important to make sure you know where to look for help and advice if you are having difficulties with your studies or if you have personal problems.

3 STUDY SKILLS

Developing good study habits, knowing how to locate materials and what you are aiming for at the end of the course are essential prerequisites for effective study. By mastering the basic study skills at an early stage as an undergraduate, you will be well prepared to perform the language tasks which are assigned to you, both while you are a student and in professional life. In this chapter guidance is given on how to acquire the skills you will need, focusing on the following:

1. Learning the techniques of skimming, scanning and reading a text for ideas and language.

2. Note-taking on reading and from lectures, with emphasis on extracting meaning and information and organising materials in note form.

3. Knowing how to abstract and summarise content, how to carry out text analysis and commentary, with particular reference to the characteristic features of different language registers.

4. Preparing for, planning and writing academic essays.

5. Oral interaction and participation in a group situation.

As for students in other subjects, especially in the social sciences and humanities, your work will be structured mainly around private study, lectures and smaller group work. You will need to master the same skills of reading and note-taking, understanding lectures and making notes, abstracting, summarising, analysing materials, planning and writing essays and working together with other students. A skill can be defined as a technique which is well practised so that the learner becomes proficient in it. Skills are said to be directed towards helping to establish a framework and a structure for study.

Compared with non-language undergraduates, in every activity there will be an additional dimension to your studies, in that your programme requires you to understand and manipulate materials and produce work in a foreign language. It is therefore all the more important for you to be competent in the basic study skills, so that you can devote enough effort to accuracy, appropriateness and style in the language. If you cannot read easily in English and make useful notes on your reading, or if you have difficulty in following a lecture and taking notes in your own language, you will find the problems are compounded when you try to do so in a foreign language.

In this chapter, guidance is given about the main study skills, but with particular reference to their linguistic dimension. They are considered in terms of a progression: you need to know how to read effectively before you can become proficient at extracting information and noting it down. Extracting is an essential step towards summarising. The ability to write an abstract is one component in the process of analysis. Critical appraisal is an important stage in preparing materials which are to be presented in an essay. Small group interaction depends upon the ability to present information and ideas orally and to be receptive to meaning and tone in listening to others. Although you may not be directly tested on each of the skills you are learning, they are all part of the cumulative process of language acquisition and contribute to the consolidation of your knowledge.

READING

Some authors of books on study skills maintain that, in the humanities, reading is the most important single skill, accounting for as much as ninety per cent of private study time. The expression 'reading for a degree', which is still in use, illustrates how central reading has always been to academic learning and how other activities can be considered as adjuncts. For language courses which place emphasis on productive skills and oral fluency, reading may not occupy such a high proportion of your time, but it is still likely to account for a substantial part of your work schedule and will underpin most of your study activities. If you can become a fast and retentive reader, then you will have a good foundation for many of the language tasks you are expected to perform.

Two main approaches to learning have been identified by researchers: some undergraduates find it easier to understand a subject if they first have an overview, or synthesis, of the whole field, before going on to look at individual topics; others find they work better by studying one concept, or section, at a time, building up to a total picture. Applied to languages, the difference would be between the student who needs to have a sound knowledge of grammar rules, syntax and lexis in order to feel confident in using the language and the student who concentrates on productive skills before mastering the subtleties of grammatical, syntactic and lexical structures.

Your preference may not correspond to the way the syllabus for your course is organised: if the serial approach is adopted, where topics are studied in series, one after another, and you feel you need to have a general overview, you may need to compensate by reading round the subject; if your preference is for the serial approach, and the lecturer follows a holistic plan, where emphasis is on the total picture, you may want to read further on into the course so that you can understand how the topics relate to one another. In both cases, the ability to read independently is a key factor in following the structure of the course.

For students who are not on language courses, reading is primarily for content or gist. For you, however, language is as important as content. Unless you are studying a language as a beginner, much of the material you are called upon to read as an undergraduate should be in your foreign language. You will want to be able to read intensively and closely, concentrating on the form (vocabulary and syntactic structures) as well as the content.

Reading techniques

Reading can have a number of purposes and may take different forms. You will find that reading lists provided by lecturers often classify books as 'required' or 'recommended' reading. Sometimes you will be directed towards a particular chapter or journal article. For projects or essays you may be expected to select from a reading list or to carry out your own library search. You will therefore want to be competent in all the reading techniques, which are generally referred to as skimming, scanning, reading for study or checking and light reading.

SKIMMING

You may want to skim through or survey a book or article in order to extract the main gist and ideas or to find out whether it is going to be of interest and use for the task in hand. For this purpose, you will be looking at the title, author's name and date of publication to see whether they are relevant, authoritative and up to date. The cover of a book, introduction or preface, table of contents, index, chapter summaries and key words will tell you whether you want to read parts of it in more detail. For journal articles there may be a summary or abstract which you can refer to, and section headings will also provide a useful reference point.

SCANNING

If you are scanning a book or article, you will be trying to find out what a particular author's opinions are on a subject or to identify and extract information which will help you answer a specific question. Scanning can be very useful in searching for specialised terminology in context. The same entry points can be used as for skimming, but you will want to focus on a particular section once you have identified it as being relevant to your query of the moment. Clues which will help you to identify opinions and facts quickly may be found in the first or last sentences of paragraphs.

READING FOR STUDY

You may be asked to study a set text critically and to assess its literary value, or you may need to read a complex text in order to grasp the details of a linguistic theory. In both cases the aim is to absorb all the major points and arguments and to be able to answer questions about the content and often the style as well. You will probably need to read the text, or parts of it, several times. After first skimming and scanning so that you have an overview, you will be ready to embark on careful selective and critical reading.

READING FOR CHECKING

This form of reading applies when you are checking, proof-reading or editing a piece of work for technical accuracy of spelling, punctuation, grammatical and syntactic structures, as well as consistency and appropriateness of tone and register. Many language students complain that they cannot see their own mistakes. To be a good proof-reader, you need to be alert and systematic and to know what you are looking for. By going back over work which you have had corrected, you should be able to identify the situations where you are most prone to make mistakes. It is always useful to plan your term-time written assignments so that you can check the final version several days after writing it, when you should be able to approach your work more objectively. Reading for checking can also apply to the work of another author. It is useful to get into the habit of selectively checking, for example, all the verbs, adverbial phrases or adjectives used in a paragraph, in order to reinforce or expand your own knowledge.

LIGHT READING

What you would normally consider as light reading in your own language may, at least until you are sufficiently experienced, be more like reading for study when the materials are in a foreign language. This may be the case for novels or the foreign press. Your tutors should be able to recommend a programme of reading, beginning with relatively straightforward novels or other general texts, which can be used to try to get yourself into the habit of reading fast and with ease. In the case of the press, you can start with some of the less intellectual papers or magazines and try to skim and scan to keep yourself up to date with events, while also focusing on specific articles which catch your interest and which you can read at first for study and later, as you become more proficient, for pleasure.

Improving your reading skills

Depending upon the purpose of your reading, and consequently the technique you are using, you will need to adapt your rate. Unless you learn to read quickly and extensively, as well as intensively, you will never be able to keep up with the sheer volume of material there is to consult.

Reading speed does vary considerably from one person to another. In English fewer than 200 words per minute for an educated person is slow, and you should be aiming at a figure nearer to 400, which represents about a page of a printed book. In your foreign language you will be trying to achieve a speed as near as possible to the average for English, which would be between about 250 and 300 words per minute.

If you think your reading is slow—and you can check by timing yourself—then you should look at ways of improving your speed. Much has been written about speed reading techniques. It is possible to reduce the number of eye fixations needed to cover a line of text, to focus eye movements on the centre of a column of text and to avoid rereading lines or sentences. Regular daily practice is recommended to improve speed, preferably at the same time every day, for about fifteen to twenty minutes. You can practise reading straightforward newspaper articles from the same paper over several weeks. You should try to read as fast as you can without sacrificing comprehension, noting the number of words and the time spent so that you can work out your rate per minute. To check whether you have understood and retained the main points, try to jot them down immediately you finish reading.

As a linguist interested in form as well as content, you should be using your reading to increase your vocabulary, your knowledge of syntactic structures and language registers. You therefore need to develop two skills in parallel: rapid or extensive reading for content; receptive or intensive reading for language. As they are mutually reinforcing, you will be doing yourself a double service if you work at improving your reading in both respects.

Reading speed is known to be affected by difficulties in understanding. These may result from problems with vocabulary and syntactic structures, from an indadequate knowledge of the material or from difficulties in understanding concepts, particularly where the writer's presuppositions are founded in a different cultural environment from that of the reader. Therefore by improving your linguistic ability you will increase your rate. By reading more extensively, because you can read faster, you will further enhance your knowledge of the language and your subject.

You should be in the habit of keeping a record of any new or unusual words and expressions, checking on their usage and learning them. You will find that it pays dividends for other language tasks if you make a point of noting frequently recurring link phrases or structures which seem characteristic of the writing in a particular context. It is worthwhile taking your time at first, with the idea that, as you build up your vocabulary and your knowledge of the subject, you will be able to read much more easily and fluently.

The literature on reading skills generally refers to a method of approaching a text called SQ3R. The system was originally designed for secondary schools and is said not to be appropriate for complex argument. It does not, however, exclude detailed and careful study of texts and it can provide a useful summary of the stages involved in effective reading:

S   The first letter is for *survey*, meaning that you skim and scan a book or article in order to gain an overall impression of it.

Q   The second letter stands for *question*, implying that you should ask yourself what you want to gain from reading a text so that you are reading with a purpose.

R   The first of the three Rs stands for *read*, meaning that you will probably first read through the text fairly quickly to identify the author's approach to the subject, before studying arguments and illustrations in more detail in order to be able to evaluate the ideas.

R   The second R is for *recall*, implying that you should note down the main points in a text, preferably as you finish each section.

R   The third R indicates *review*, suggesting that you check back over a section and make sure you have accurately recorded the main points.

L   Rather than being an extra stage, you might frame your SQ3R with an L for *language* to remind yourself that you should always be checking for new vocabulary or idiomatic usage and noting it down as you go along:

$$\underline{|\text{SQ3R}}$$

NOTE-TAKING

Research shows that students who make notes retain more information than those who do not. By making notes, you have a record which you can refer back to at a later stage, and you are likely to adopt a more active attitude towards your reading. The advantage of taking notes is that they force you to summarise ideas and arguments, and therefore to select relevant points and see the relationship between ideas. They will help you to understand and interpret source materials and encourage you to clarify and adjust your own perspectives on a topic. Since your visual memory will be activated, notes can also provide a valuable means of reinforcement of knowledge.

Even when reading is not in preparation for a particular assignment, it is important to develop the habit of taking notes on content which will be understandable and usable for reference and revision. If you have your own copies of books, you can mark key sections, but it is still useful to keep notes so that you can trace references when you need them.

The notes you take on lectures will involve the same basic techniques. Language tasks, such as abstracting and summarising, will also call on the same skills for selecting and recording essential information.

The characteristics of good notes are that they are concise, clear and in a form which can be easily understood. Notes, like study habits, are very personal, and it is therefore unusual for one student to find another student's notes helpful. The onus is on you to develop your own note-taking practices through a personalised system.

Content and organisation

The point of having a good set of notes, whether they are based on your reading or on lectures, is that they will enable you to bring together information from different sources and to reconstruct the rest of the material as needed. It is important to establish a note-taking technique which will enable you afterwards to pick out the main points, follow any leads and elaborate on the material under discussion from your own reading. Most authors on study skills recommend getting into the habit of using loose-leaf sheets, writing on one side of the paper, being generous over spacing and always starting a new page for a new subject.

To avoid making copious notes from books or journals which you may never want to use, you should start by reading according to the scheme outlined above, identifying the sections and the aspects of a text which are likely to be most relevant. All the points which you extract initially, in order to understand the text, may not be needed in the longer term, and you may want to add some cross-references of your own to other works as part of the process of critical appraisal. It is therefore important to spend time rearranging your notes, to leave space for additions and to check back through them while you still have the source text available to see whether they enable you to make a logical reconstruction of the argument.

There are three categories of information contained in reading matter and lectures:

- *Facts* You will probably find it is easy to identify and record factual information using chapter headings and indexes and illustrative materials.

- *Concepts* Concepts, like theories, argument and ideas, are more difficult to handle. Conclusions to chapters or summaries may help you to pick out the main ideas and the stages in their development, as well as supporting evidence.

- *References* It is important to be in the habit of noting down any useful references within chapters, taking full details from the bibliography so that you can subsequently follow them up. You will want to record the essential information already mentioned in the previous chapter: author's name, initial, title of book or article, publisher, date and place of publication and relevant page numbers, as well as the library catalogue reference if appropriate.

Although you will probably make your notes on loose-leaf sheets of paper, it might be useful to consider keeping a card index (organised alphabetically and/or by topic) for references. You might also keep a note on your cards of the main topics covered in a book or any other useful information, together with an indication of the place where you have filed your notes on a particular book.

The form of notes

Notes which are simply a summary of material may not be very useful when it comes to writing an assignment or revising for an examination. Note-taking affords the opportunity to rearrange material in a way which will be useful at a later date. This implies that you are reading with a specific purpose in mind, such as gaining an insight into the thinking of different individuals on a particular topic, documenting the events which provide the background to an understanding of contemporary affairs or preparing for an essay on a specific theme.

It is better to take notes which record the essential points rather than copying out sentences or paragraphs from the original text, except if you intend to quote them verbatim. Unlike the abstract or summary, which you may be required to write as a language exercise, your notes do not need to be in the form of complete sentences. You will normally omit articles and other grammar words where they do not add anything to the meaning. You will want to pay attention to layout which should be used, rather than punctuation, to indicate new points and stages in an argument. You will need to develop your own set of abbreviations or symbols, which will stay with you throughout your undergraduate career and possibly beyond, and you should give consideration to the language in which you take your notes.

LAYOUT

The clarity of notes can be greatly improved by getting into the habit of organising information so that the visual display is meaningful. If you use different levels of subheading, indentation and numbering systems, you will quickly be able to spot important points as well as the relationship between them. Underlining, circling and highlighting of key words with different coloured pens will also help you to identify the structure of the main ideas. It is useful to leave space where you can add other relevant points or critical notes derived from your own reflection on the subject and from other reading. A typical set of notes, using what is fast becoming the most popular numbering system, might be set out as follows:

LINEAR NOTES

<u>GENERAL TOPIC AREA</u> *Author's name, bibliographical details* *and other general information*	<u>Notes</u> *For your own* *comments*

1 FIRST MAIN HEADING	Linguistic
for an outline of the general	points
approach to a topic	References

1.1 *First level of subheading*
    to indicate each of the main
    arguments

1.1.1 *Second level of subheading*
      for examples or illustrations,
      e.g. using further levels
      of indentation

2 SECOND MAIN HEADING
  for the second main point or idea

2.1 *First level of subheading*
    for further arguments

Most authors on study skills suggest students should experiment with alternatives to the standard linear form of notes, by using diagrammatic notes, or what have come to be known as patterned notes from a system described by Buzan (1982).

Unlike linear notes which run from the top to the bottom of a page, patterned notes start in the centre and radiate outwards. The main heading, concept or idea is placed in the middle and what, in the linear system, would be different levels of subheading become the radials which can further branch in other directions.

This system is said to have the advantage of being open-ended, which means that more materials can be added, and any one line of argument can be developed as required. Since the pattern is easy to memorise and recall, a set of patterned notes can serve as a useful aid in revision. Critics of the system argue that it lacks a sense of sequence, coherence and hierarchy and that the overall pattern may only become visible when the notes are complete.

A variation on patterning is provided by diagrammatic notes which may take the form of a tree branching out in different directions. New branches or a root system can be created as required in the same way as for patterned notes. Some people recommend a hybrid system whereby headings are presented down the page with branches leading out from them.

The following is an example of patterned notes showing the different levels of heading and the way in which new radials can be added when necessary:

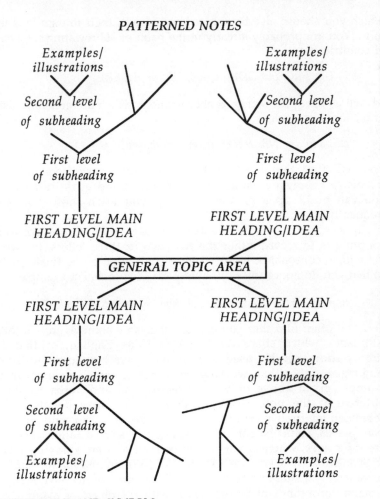

ABBREVIATIONS AND SYMBOLS

Any abbreviations and symbols in notes must be immediately recognisable, unambiguous and meaningful. There is no point in using them if several months later you can no longer decipher your notes.

Abbreviations and symbols fall into two categories: those which are standard or conventional and widely used; those which are *ad hoc* and personal which you work out for yourself. Standard abbreviations would include acronyms such as:

NATO or *UNESCO*

which you should also be able to recognise in their foreign language form. You are probably already in the habit of abbreviating the names of countries to:

F, GB, FRG and GDR, It, Jap, NL, Sp, USSR,

as well as using the standard abbreviations which are generally listed in dictionaries, such as:

adj, adv, eg, NB, etc, cf, ie, et seq, ibid, viz, p.

You will find that the French, for example, very frequently use initials to abbreviate names of organisations and qualifications, and you can build up a glossary to help you learn those you meet frequently.

In deciding on your own abbreviations of words, a practice worth adopting is to record either the first two or three letters, or two or three main consonants, followed by an indication of the final syllable, so that you do not confuse different parts of speech. For example:

Imp of understd^g soc, ec, pol dvp^t for incrs^g int colbr^n

You will often find that you can use the same abbreviations in other languages which share the same roots as English, or that one abbreviation can be used almost as a symbol across different languages, rather than working out a new form every time. In the example given above only the prepositions and verbs would be different if the notes were in French. You may decide to use abbreviations from your different languages to avoid ambiguity: for example *wk* could be confusing in English, so you might choose to use it for *week*, whereas *work* could be *tr*, if you are studying French or Spanish, *Arbt* if you are a student of German and *lvr* for students of Italian. You should also try to think in terms of near-synonyms or semantic groupings of words, again with the object of avoiding the need to look for new abbreviations all the time.

Symbols have the advantage of being translingual and also of conveying meaning rather than sounds, which is useful because it makes you concentrate on understanding a text or a lecture. There are a few commonly used symbols, which you probably already know, such as:

∴	therefore		∵	because
<	less than		>	greater than
)(	unlike		//	similarly
/	for an alternative			

Various forms and directions of arrows can be used to show that one point follows from or leads on to another.

You can develop other symbols for yourself to denote words or expressions and also concepts which are common currency in your topic area. Some further suggestions are made in the next chapter with reference to note-taking for interpreting (see pages 147-9).

LANGUAGE AND NOTE-TAKING

Students in other disciplines are often advised to try to use their own words in their notes because it forces them to think about meaning rather than form. Many of the points made above suggest how notes which focus on meaning transcend language. This is not to say that the language in which you make your notes is irrelevant. You will want to use every opportunity to improve your linguistic proficiency. The underlying principle should be that you always make your notes in the language in which you are reading or to which you are listening, except perhaps for interpreting (see page 147).

There is also a case for arguing that, when you are reading in a foreign language, you should aim to make a note of at least some of the vocabulary and phraseology of the original text, for this is a way of extending your own language range, provided that you do understand and subsequently make an effort to learn what you have written down. There may be a case too for including grammar words and other linguistic information in your notes, so that you have a record of genders, for example. Lecturers will form a poor impression of a student who is unable to use the appropriate vocabulary and accurately produce the morphology of the language in work based on foreign source materials. A possible compromise might be to have two sets of notes: one for content and one for linguistic points, or to reserve a column in your notes for language, as suggested in the example of linear notes (pages 73-4).

Taking notes on lectures

Your other main source of information about facts and concepts will be lecture courses. Although the terminology used may vary, by 'lectures' most academics mean the hours spent delivering a monologue before a large group of students, where the purpose is mainly expository and with minimal opportunity for interaction or feedback. The advantages of lectures are that students can be kept abreast of recent developments. Lecturers can help them to adopt a critical approach to a topic by succinctly reviewing an issue and commenting on different bodies of material. Also, a large group of students can all be given the same information at one time.

Attendance at lectures is likely to be voluntary, but since they are generally used to set the pattern of study for small follow-up classes, such as tutorials or seminars, they should be worth attending. Where lectures are given in the foreign language, it is all the more important to use the opportunity of hearing a topic presented orally in a formal language register.

Many students complain that they find it difficult to listen and take notes at the same time, even in English. Yet, without notes, it is well known that the amount retained by memory from a lecture is very small. The more you practise taking notes, the more automatic they will become, so that you will be able to listen carefully without being distracted by thinking about what you are going to write down.

Most lecturers will respond to students looking blank or bewildered by offering additional explanations, and some may help by providing a lecture plan or outline. If there is a plan available, you should try to look at it beforehand so that you have an idea of how the lecture will be structured and know what the main headings will be to which you can peg information.

Lecturers, particularly in a foreign language, will normally make use of verbal signposting or pointers to indicate what is worth noting down, but they may also try to keep the interest of their audience by introducing material intended as entertainment rather than for information. Some of the most important features to look out for are:

- *Repetition* This is used as an important form of oral reinforcement. You should learn to recognise redundancy and repetition so that you do not write down the same thing twice.

- *Rephrasing* Lecturers often express the same point in more than one way to ensure that it is clear, and again you need not take it down twice in your notes.

- *Structuring* You need to be able to identify the message and the way it is structured. The classic structure for a lecture is to begin by giving an outline of the topic, then to present and discuss materials and arguments and, finally, to summarise the main points and suggest follow-up work.

- *Anecdotes* Lecturers sometimes recount anecdotes or give several examples or illustrations, many of which do not need to be recorded in your notes.

- *References* If you are told a reference is on a reading list, you will not need to copy down all the details.

- *Spelling* If you cannot spell a word, try to take it down phonetically so that you can check afterwards. It is worth making a note in the margin of any point you want to clarify.

The main difference between note-taking from reading and from lectures is that you can always reread a passage, whereas you normally only hear a lecture once. Occasionally, lectures are recorded on audio or video tape. Even if you cannot listen to a lecture again, by checking your notes as soon as possible after the lecture, preferably with other students, you should be able to identify any omissions or points you do not understand properly and you can ask for clarification in seminars. By spending considerable time at the beginning of the year going back over lecture notes while they are still fresh in your mind, you will find you can improve your understanding as well as the quality of the notes you take.

Although you may not be called upon to deal with many figures or proper names, most lecturers will refer to dates and names of key individuals or organisations. It is worth practising with a friend jotting down numbers or spelling out names or titles in a foreign language. Otherwise you may find you become so preoccupied with a figure that you miss the argument it was intended to illustrate.

Many of these points are relevant to other written and aural tasks or to those where you are moving between the two channels of expression. Note-taking from a lecture involves the same basic skills as extracting information from a radio or television broadcast, perhaps with the purpose of writing a summary. The different forms of interpreting involve working from aural comprehension through notes to oral production. Practising note-taking from lectures and from reading will help to prepare you for abstracting exercises or essay work and for an oral presentation. If you have not mastered this and other basic skills, it will be much more difficult for you to perform many of the tasks you are assigned.

ABSTRACTING AND ANALYSIS

If you have learnt how to read a text for content and structure, are used to listening to lectures and taped materials and know how to take notes in your own words, you will be in a position to move on to tasks which require you to abstract information, summarise essential ideas and the links between them and analyse texts for content, form and purpose.

Many graduates find that, even if they are not employed professionally in an abstracting service, they are called upon to process large amounts of information in a foreign language, by extracting the essentials and conveying them to others in a form which can be quickly and easily assimilated. This skill is considered to be so important that it is used in one of the tests for candidates at the competitive entrance examinations which are part of the selection process in the elitist sector of higher education in France. There are consequently a number of books in French which give guidance and worked examples both for summarising and analysing texts. These two skills are, moreover, closely related, since abstracting can be considered as one of the components of analysis.

Abstracting and summary writing

The term 'abstract' tends to appear in references to professional contexts, whereas 'summary' is generally used to describe the skill acquired by undergraduates, and this is the distinction made in this section.

An abstract or summary will normally follow the order of the original text and reproduce faithfully and in a condensed form the information and the process of reasoning it contains, without distortion or the omission of any points which are needed for the argument. The author of an abstract or summary should not comment on the text, express his or her own opinions, amplify any points or simply paraphrase. One criterion which has been suggested for judging the quality of the text produced is whether the comments which can be made on it are the same as those which could have been made about the original passage.

The stages which are involved in preparing a summary of a written text are the following:

1. Read through the text quickly to gain an *overall impression* of the content, the author's approach to the subject and the general structure of the passage, making sure you understand what the author is saying and the type of text you are dealing with (technical information, ideas, creative or persuasive discourse).

2. Reread the text slowly underlining or highlighting the *key words* (generally nouns) which most clearly express the author's line of thought and also any important phrases which indicate the main ideas.

3. Make a plan of the text in note form, showing the *hierarchy of points* by using different levels of heading in such a way that you reproduce the structure of the text and the logic behind it, while paying special attention to the paragraphs in the original which will each contain a main idea.

4. Write out your *concluding sentence* to ensure that your summary will follow the right direction.

5. Write out a *summary* from the plan, ensuring you eliminate any details which are not essential. Illustrations and examples used in support of an argument should be synthesised.

6. *Check* your work carefully to make sure you have not exceeded the word limit, that there is no unnecessary information, that you have used the most succinct form of expression, that the spelling and grammar are correct and sentences are linked logically.

If you are working under pressure of time, it may not be practical to follow all these stages. As you gain experience, you should be able to combine the first three by taking notes on the first reading and devoting most of the remaining time to refining your initial draft.

Where you are working from an oral source text to a written summary, you will probably hear the text twice and will be allowed to make notes while you are listening. As with a written source text, you should be identifying the structure of the passage and the author's message and recording key words and the main ideas. You can then follow stages 3 to 6 described above.

When used as an academic exercise the required length of a summary is sometimes specified. Otherwise, the expectation is that the text should be reduced to between a quarter and a third of the original.

There are different views about the style of the summary. You may be expected to reproduce the form, register and tone of the original text, or you may be instructed to use your own style. It is important to follow the instructions scrupulously. Otherwise, you may find that a piece of work which might have qualified as a good summary on many criteria is not awarded the mark you thought you deserved, perhaps simply because you have written fifty words over the prescribed limit or because you have used the wording of the original, or even, as occasionally happens, because the summary has been produced in the wrong language.

Text analysis and commentary

Text analysis and commentary can be considered as an extension of the initial stages of abstracting and summary writing. The two tasks have in common that they require you to understand the text, to identify its structure and the author's intentions, to approach it objectively and to study it rigorously. The main differences between summarising and analysis are that in the latter case you do not have to follow the same linear order in discussing the text and you are expected to comment on the content and form.

You will probably be introduced to text analysis and commentary in your first year as an undergraduate, and it may recur in later years in different forms, involving tasks of different levels of difficulty and complexity. At the beginning of the course you may simply be asked to identify the message the author is trying to convey. At the other extreme, the purpose of the exercise may be to analyse the communicative process as a whole, comparing a particular text with others from the same or different language varieties.

A fundamental exercise which has long been used by the French as an approach to the study of literary texts is the *explication de texte*. More recently it has been replaced, at least in name, by the *analyse de texte*. The main purpose of this exercise is to identify and contextualise the logical structure of a text by analysing the main and secondary ideas and the way they relate to one another, in order to demonstrate the thought process of the author. This may be what you are asked to do on some French courses. Students of German may find that the influence of the German philosophical tradition shapes the approach to text analysis, and that they are required to undertake a critical appraisal which reflects this tradition.

Text analysis, as it is presented in this section, has a much more general application and should help you to learn how to relate a given text to a wider frame of reference by being able to identify its functions, structure and the language norms attributable to different varieties and situations. The diagram presented in the first chapter (page 24) to illustrate the communicative process expresses visually the relationship described here between the author and the reader.

APPROACHES TO TEXT ANALYSIS

Whatever the nature of the text and whether it is written or oral, there are several key questions which you should ask yourself. This also applies to the reading of texts or when you are listening to recorded materials for other purposes, such as discussion or in preparation for essay writing:

1. What is the *source* of the text both in terms of the event which inspired it and the medium and channel through which it is presented to the reader or listener? What is the political persuasion and what is the intellectual level of the book, review, newspaper, magazine, radio or television broadcast concerned?

2. Who is the *sender* of the message, the author of the article or who are the presenters and participants in a broadcast? Are they well

known political figures, artists or journalists? What are their characteristics?

3. Who are the *receivers* of the message likely to be? Will they be well educated and well informed? Will they be looking for facts or comment or an emotional stimulus?

4. In what *context* or circumstances are they likely to be reading the material? Do they have to read or listen to it or can they simply ignore a text if it does not hold their interest?

5. What is the author's *purpose*? Does he or she want to describe, inform, provide a synthesis, debate a subject, convince, persuade, move, entertain, explain, interpret or stimulate reflection?

6. What *form* does the text take? How is it presented physically on the page? Or what are the features of pitch and speed of delivery in the spoken text?

7. What is the *starting point* of the text? Does it begin by a question, a hypothesis, a statement of fact or opinion, a comment, criticism or analysis of an idea? What themes are introduced?

8. What is the *structure* of the text? How are the points organised and sequenced?

9. What *conclusions* does the author draw? Do the arguments justify these conclusions?

10. What is the *tone* of the text? Is it a personalised account of events, or is it objective, didactic, rhetorical or polemical? Is the author negative or positive, enquiring or assertive, satirical, ironic or sarcastic?

11. What *linguistic tools* are exploited by the author both to convey a message and to ensure that it is received by the readers or listeners in the way intended? How does the author present information and ideas? How are the links made between points? What use is made of rhetorical devices and, in some instances, especially figurative language? Which personal pronouns and parts of speech does the author favour? Is the vocabulary specialised, technical, colloquial, unusual? What are the key words or frequently recurring vocabulary items? Is the vocabulary varied? Is the emphasis on the use of content-bearing words or grammatical items, and what does this tell you about the author and potential recipients of the message? Is the sentence structure

complex or simple? Does the author favour subordination or coordination, and to what effect? What are the most commonly used verbal structures, what tense and mood are dominant? For oral and video recordings, what are the extralinguistic features, such as tone of voice, pauses, facial and other physical gestures, which are used to reinforce the message?

In conclusion, you will also want to ask yourself what effect the text has on you, although you will probably not be the target reader. More importantly, you should try to assess to what extent the text fulfils the objectives it sets out to achieve in relation to the readership or audience for which it was composed. In other words, does it succeed in its communicative task?

If you get into the habit of working through these questions in all your reading, you will find that you develop a sensitivity to different styles of writing and that text commentary becomes a relatively straightforward exercise.

UNDERSTANDING THE FUNCTIONS OF TEXTS

As emphasis has shifted towards communicative approaches to language learning, an aspect of text analysis which has been given much more attention by linguists is the identification of the functions of language in different contexts. A number of classification systems have been developed which distinguish the functions operating in specific situations. Those which will be of most relevance for you in analysing texts can be summarised as:

- *Referential or denotative*, imparting and seeking factual information.
- *Emotive or expressive*, where the sender of the message gives expression to intellectual, emotional and moral attitudes.
- *Conative or directive*, finding out the attitudes of the receiver of the message and provoking a reaction.
- *Phatic, discursive or social*, establishing, maintaining and breaking off contact in social interaction.
- *Aesthetic or poetic*, described as the relationship between the message and itself and with the capacity for conveying insights.
- *Metalinguistic*, defining and referring to the meaning of the linguistic code.

Some types of communication involve several or all of these functions, whereas others will be confined to one of them. A spontaneous conversation with a friend might simply have the purpose of socialising, whereas a political interview or a business transaction may involve several different functions.

Discourse markers, which include cohesive devices, serve to indicate the functions of an utterance and the way a text is organised. You will need to be able to recognise markers in order to help you to identify the purpose of a text that you are analysing. They are present in written as well as spoken language, but their role is probably more important in spoken language, where it may be difficult to convey the structure of the message and retain the attention and interest of the listener. The following list provides some useful examples of discourse markers, with French, German and Spanish equivalents:

DISCOURSE MARKERS

Sequencing
  first of all, next, in conclusion
  tout d'abord, ensuite, en conclusion
  zuerst, zunächst, schließlich
  para empezar, luego, finalmente/por último

Adding information
  and, moreover, incidentally, likewise
  et, en outre, au fait, de même
  und, noch dazu, übrigens, ebenfalls
  y, además, no obstante, por cierto, asimismo

Contradicting
  though, however, rather, on the other hand, in any case
  quoique, pourtant, plutôt, de l'autre côté, de toute manière
  doch, jedoch, vielmehr, andrerseits, auf jeden Fall
  aunque, sin embargo, más bien, en cambio, de todas
    formas

Re-expressing
  to put it another way, in other words
  autrement dit, en d'autres termes
  das bedeutet, mit anderen Worten
  es decir, o sea

Specifying
  namely, that is to say, firstly, secondly
  à savoir, c'est-à-dire, en premier lieu, deuxièmement
  nämlich, das heißt, zuerst/erstens, zweitens
  a saber, es decir, en primer lugar, en segundo lugar

Linking
for, therefore, because, in order to, so that, as a result, if, unless, otherwise
car, ainsi, parce que, afin de, de manière à ce que, en conséquence, si, à moins que, autrement
denn, deswegen, weil, um...zu, so daß, die Folge ist, wenn, wofern, anders
puesto que, por eso, porque, para, para que, por eso, si, a menos que, si no/de otro modo

Referring
as already mentioned, in this connection
comme nous l'avons déjà dit, à ce propos
wie schon gesagt, in dieser Beziehung
como queda dicho, tocante a esto

Exemplifying
for example, to illustrate this point
à titre d'exemple, pour en donner un exemple
zum Beispiel, um diesen Punkt zu erklären
por ejemplo, para ilustrar esto

Summarising
to sum up, to recap, having shown that
en résumé, pour reprendre, ayant démontré que
zusammenfassend, um kurz zu wiederholen, es wurde gezeigt, daß
para concluir, para recapitular, habiendo demostrado que

Focusing or signposting
now I want to turn to, I should like to begin by, now I want to move on to look at...in more detail
maintenant je voudrais aborder, j'aimerais commencer par, je voudrais ensuite regarder...en plus de détail
jetzt möchte ich ein anderes Thema behandeln, zum Anfang möchte ich, jetzt können wir dieses Thema ausführlicher erörtern
ahora quiero tratar de, quisiera empezar...ando, ahora quiero pasar a...más detalladamente

It is usually easy to identify these markers when you are reading a text or listening to somebody speaking, although you will probably not be in the habit of recording them within the body of your notes if you are concerned with the message. Markers do not mean very much in themselves, but, as you will see when you are interpreting, without these links it may be difficult to convey the thrust and purpose of a message.

COMMENTING ON STRUCTURE

Cohesive devices are equally important, if not more so, when you are trying to analyse the structure of a text. One of the aspects of textual commentary which students often find particularly difficult is identifying how an author structures a message. In abstracting or summarising, you are expected to look for the main points and reproduce them in a shorter form, generally in your own words. In the commentary you should not 'tell the story'. It is not so much the content of the text *per se* which is important but a critical appraisal of how the author uses the medium to convey a particular message. You will therefore need to identify the starting point taken by the author, how he or she follows through from one stage to another and how the conclusions are drawn out.

You will want to ask yourself, for example, whether the argument follows a logical and linear development or whether the author proceeds according to what is generally considered as a classical French structure, namely the dialectical plan (these and other examples of text structure are outlined in the discussion on essays in the next section). Other questions you should be asking might be: Is each point elucidated by illustrations and examples? How balanced is the argument? Does the author get side-tracked from the central point being made? Is the structure explicit?

Some authors, particularly in didactic writing or in speeches, announce clearly how they are going to set out their points and then summarise them at the end. The standard feature article will present information point by point, with a new paragraph for each element. There may be no conclusion or the conclusion may be at the beginning, so the end of the text can be cut without loss of meaning if the editor decides there is not enough space to publish an article in its entirety. A political speech may begin with an attack on the policy or action of an opposing party and then present a positive statement of the speaker's own policies, leading to exhortations to vote for a particular candidate or party. A scientific or technical paper is likely to have a clearly recognisable structure: it will first set out the problem and comment on previous research; then it will describe the method of investigation; finally, the results will be presented, analysed and evaluated.

RECOGNISING NORMS AND LANGUAGE VARIETIES

When analysing a text it is important to remember, firstly, that most authors will be following well-established norms for a given language variety and register; secondly, that within these norms there is always some degree of choice. A language variety can be defined as the language associated with a particular individual or group, whereas register is said to refer to the language associated with an occasion or the context within which it is used.

Norms serve to facilitate the task of the reader or listener: if expectations are met, the recipient will be able to make the most effective and economic use of a text. If you are interested in the results of football matches and your regular paper always publishes them on the penultimate page, using a standard format, you will know where to look and how to interpret the information. Norms are also the outcome of studying the communicative process: the advertiser will know how to catch and hold the attention of the target readers or audience because market research has shown that different categories of people react in different ways to a particular stimulus. The norms which you will want to identify will be concerned with such aspects as:

- The length of the text, paragraphs and sentences.
- Internal structure and sequencing.
- The physical or visual presentation of the text.
- The choice of vocabulary and syntax and the freedom the author has to present personal views.

The amount of choice may be very limited in the case of administrative documents or in a political speech broadcast by the media; it will be greatest for creative writing. The literary critic offers an interesting example of an intermediate stage, where many of the characteristics of a literary style will merge with the constraining norms of the newspaper or magazine in which the review is published.

Once you have identified the norms, or expectations, of a particular language variety and register, you will be able to consider how an individual text conforms to them. You will also be able to compare different language registers with one another. Courses vary in the range of text types to which students are exposed. In analysing the communicative process, you will normally be required to be familiar with a range of different source materials. You should at some stage in your career as an undergraduate come into contact with the foreign press, administrative documents, political texts, commercial advertising, technical exposition and literary works.

In most of the non-literary courses, a major source of information is the press and broadcasting, and you will generally have access to several newspapers and magazines, radio stations and television channels. It is important not to consider the contents of any one paper as homogeneous: a feature article is distinguishable from a leader, and the review section will call on another category of journalists. The same applies to broadcasting. Journalism is never neutral. The way that the same basic information, as supplied by a news agency, is presented will differ markedly from one paper to another or one national news broadcast to another and even from one section of a paper or programme to another: the same event, reported in the local or national press, in a daily or a weekly paper, in the serious or the popular press will look very different. Although the major function of the press is to report and inform, some papers will represent a strong political line and will also seek to persuade. Political bias may also be apparent in broadcasting.

Your task as an analyst will be to discover what the differences are, to understand what has happened to the original information and why and how the process operates. Your knowledge of the wider social and cultural environment within which your particular text is located, in combination with an ability to identify the linguistic markers, will give you an understanding of the author's intentions and the ways in which the communicative act is taking place.

When you have studied a number of texts from the same language variety and register and mastered the analytical framework, you will know what to look out for and what is standard or departs from the norm. You will also have a sound basis for producing texts yourself which can be recognised and accepted as belonging to a prescribed text type.

ACADEMIC ESSAY WRITING

The different types of language degree programme described in Chapter 1 ranged from the study of a language with another subject, belonging to a different and separate discipline, to language courses which are themselves interdisciplinary. When a degree title implies the combination of different disciplines, for example politics, economics or sociology with French, German or Spanish, within a European studies programme, or where business administration is studied as one subject in a combined degree with a language, students will not necessarily be learning about the French economy, German politics or Japanese business. Even if they are, the teaching may be done by experts on the French economy or German politics who are not linguists and are not competent to lecture or mark written work in the foreign language. Similarly, courses in literature or linguistics will often be taught almost entirely in English, and assignments, generally in the form of an essay or analysis, will also be written in English.

Where the foreign language is treated as a separate entity from its societal and cultural contexts, you may never be required to write an academic essay in a foreign language on a political, economic, sociological, management, literary or linguistic topic. You will probably be left to make your own linkages between language and content. Your final examination may involve writing an essay in the foreign language, but on an esoteric or discursive subject unrelated to the content of the course. While many of the principles involved are the same as for what is referred to in this section as the 'academic' essay, the general essay probably leaves more room for displaying imagination and personal creative thought. Even here, a well structured and carefully supported argument will be favourably received by examiners, and many of the points suggested below should have some relevance.

The present section examines the purposes of essay writing and the procedures involved. The guidelines are intended primarily for undergraduates who are expected to write substantive term-time essays on their disciplinary studies in a foreign language as part of an integrated degree programme. These assignments may count towards the assessment or they may be used as a learning tool and a preparation for the essays written under examination conditions without reference materials at the end of the year. As with reading and note-taking, many of the basic principles will apply irrespective of the language in which you are writing, but where the foreign language is the medium of expression there is always an extra dimension.

The academic essay is a very popular topic in the study skills literature. Most books include at least a section on the subject, and some authors devote whole works to it and provide illustrations taken from students' essays. The most frequently recurring themes include: the reasons for learning to write an academic essay; the stages in preparing the essay, from choosing a topic to assembling and adapting information and ideas, planning, preparing and checking a draft; and finally the presentation of reference materials.

The purpose of academic essay writing

Whether the essay is written in English or in a foreign language, most of the aims are similar. The primary purpose of the academic essay is to enable you to demonstrate that you have researched and thought through a question, understood the issues, know how to handle concepts, structure information and ideas, relate general theory to specific examples, present points and arguments cogently and logically and draw out well-substantiated conclusions.

If the essay is to be written in the foreign language, then it also becomes an exercise in manipulating appropriate terminology and phraseology and expressing yourself accurately and fluently in an academic register in another language.

Essays may be used in examinations to test your ability to write well under pressure and without supporting materials and reference tools. Since you are generally given a word limit to respect, you will also be tested on your ability to structure material within certain constraints.

An important function of essays, both for you personally and for those who teach you, is that they provide a means of generating feedback and measuring progress. The comments you receive should give some guidance on how well you have understood what is expected of you in quite a complex task and they should help you to improve your performance. For tutors a sustained piece of written work, which tests several basic skills, is a useful indicator of whether students are reaching the required standards.

Stages in essay writing

You can make yourself a mental checklist of the different steps in essay writing which should include:

- Careful selection of the question you are going to treat.
- Planning the process and making a plan.
- Writing out the essay
- Checking and editing your drafts.

SELECTING ESSAY TOPICS

In the British educational system, the aim in assignments is normally to give students a chance to show what they know. You are therefore likely to have maximum choice, and questions are not designed deliberately to catch you out. It is essential, nonetheless, to follow closely any instructions given in the rubric about length and presentation and to study carefully the way questions are phrased.

The length of the essay may not seem particularly important at this stage, but it can help in selecting a question if you try to envisage the amount of detail which will be required. Essays range from 500 to 5,000 words, and you may want to reserve a more complex topic for a longer piece of work. Lecturers are usually quick to spot any information which is irrelevant, particularly if you seem to be over the word limit. It is important to make sure you have the right amount of relevant material to treat the topic in sufficient depth within the prescribed length.

In choosing the question you are going to tackle, you need to be able to identify and define all the key terms in the title and understand perfectly what is involved when you are asked to summarise, examine or discuss, analyse, compare or contrast or evaluate the elements in a statement, hypothesis or description. Although a particular theme may look attractive, the way the question is phrased may not suggest an approach which you find easy to handle. However much effort you put into researching the topic and drafting your essay, if you do not answer the question, you will not receive the rewards for your efforts.

In selecting your topic, you should bear in mind that there are three basic types of essay:

- *Descriptive* It is rare, except perhaps in the very early stages of a degree, for students to be asked simply to summarise, define, explain or describe theories, concepts, facts or opinions in the context of an essay.
- *Analytical* In most academic essays analysis will be a central focus. Analysis means that you should consider the different elements making up the whole and that you should be able to show how they relate to one another, while distinguishing between facts and opinions.
- *Argumentative* An academic essay will generally require you to begin by analysing a topic and then compare or contrast certain aspects of it. In this case, you are being asked to confront and weigh up the various factors you have identified by looking for similarities or differences in the objects concerned. You are thereby led into an argumentative approach, where you are required to consider different and often competing or contrasting perspectives on a particular issue. Discussion also requires you to examine the many facets of a question, which could be expressed in terms of a controversy. Evaluation implies that you should go

on from analysis to present a reasoned judgement based on different factors or opinions. In the argumentative essay, you are encouraged to show that you understand the relations between different bodies of information and that you have a good command of a wide range of materials.

Not only should you choose a question which you fully understand but you will also want to write on a topic which you know you are able to treat in an interesting way. This will depend to some extent on the reading you have already done and on the notes you have assembled on the subject. If you were given your essay titles early in the year, you will have had time to think about their feasibility, and your reading may have been focused accordingly.

Initially it may be worthwhile pursuing more than one question until you are sure that you have enough material to finalise your choice. If you discover that the books you need are not available or that you quickly come up against a problem of interpretation, you may be glad to have another topic in reserve.

Some authors suggest that you should try brainstorming around the essay question. By trying to write down everything that comes into your head in relation to a particular topic, you will soon discover whether it has much potential for you, and this may be another way of eliminating unsuitable or dead-end questions.

PLANNING FOR THE ESSAY

You may have used your prescribed reading and lecture notes already to pick out information and ideas which are going to be of relevance for your essay. This is part of the planning process, which can be distinguished from writing a plan of the essay.

You will be expected to give evidence of having read widely and critically and to be able to show that you can relate the specific to more general concepts and to a wider context. In reading round the subject, you should use the search, scanning and skimming techniques you have learnt to ensure that you have covered the ground, identified the range of viewpoints and can show that you are aware of the available literature. It is important as you proceed to note any useful references you may want to bring in or pursue further.

Planning involves, firstly, assembling information, then organising and evaluating materials and ideas. In many institutions essays will be on topics which you have treated in lectures and seminars. You should remember, however, that lectures are generally intended as a means of presenting concepts and approaches to a topic. Also, lecturers will not want to read a synopsis of their own words.

Your notes from reading and lectures are the raw materials, and you should plan to spend some time sifting through them to pick out any useful points, which you can list thematically on different sheets of paper or cards, so that they can easily be sorted.

The essay requires you to select aspects which are relevant to a particular question, analyse and synthesise them and justify their inclusion by demonstrating how they relate to the title. An important stage in the process is therefore adapting the material you have assembled from the purpose for which it was originally intended to that which is suggested by the question you are examining, according to the plan you decide to adopt.

THE ESSAY PLAN

Although you may feel you know exactly what you want to say, it is still essential to plan your essay in detail. The plan should set out the steps in the argument and be presented in such a way that it is possible for somebody else to deduce what the links are and how you are going to arrive at your conclusion. The academic essay comes nearer to scientific exposition than to creative writing in that the qualities looked for are organisation, rigorous logic and progression towards an irrefutable conclusion on the basis of the evidence presented.

Depending upon the type of essay you are writing (descriptive, analytical, argumentative), there are several different structures which can be used. The list below briefly summarises some of the suggestions made in the study skills literature in both English and other languages:

- The *chronological plan* is probably the simplest structure, but it is only suitable for topics asking for an account or a description. As its name suggests, the essay takes the form of a series of stages, following the sequence in which events occurred.

- The *random sequence plan*, rather than progressing through a sequence of events or a series of arguments, randomly juxtaposes accounts, which may be of equal or different weight, without an internal logic or rationale. Again this pattern is likely to suit a descriptive essay.

- The *periodised chronological plan* is a variant on the chronological plan which is more appropriate for looking at problems, their causes and solutions, as required in an analytical essay. Periods within which events occurred provide the main framework for studying themes and arguments.

- The *linear plan* involves a tightly argued and logical development from a relatively straightforward point through a series of stages, where each argument is expanded, leading to a more complex and cumulative conclusion. This plan is likely to be suited to the argumentative essay. A useful variation on the linear plan is to present a series of arguments, each accompanied by the relevant counter-argument.

- The *dialectical plan*, which relies on the progression from thesis through antithesis to synthesis, is considered by the French as the classical essay plan and is clearly appropriate for the argumentative essay. A problem is posed in the introduction, then one body of opinion is set out and developed, followed by opposing views which underline the contradictions between the two sets of argument. In the synthesis, an attempt is made to resolve the contradiction through compromise or by introducing new ideas. The French have made the dialectical essay into a fine art which you may have difficulty in imitating, but it does provide a useful model.

DRAFTING THE ESSAY

Whatever plan you decide to adopt, the essay will be structured around an introduction, the body of the essay and a conclusion. As the introduction is going to create the first impression of your work, and the conclusion is going to be foremost in the mind of the reader when he or she prepares comments, it is worth spending some time ensuring that they fulfil their respective purposes:

1. It is sometimes said that the *introduction* can be written last of all, but in an academic essay, the introduction, if written before the rest of the essay, can serve a very useful function by forcing you to state—and therefore think carefully about—how you intend to interpret the terms of the title and how you will develop and sequence the ideas. It should not state what your conclusion will be. Rather it should indicate the direction you will be taking. In the introduction you should define what you understand the title to mean, set it in relation to its wider context and outline your approach in very general terms, indicating the main points you are going to make and the order in which you intend to present them.

2. As for the summary, you may find that you are well advised to think about the *conclusion* before writing the rest of the essay to ensure you know where all the arguments are leading. It should

offer a synthesis of the body of the essay, while drawing out the findings and possibly suggesting solutions and future directions but not introducing new material.

3. For shorter essays, particularly those which are written under examination conditions, authors on study skills generally suggest that you should aim to produce about seven or eight paragraphs in the main *body of the essay*, each making one point clearly, probably by introducing it in the first sentence.

You will want to illustrate and document every point you make with supporting evidence which may take the form of quotations, but you should avoid stringing together a series of quotations. They are no substitute for your own analysis. You should always make sure that the reader can distinguish between what you have found in your source materials and your own interpretations (the dangers of plagiarism were discussed in the previous chapter, pages 55-6). In an essay written in a foreign language, it is easy for a lecturer to detect when students are not using their own words. Yet it is not difficult to learn how to use quotations properly or how to introduce somebody else's views and attribute them to the person concerned. The essay should demonstrate that you are capable of taking ideas and information and transforming them into your own arguments.

Where you are asked to present a case, you must ensure that you balance your points. The weight of the arguments should dictate the conclusion, rather than a view of your own which has not been properly documented. There is unlikely to be a single solution to any question or an answer which is right or wrong. Your lecturer may not agree with your conclusion, but if your argument is carefully conceived, convincing, informed, well structured, rational and clearly presented you will not be penalised.

LANGUAGE AND STYLE

In an academic essay you are expected to express views objectively. You will therefore want to avoid using the first person singular of verbs. Your aim is to convince an informed and critical reader, which is not to be achieved by using dogmatic, polemical or emotive language. Rather you must convince by the force of the argument, its coherence, clarity and logic.

Language appropriate to a formal register, such as that required in an academic essay, will avoid the use of slang or colloquial expressions. It will be unemotional and relatively complex, demonstrating that you know the technical vocabulary of the topic as well as the discourse markers needed to introduce arguments and references to the opinions of different authors. You will be expected to show that you know how to signpost transitions between ideas, handle statistics and analyse diagrams and tables.

Although you should aim to start a new paragraph for every idea and use the opening sentence to indicate what it is about, you should avoid the practice which has become common in journalism whereby every sentence is presented as a new paragraph. You may be instructed that you can use subheadings as organising devices, particularly in longer essays or projects. If you choose your headings carefully so that they suggest the development of the essay, the reader will find them useful in identifying the stages in your plan and in reviewing what you have written.

CHECKING AND EDITING

The comments students receive on their essays usually focus on the range of source materials and the use made of them, the overall structure and coherence of the essay, the quality and depth of the argument, the style of presentation and the accuracy, appropriateness and fluency of the language. The best way of checking through your essay is by asking yourself the following series of questions:

1. *Have you answered the question?*
   If your conclusion follows logically from your arguments and if it brings you back to the question, the answer is probably yes.

2. *Is everything relevant?*
   By checking paragraph by paragraph whether each one helps to bring you nearer to answering the question, you should be able to reply in the affirmative.

3. *Are the arguments justified?*
   You need to be sure that you can defend the arguments you have used and that they are adequately supported by evidence and examples.

4. *Is your essay balanced?*
   Even though you may not have chosen a dialectical plan, you should ensure that you have not ignored alternatives and counter-arguments.

5. *Is what you say accurate?*
   This applies both for the content, or information, and for the references to secondary materials. It is useful to select a few statements, quotations, figures and references at random and

check them. If they are all correct, then you can be fairly confident about the rest. If you detect any errors, you will need to check the whole of the essay systematically.

6. *Have you acknowledged all your sources?*
Particularly in essays written in a foreign language, lecturers can easily detect any changes in style if students are remaining too close to their sources or indulging in unacknowledged borrowing.

7. *Is the language accurate both in terms of grammar and appropriateness?*
From language work you should know what your common mistakes are. In learning how to read for the purpose of systematically checking work, you should have found out how to set about proof-reading (see page 68). Your reader will soon become alienated and may lose sight of the qualities in your argument if he or she is distracted by inaccuracies in the language. The same applies for lack of clarity and precision or for expressions which are not appropriate for the context. The way you use linguistic signposts is also important in helping your reader to follow the development of the essay.

Referencing and presenting source materials

An important skill required in essay writing is the referencing of source materials. In the advice on note-taking (page 72) it was suggested that full details of books and articles should be carefully recorded as you read. An academic essay will be based on information and also opinions presented in books and other reference materials. It is essential to know how to use these sources intelligently and how to refer to them both in the body of the essay and in the list of references you provide at the end of the essay.

PRESENTATION OF REFERENCES

You may be asked to present a bibliography, which will include all the works you have consulted, or a list of references, which will cover all the books or other materials you have referred to directly in the essay. The bibliography and end references can be presented in the same way, using one of the widely accepted referencing systems to list works ordered alphabetically under the authors' names. There is some variation in the use of punctuation and the exact ordering within an entry, but the following system should be acceptable to most lecturers:

PRESENTATION OF REFERENCES

For a book
Surname, initials separated by full stops, date of publication in brackets, or alternatively the date can be put at the end of the reference without brackets, title of book in italics or underlined, place of publication, publisher:
    Dunleavy, P. (1986) <u>Studying for a Degree in the Humanities and Social Sciences</u>, London, Macmillan.

For a chapter in an edited book
Surname, initials separated by full stops, date of publication in brackets, title of chapter in single inverted commas, initials and name of editor followed by (ed), title of book in italics or underlined, place of publication, publisher, pp. followed by page numbers, or pp. may be omitted.
    Taylor, S.S.B. (1988) 'The assessment of writing skills', in D.E. Ager (ed), <u>Written Skills in the Modern Languages Degree</u>, Birmingham and London, AMLC and CILT, pp.110-26.

For a journal article
Surname, initials separated by full stops, date of publication in brackets, title of article in single inverted commas, title of journal in italics or underlined, vol followed by the volume number, no followed by the issue number, or these may be indicated in a shortened from as 61(3), pp. followed by page numbers, or pp. may be omitted.
    Morris, C. (1980) 'Are modern languages of any use? A limited survey of job opportunities for modern linguists', <u>Modern Languages</u>, vol 61, no 3, pp.109-12.

When you are referring to an author's work in an essay, the Harvard system of referencing, which is now extensively used, offers a good alternative to what may otherwise be cumbersome footnotes. You simply insert the author's surname followed by a comma and the date of publication in your main text within brackets, and if relevant a colon and page reference, for example (Dunleavy, 1986:126), or the comma may be omitted and the colon replaced by a comma. The reader can easily find the full details in your list of references.

Practice differs from one language to another in the use of capital letters in the titles of books and journals. In English, generally all the content words have capital letters throughout a title; German uses capitals for nouns and pronouns which would normally be capitalised in the written language; in French the practice of using a capital letter for only the first word in a title has now been widely adopted, and the tendency in Spanish is also to use fewer capital letters than in English.

FOOTNOTES

Footnotes should be used sparingly in essays. When necessary, they can be presented at the end of a chapter, numbered consecutively within chapters and in single spacing. They are required in a number of instances:

- To explain any specialist terms at the point where they first occur (unless there are several such terms which can be grouped in a glossary).
- For any translation of quotations and foreign terms included in the body of the text (quote in the original language in the text).
- For any references to sources other than those covered by the Harvard system.
- For any points which would interrupt the flow of the argument if included in the body of the text.

QUOTATIONS

Short quotations of less than three lines can be presented in the main text, distinguished by double quotation marks. Quotations of more than three lines should be separated from the body of the text, inset and single spaced. Any sections you want to omit from a quotation should be denoted by .... Square brackets should be used for any insertion, for example to clarify the meaning of a pronoun. You should always make sure that you give the reference at the end of a quotation, including the page number. The same applies to tables and other illustrative materials.

Evaluation of essay writing

As you will be aware from reading this section and from your own attempts at writing academic essays, the exercise is very demanding. Despite the case made earlier in this section justifying essay writing, you may wonder why lecturers persist in asking you to produce a piece of work which apparently has no direct application outside the academic world.

The answer is that they want to know whether you have understood concepts and ideas and are able to handle them with a specific purpose in mind. They will be looking for relevance, evidence of critical reading, reasoned and documented argument and a competent presentation.

It is not, however, so much the product of your efforts which is of value, but rather the skills involved and the process of self-discipline and organisation which are called into play during the process of preparing and writing the essay. If you learn from the feedback you receive and succeed in achieving high marks for your essays, you will have an indication that you have mastered a number of important skills which will serve you throughout your undergraduate studies and in professional life.

GROUP INTERACTION

Although you will find that, as an undergraduate, you are part of a much larger community than that which you were used to as a sixth former, British higher education provides a relatively sheltered environment in which you should be able easily to build a new circle of friends, while also getting to know students on your own course. Learning to interact both socially with your peers and also academically with staff and fellow students is another way in which your education will contribute to your personal development.

Whereas the topics of reading, note-taking and essay writing all figure prominently in the study skills literature, less attention is devoted to a skill which is very important for language students: group interaction and interpersonal communication.

Traditionally in the Oxbridge system, interaction was in a face to face situation with an academic tutor discussing a student's essay, and tutorials are still organised on this model in a number of institutions. In the more widespread context of seminars, the practice is for a student to present a paper or essay orally with a lecturer or tutor leading the discussion. For language students, it is common in written language activities for practical classes to be organised around smaller groups of students than is the case for lectures. Oral classes, generally with a native speaker, may take place with a very small number of students, generally in single figures.

While the British educational system has long encouraged team work through sports and social clubs, it has only recently begun to promote group projects as part of the academic curriculum. Higher education, in particular, has tended to favour the concept of private study, where the main interaction is between the individual and his or her learning materials, mostly in the form of books, pens and paper. The fact that so much of a student's time is said to be taken up with reading is an indication of the importance attributed to this mode of learning.

Many of the language programmes created in the 1960s and 70s tried to break away from the traditional mould by emphasising practical language skills, and particularly oral work. More recently communicative approaches to language learning have stressed, to an even greater extent, the importance of being able to operate in communicative situations, implying that an attempt is made to simulate real life contexts in order to understand the strategies needed for effective communication.

The net effect is that tutorials, seminars, practical language classes and discussion groups, which enable group project work, exchange and debate, have been recognised as important methods in language learning. It has become legitimate to prepare assignments in collaboration with other students. Group work has been shown to improve motivation and stimulate interest. Discussion can help you to understand different perspectives and viewpoints, to learn techniques of persuasion and how to resolve conflicts, as well as encouraging an appreciation of the positive outcomes of collective endeavour.

Characteristics of oral interaction

There are a number of important differences between oral and written language which you need to be able to identify as the first stage in learning how to reproduce language appropriate to specific situations.

Sometimes when you read a text, you will be aware that it is a transcription of an oral text which was not intended for the printed page. For example, when conference papers are published, the editor may simply reproduce a transcription of what the speakers said without adapting it for the written channel. The shift between oral and written language may be in the other direction. Lecturers may make written notes as a basis for their lecture, but, when delivering a lecture, they take account of the medium of presentation by inserting appropriate phraseology to indicate the direction they are following and the points they wish to emphasise. Politicians rarely make impromptu speeches, and even a televised interview will be carefully prepared and tailored to suit an audience of known characteristics in a specific context. Even if the text is subsequently to be reproduced in a newspaper, the orator will exploit rhetorical devices to ensure that his message is conveyed effectively in the oral channel.

Whereas three main registers are normally identified for written language (formal, neutral and informal), five are recognised in spoken language, since a distinction is made between spontaneous and non-spontaneous speech. Spontaneous spoken language has been classified into three levels: very informal, informal and neutral. Informal language would be used with friends or close acquaintances. Non-spontaneous language has a formal and very formal level.

Most speakers can move between the different levels. Politicians know how to vary the language used to present a message in a mass meeting or when speaking to the public in their own homes through a television broadcast. A student in an oral examination will use a different language register from that in a telephone conversation, and a telephone call to a friend will be very different from that to a client. A lecturer addressing students in a lecture theatre will not use the same language as in a tutorial. Situations arise in both written and oral contexts where authors or speakers move from one register to another, as for example when the words used by another person in a different context are quoted.

The main differences between the spoken and the written word can be summarised as follows:

- The speaker knows that he or she has to make an *immediate impact*. In theory the listener will only hear the message once, whereas most written texts can be re-read if necessary. Consequently the speaker has to ensure that the attention of the audience is captured and retained and that the message is accessible to the listeners for whom it is intended. In a live situation involving a debate or discussion, unlike correspondence, the success of the interaction depends upon immediate responses and each speaker's ability and willingness to react to any clues provided by the other.

- Different *linguistic strategies* are deployed to ensure that attention is held, that the direction of the argument is clear, that the message is seized and that the listener is left in no doubt about the speaker's intentions. Attention is gained by directly addressing the listener by an appropriate salutation. It is held by using phatic language, such as *you know, obviously,* or by introducing an unusual word order or devices such as rhetorical questions. The message is reinforced through repetition or the use of near synonyms, redundancy, exaggeration, supported by variations in the speed of delivery. Clarity may be achieved by using relatively simple syntactic structures and by alternating them with longer sentences.

- An oral text will probably use different *forms of address*. It is more likely to be characterised by the first person singular and second person plural, whereas a written version would normally be more impersonal: the conference speaker may address his or her listeners directly, with references to discussions or points made by other speakers earlier in the day which will not be reproduced in the written version.

- Spoken language, particularly at its less formal levels, is characterised by *simplification of structures*. Elliptical forms are more common, such as *j' sais pas* in French, and rising intonation may be used to express a question rather than the more complex interrogative form. In German abridged forms are used such as *stimmt's, weiß nicht*. In Spanish *que* may be omitted, as for example in *dice vendrá mañana*. Grammatical accuracy will be less important than in the written medium, since incorrect forms are less likely to obscure meaning. Sentence structure will be shorter and often incomplete, and juxtaposition may be used in preference to subordination. Exclamation may replace argument.

Understanding para-language

Another difference between the oral and the written channels can be found in para-language, or non-verbal communication, which is normally closely synchronised with speech. Para-language involves the use of gestures, voice modulation, eye and body movements, facial expressions and posture. These signs can be used in analysis, like linguistic clues, to identify the characteristics of the speaker, the purpose of the discourse and its probable effects. Politicians now have to work at their image if they are to appeal to the electorate. Dress and manner are important considerations, and it is in the interest of public speakers to practise in front of a video camera and follow expert advice on how to improve their performance in the same way as actors.

Perhaps even more than in the written medium, there are national differences in what is expected in oral communication. These are particularly noticeable in para-language. Cross-national comparisons indicate that differences in para-linguistic behaviour are perhaps most marked between the nations of the North and the South of Europe. The British are more likely to give an impression of self-control, whereas it is considered legitimate for Italians to display passion and other emotions verbally and visually in public.

Differences can easily be identified in the way in which people greet each other. The custom in continental Europe is to shake hands on every occasion when you meet somebody and when you say goodbye. In France a student joining a group of young people will embrace (*faire la bise*) them all, whereas Germans would shake hands. In Spain friends may embrace, particularly if they have not seen each other for some time, and a kiss on the cheek is not uncommon between women friends and between the sexes. The British habit of shaking hands only when you are introduced for the first time gives foreigners the impression of being impolite and stand-offish.

There are differences from one country to another in the distance between speakers in an exchange: in the Mediterranean countries, such as Spain, speakers tend to stand closer together when holding a conversation. To move back may cause offence. An exchange is likely to be conducted in a loud voice, giving the impression to onlookers that an argument is in progress. Speech also tends to be less regular, and one speaker may not wait until the previous one has completely finished before intervening. In Britain it is customary for two people engaged in conversation not to talk at the same time. Rather they will take turns. The British observer watching an exchange between two French or Spanish people will get the impression that they are interrupting one another, which may in fact be the case. The French observer, on the other hand, watching a conversation between two British people will find the process very laboured and may get impatient with the slow pace of the exchange.

Whereas a Spaniard may expect to talk at great length without taking much account of the reaction of listeners, speakers elsewhere are more likely to use eye contact and look out for appropriate vocal sounds to gain assurance that the listener is being attentive. In cross-cultural communication, the British person may never manage to participate in a conversation, if he or she patiently awaits a turn, trying to signal by eye contact and smiling or leaning forward that he or she is ready to intervene. In a group situation, whereas the Northerner tends to listen while one person holds the floor, the Southerner will quickly start up secondary conversations and probably participate in more than one conversation at a time.

Physical gesturing is also more common in the South. There are standard gestures which are recognised by all members of a language community. Tapping on the palm of the hand or a table with the forefinger is used in Spain, for example, to underline important points or to issue a warning. The Germans tend to drum on the table rather than clap to indicate approval. Upturned and trailing palms and shrugged shoulders in France are used to say: *j' sais pas, moi*; a raise of the eyebrows serves to invite a response; or the right hand drawn across the forehead and then shaken lightly signals relief. In Spain a wave of the hand at chest level could signify dismissal of an opinion or comment as unimportant. Gestures may be used as a form of mime to beat time with the rhythm of speech or to illustrate a movement or shape which is difficult to describe in words.

If you cannot recognise and use appropriate para-language, you will not be fully integrated into another speech community. It is therefore worthwhile making a special point of observing interaction within groups of native speakers and learning the visual clues which they use automatically amongst themselves and which you can try to imitate in your own group work.

Learning from oral interaction

In learning how to take the best advantage of opportunities for oral work the following points may be worth remembering:

- It is important to know how to *listen* and learn from what you hear. You need to be receptive to the views of others. Your own ideas should not be shaped on the basis of reading one author or listening to a particular lecturer. Group discussion should help you to clarify your own opinions.
- Listening is only one part of the interactive learning. You will not acquire the ability to communicate effectively, unless you engage in a two-way process. You should aim to take advantage of small group sessions and of other opportunities for interaction with native speakers by *participating actively*.
- Other people will only want to listen if you have something interesting and relevant to say. It is therefore essential to *prepare for a discussion* by working through the topics or other materials which have been handed out in advance, by deciding what you want to say or which points you find most difficult or interesting and by being able to support your own ideas with facts and well-founded argument.
- It is not enough to have something to say, you also need to know how to *express yourself*, by being able to interrupt, frame questions or respond to them and hold the floor.
- You may not have many opportunities for small group work, and it is therefore worth ensuring that everybody gains from the experience. It is useful to spend several minutes at the end of a discussion group, summing up what has been said and trying to *assess* why interaction within a particular group is effective whereas in another it does not seem to work successfully.
- It is worthwhile trying both to *observe* group interaction from the outside, by looking for the different forms of non-verbal communication, and to *understand your own reactions* in the group situation.

Structured group activities can be seen as a means of testing out your proficiency in the basic study skills you are learning: the reading techniques you have mastered will provide you with the information, concepts and ideas required for purposeful discussion; efficient note-taking will enable you to sort and select relevant facts and arguments; knowing how to abstract and summarise will make it easy for you to present views and evidence succinctly; analytical techniques will give you a good understanding of the materials and the interactional situation, as well as the ability to identify the purpose of other speakers, the appropriate level of language and the cohesive devices needed to ensure that the message is conveyed effectively; finally, from learning how arguments are structured, you will be able to analyse how the discussion is developing and possibly help to direct it.

SUMMARY OF SUGGESTIONS

1. You will need to acquire the same study skills as students in other disciplines but, because languages add an extra dimension, it is particularly important to ensure that you are really competent in the basic skills.

2. It is worth remembering that study skills are cumulative and mutually reinforcing.

3. For the linguist reading is for form and content. If you understand your material and know what you are looking for, you will be able to read more efficiently and consolidate your knowledge of information, ideas and arguments and the way they are expressed.

4. You should be aware of the different reading techniques and know how to adapt your reading according to your purpose and your material.

5. You can learn from intensive reading and can also improve your own work by checking carefully for accuracy, fluency and appropriateness.

6. It is important to work at your note-taking skills since they help you to retain information in the form of facts, concepts and references. They are a major organising device and a useful resource for essay writing. The main qualities to perfect are concision and clarity. You

should aim to develop a personalised system, which must become automatic.

7. The techniques of abstracting information and summarising, analysing and commenting on texts will help you to develop a critical awareness of content and form. By learning to recognise structure and the language norms of different varieties and registers of texts, you should be able to gain a better understanding of the communicative process.

8. The academic essay involves a combination of skills, including reading, understanding what is required, assembling and processing information and ideas, selecting, organising, planning, interpreting and evaluating material, and expressing points clearly, succinctly, logically and coherently.

9. In whatever way you are required to apply your skills, you should ensure that you follow instructions carefully and that you know how to reference your materials.

10. Small group work provides an opportunity to develop interpersonal skills which are particularly valued in courses which stress communicative competence.

11. In the oral and aural channel you need to be aware of the functions of language and of the discourse markers and para-linguistic clues which help the speaker and the receiver of the message to interact effectively.

4 TASK-BASED LANGUAGE EXERCISES

In the process of learning the basic study skills of reading, note-taking, abstracting, analysis, academic essay writing and group interaction, you will be called upon to perform various language exercises, many of which are based on the real life tasks which you may need to carry out when spending a period of residence abroad and after graduation. Some of the more common task-based exercises are examined in this chapter, covering:

1. Different forms of written text manipulation and production, which involve intra-lingual transfer, as in correspondence, responses to official documents and report-writing.

2. Self-presentation in the written and spoken channels in a *curriculum vitae* and job interview.

3. Oral presentation and interaction when conducting an interview and telephoning.

4. Inter-lingual transfer through translation both from and into a foreign language.

5. The different forms of interpreting, with reference to conference and simultaneous but focusing particularly on *ad hoc* or liaison interpreting.

An explicit distinction was made in previous chapters between the general study skills, which have to be mastered by undergraduates in all humanities and social science disciplines, and their linguistic applications, which were said to add an extra dimension to the work of language students. In learning basic study skills undergraduates receive intellectual training in analysis, logical argument and independent thinking, they develop their powers of observation and judgement and find out how to handle materials and present them clearly both in writing and orally. All students who obtain a degree demonstrate that they know how to study and learn. By successfully completing a degree in languages, you will also show that you possess a number of practical skills with professional applications, which may give you the edge on other graduates on the labour market.

The exercises presented in this chapter are unlikely to be included on syllabuses for non-language degree subjects. Nor will they necessarily be part of every language programme. Some are even less likely to be examined formally at the end of a language degree course, for assessment, particularly on the literature-based courses, is still predominantly based on translation into English, prose composition or translation into the foreign language, the general essay and a formal oral. In adopting a communicative approach to language learning, the non-literary courses have often sought to develop alternatives, at least for teaching purposes and sometimes also for assessment. Even though preparing a *curriculum vitae*, writing a report in a foreign language, conducting an interview or interpreting may not be part of the undergraduate syllabus, the exercises described in this chapter do all relate to specific tasks which, as a language student living or working abroad or as a graduate, you may be expected to perform in real life.

Some of the tasks examined, although they may be needed only on a few occasions, will figure prominently when you are preparing for, or carrying out, your period of residence abroad: whatever type of placement you have, you will probably need to know how to present yourself in a *curriculum vitae*, deal with administrative correspondence and complete formalities by responding to official documents; if you are required to write a project (discussed in the next chapter), you may want to arrange and conduct interviews and gain access to secondary materials; alternatively, you may be required to write a report on a work placement.

If you use your languages in your career or in a work placement during the period of residence abroad, you could be called upon to manipulate text-based information, for example by drafting reports on meetings or on visits to clients in another country or by extracting and presenting market information from trade journals; you may be required to translate publicity materials, conduct interviews, act as an interpreter for foreign visitors or handle queries from clients by telephone or in correspondence. Many of these tasks are being introduced into degree syllabuses for language and business.

As outlined in the first chapter, your primary aim in learning the strategies for carrying out particular language tasks is to be able to interact as a credible partner with educated native speakers of the foreign language in a range of situations both orally and in writing. The means of achieving this aim and the skills called into play are many and varied and are not easy to attain. The relevance of some exercises may not always be immediately obvious, but it is worth keeping your final objective in mind and trying to see all task-based language learning exercises as part of a cumulative learning process.

It is sometimes argued that students could be assessed on their performance at the same exercises, even using the same materials, in every year of a course, but that the level of performance expected and achieved would be different, in terms of the sophistication of the work produced, its accuracy and effectiveness. It is also argued that some exercises are inherently simpler or less demanding. For example, it is probably easier to extract information and note it down than to manipulate and reproduce it in another form. Some texts are more densely written than others, and their vocabulary, syntax and ideas are more complex.

The exercises presented in this chapter can be, and often are, included at various stages in a language course, possibly using graded texts so that the level of difficulty matches the student's progress. Some exercises would seem to be more suitable at a later point in the course, when the command of the language is greater: it is rare for interpreting, to take one example, to be studied before the end of the second year of an undergraduate course. Introduced into the first year of a degree programme, materials or exercises which are too difficult might be discouraging, but they can also have the effect of showing what the targets are for later years.

Where the logic behind syllabus design is task-based, some exercises, irrespective of their inherent difficulty, will be particularly appropriate when students are preparing for the experience of living and working abroad. As has already been suggested, the language tasks which undergraduates are set should be intellectually challenging. Otherwise, they do not have a legitimate place on a degree syllabus. It may be possible to write an acceptable letter in another language by slavishly following a prescribed model, but it is much more intellectually demanding to try to assess the effect that the choice of a particular word order or verb form will have on a reader in a defined context. It is also important to know how to attenuate or reinforce a message without provoking an unwanted reaction, for example in a *curriculum vitae* and in oral self-presentation.

In this chapter the sections are organised around different categories of exercises, according to the type of task and strategy involved rather than the level of difficulty: exercises requiring intralingual text manipulation, concentrating particularly on the administrative context, are treated separately from those where interlingual transfer is needed as in translating and interpreting.

With the exception of self-presentation, the written and oral channels are dealt with in different sections. This is for reasons of clarity and because most courses do tend to make this separation, at least in the naming of course components. It is, however, rare nowadays to study a language to degree level without using the two channels of communication to reinforce one another: interpreting relies on note-taking as a support for memory; different options in a translation are generally discussed orally; in an aural comprehension exercise, you may be required to transfer from the aural to the written medium; and an oral presentation may be made from written notes you have prepared. Because of the movement between the two, it is important to learn to identify the differences between language intended for the written or the spoken channel (a topic examined in the previous chapter, pages 103-4) and to be able to use appropriate discourse markers yourself (see pages 85-7).

A constant concern in all the language tasks you are performing should be to check for accuracy and appropriateness of language and to look for ways of extending your vocabulary and knowledge of idiomatic expressions. Audio-visual and computerised materials provide an important means of acquiring and reinforcing knowledge of vocabulary and syntax.

A separate section is not devoted to grammar exercises, although you may find that classes are set aside for the systematic study of grammar. On some language courses grammatical points are examined as they arise, or the assumption, for more advanced language learners, may be that you should check any difficulties you have for yourself. Regular use of a good grammar reference book, a dictionary in the foreign language and dictionaries of synonyms and specialised terminology is essential, whatever your level of proficiency. Suggestions for identifying and using reference tools were made in the second chapter (pages 44-5).

TEXT MANIPULATION IN INTRA-LANGUAGE TRANSFER

Abstracting, text analysis and commentary were presented in the previous chapter as part of the process of learning how to read, extract and summarise information and evaluate it critically. At the same time their importance in helping to identify and characterise different language varieties and registers was stressed. Another form of text analysis and commentary, requiring the same basic skills, is the comparison of the styles of writing of different authors or source materials on the same topic. The ability to recognise and describe the stylistic features and target readership of a text is also a prerequisite for the manipulation of materials in order to produce a text in another language variety or register.

TASK-BASED LANGUAGE EXERCISES   113

There are many text production tasks which you can work on once you have understood the features of particular styles of writing. These range from the creation of an election manifesto, based on the information contained in an administrative report, to an advertisement for a product or company, using a newspaper editorial as a starting point. In the limited space available here, only a few of what are likely to be the most useful written text types are covered: formal correspondence, administrative documents and reports. The focus is particularly on their applications in French, German and Spanish. The references in the bibliography will direct you to more detailed accounts and worked examples of these and other exercises and to a wider range of language registers.

Formal correspondence

Nowadays the main means of communication in many professional contexts is by telephone. Telexes and fax messages are also becoming increasingly widespread as substitutes for letters sent through the post. There are, nonetheless, still occasions when it is necessary to write formal letters, particularly to administrative authorities or in business dealings. It is important to know how to handle the appropriate language register and tone and observe the norms for layout, if communication is to be effective.

As you have learnt from the section on analysis and commentary, any text must be appropriate for the purpose for which it is written, the person to whom it is addressed and the situation for which it is produced. The correspondence with which you are likely to come into contact can be grouped into three main types: personal, official and business. You are probably already familiar with styles of writing in personal correspondence, and it should present no problems. Business and administrative correspondence are similar in form and tone. The French, for example, adopt a very formal style in their correspondence, and you could give offence, or at least not receive the response you want, if you do not use the correct form of address, an appropriate tone and suitable phraseology for opening and closing a letter. The set openings and endings may seem excessively flowery, compared with the more straightforward British, German or Spanish formulae, but without them, a letter will not conform to the norms of the relevant language variety.

There are numerous books on the subject of letter-writing, some of which provide model letters for every conceivable occasion as well as information about the contexts for which they are written. The guidelines below apply for correspondence with a person you do not know, for French, German and Spanish. They are intended to help you to understand the technicalities of drafting a letter by suggesting the strategies you would need to deploy in order to achieve a particular effect. They should give you an idea of what to aim for, especially as far as linguistic features are concerned.

DRAFTING A FORMAL LETTER

POSITION AND LAYOUT OF THE ADDRESS OF THE SENDER AND THE RECIPIENT

Adresse de l'expéditeur:
In France the position of the sender's name and address is shifting and may sometimes (in the case of a company or organisation) be placed in the centre of the page or, alternatively, at the bottom. The postal code is always put before the name of the town in France.

Adresse des Absenders:
In correspondence to Germany the sender's address is normally written at the top lefthand side of the letter. The street number follows its name. It is now usual in typed correspondence to leave a space before the name of the town, which is preceded by its postal sorting code (**Postleitzahl**). *The number following the name indicates the area within the city. A variant is to put your name at the top lefthand side of the page and your address at the top righthand side, or both can be put on the right. In the past the name of the town would have been underlined, but this is no longer the practice, and the trend is towards simplification of presentation.*

Remitente:
For a business letter in Spanish, the full address of the sender is sometimes put at the top of the page on the right, with the date, as in English. The writer's name and address are always given on the back of the envelope, preceded by the heading **remitente** *or the letters,* **Rte**, *and the address* (**dirección**). *It is therefore worthwhile making sure you open the envelope with care so as not to destroy the address.*

Nom et adresse du destinataire:
In France the name and address of the recipient of the letter are normally placed on the righthand side of the page, but the Anglo-Saxon influence and new technology are tending to encourage a shift to the left. Sometimes they appear at the bottom of the letter on the left. The position of the window on

envelopes will obviously dictate where the address should be written.

If you are writing to a business or large organisation, you may find that the postal code and name of the town is followed by a **Cedex** reference, meaning **courrier d'entreprise à distributions exceptionnelles**, which is an additional sorting code, similar to the P.O. Box numbers used in Britain, and intended to speed up delivery for heavy users of the postal service. **Cedex** is not, however, always followed by a number.

Anschrift:
In German the name of the organisation to which you are writing usually appears before the name of the individual to whom your letter is addressed. Most large organisations or firms will have a **Postfach** number, which will help to speed up delivery.

Destinatario:
In Spanish the name and address of the recipient are placed on the lefthand side of the page.

DATE OF COMPOSITION

Lieu et date d'envoi:
The French usually include the name of the place where the letter is written. The name of the month should not begin with a capital letter.

Datumsangabe:
In a letter in German the date may appear above the name of the recipient of the letter as six figures, where the first two indicate the day and the second two the month. The name of the month is no longer written out in full, except in very formal correspondence. Alternatively, the date and place where the letter is written can appear at the top righthand side of the letter.

Fecha:
In Spanish in most cases the name of the town is written above the date. The date is given as figures, ordered by day, month and year, or the month is written out in full without a capital letter. Latin American letters tend to follow the North American practice of putting the month before the day.

REFERENCE OR HEADING

Référence du destinataire:
The sender's reference can be given if applicable. When you are writing to an organisation, you may want to specify the name of the recipient by stating: **à l'attention de....**

Bezugszeile *or* **Bezugszeichen/Referencia:**
References are rarely used nowadays in German and Spanish, and it is sufficient to refer to the date of the correspondence you have received within the body of the letter together with the reason for writing.

STANDARD SALUTATION

Forme d'adresse:
Officials should be addressed by their title. A headmaster in a school would be **Monsieur le Directeur** *or a headmistress* **Madame la Directrice.** *The French respect a strict hierarchy in their forms of address.* **Monsieur/Madame** *should be used where there is no official title.* **Cher Monsieur** *or* **Chère Madame** *is possible for somebody you know, belonging to the same sex and generation or for somebody younger, but not the Anglicised form with the surname. The amount of space left before the first line is sometimes said to be determined by the degree of respect being shown for the recipient of the letter. The first line should, however, begin before the middle of the page. If in doubt about whether or not a woman is married always use* **Madame**, *and normally this form of address is preferred for an older woman, even if you know she is single.*

Anreden:
When a person has a title, this should always be used, and the name is then omitted, as in **Sehr geehrter Herr Doktor/Direktor.** *In the past the name would have been followed by an exclamation mark. Now it is sufficient to use a comma or nothing at all. Full stops are generally omitted from abbreviations, as in GmbH* **(Gesellschaft mit beschränkter Haftung)** *which indicates a limited company.*

Encabezamiento:
In Spanish for a formal or business letter, it is sufficient to say **Muy señor mío/Muy señora mía.** *Normally the salutation is followed by a colon.*

OPENING

Entrée en matière/Anfang/Para empezar:

In any language you should avoid beginning a letter with the first person singular. The first paragraph will normally refer to previous correspondence or to the purpose of the present letter.

Note that in German you should not use a capital for the first word in the letter. The custom of indenting the beginning of paragraphs is also disappearing. You are advised to come straight to the point and avoid circumlocutions.

In Spanish it is customary to mention the receipt of a letter rather than thank the person for replying to the sender's letter.

THE MAIN BODY OF THE LETTER

Les alinéas/Hauptteil des Briefes/Principio:

The term **alinéa** *is used in French to indicate a new paragraph or indented line. Often there is only one idea or point to a paragraph, expressed in a single sentence.*

The primary requirement of a letter in any language is clarity and conciseness. Complex syntax is therefore best avoided. The structure should be easy to follow, and the points should be presented in a logical order. The language should be succinct, avoiding the use of the passive and too many subordinate clauses.

Advice given in the German literature about letter writing particularly stresses the importance of using simple, clear and unemotional language, only stating a point once, being logical, objective and factual, avoiding lengthy and complex sentences and inviting positive reactions and confidence from the reader.

The last paragraph of a letter will normally refer to the action expected and any other responses looked for. The conditional is commonly used in this context in French to express formality: **je vous serais reconnaissant(e) de bien vouloir** *is a polite way of making a request, as is the use of* **veuillez**. *Both expressions are much more likely to provoke a favourable response than a more direct phrase like* **je vous demande de m'envoyer**.

In all languages you are advised to try to end a letter on a positive note.

CLOSING FORMULAE

Formules de politesse:
In French the closing formulae vary according to the relationship between the author and the recipient of the letter. The same form of address as that used in the initial salutation is reiterated (between commas). The verb **agréer** is frequently used instead of **croire à**. A woman would not normally refer to her **sentiments** in closing a letter to a man. Increasingly, shorter formulae are being used and are appropriate for somebody with whom you are on more friendly terms, for example: **Amicalement à vous.**

Schlußfloskel:
Closing formulae in German are much less elaborate than in French, and it is sufficient to say: **Mit besten freundlichen Grüßen.** In a letter to a friend, you would use an expression such as **Mit herzlichen Grüßen.**

Final:
Closing remarks in Spanish usually make reference to the subject dealt with in the main part of the letter. The accepted ending to a formal letter must be in the third person, as in **Le saluda atentamente** and will usually be followed by the signature without further punctuation since the signatory is the subject of the verb.

SIGNATURE AND NAME

Signature et nom/Unterschrift und Name/Firma y nombre:
In all three languages the signature is normally written in ink at the bottom lefthand side of the page, but in Spanish it is not unusual for it to be written on the right.

In French sometimes a woman will insert (**Madame**) after her name to avoid confusion. The status of the sender is also generally indicated after the name, for example: **Le Directeur**, and a common practice is to print out the name in full after the signature to ensure it is legible.

ENCLOSURES

Pièces jointes/Anlage/Anexos:
Enclosures are generally indicated, where appropriate, normally with a reference to the number of items concerned.

It is perhaps worth noting that the French and Spanish have tended to become even less enthusiastic letter-writers than the British, and it is not uncommon for letters to go unanswered. The Spanish, in particular, may be very casual about responding to letters. It is therefore important to know how to follow up written correspondence with a telephone call, in which you refer to any letter, and to try to obtain a response or a visit in person where appropriate.

Official documents

You may come into contact with a whole range of different types of administrative documents other than formal correspondence. They could, for example, be introduced as supporting materials for a course focusing on the study of political and legal institutions. You could be asked to analyse or, on some of the more specialised courses, even produce documents which fall into the categories of legal texts, including court decisions, parliamentary debates, committee minutes or administrative reports and what the French describe as *notes de synthèse*. When you are preparing for residence abroad, you will be expected to complete various formalities (see particularly pages 171-80). In the context of employment, either during the period of residence abroad or on graduation, you may be required to observe different administrative procedures, such as obtaining a residence permit or opening a bank account. If you are unwell, you may need to complete a social security claim form.

Whole books have been devoted to the language of administration, and the French regularly produce useful guides to help the man-in-the-street understand how the country is administered. Some of these works are noted in the bibliography. In the limited space available here, reference is made to a few of the contexts which may be relevant to you personally when you are spending a period of residence abroad.

If you are applying for a place on a university course abroad, if you are registering for social security or completing the formalities for a residence permit or other official documents, you will be expected to follow instructions for filling in forms and to present the appropriate documents at the right time and in the right place. As a student in Britain, you may not realise how well you are protected both by and from the system. If you are ill, you make an appointment to see a doctor, collect any drugs which may be prescribed from a chemist and pay a minimal and fixed contribution towards their cost. At no stage do you need to ask yourself, nor are you asked, whether you are covered and to what extent by an insurance scheme. Nor do you have to think about paying doctors' bills, the commercial price of medicines, and how to ensure you are subsequently reimbursed by completing and sending off the appropriate forms.

The points treated below are those which students generally find difficult to handle and are taken from categories of administrative documents which you are likely to encounter. The difficulties which arise are often due not only to problems in understanding terminology but also because the system is very different from that in Britain. This is why socio-cultural or background knowledge of another country is so important.

ADMINISTRATIVE PROCEDURES

Completing official forms in France

Numerous attempts have been made in France to simplify administrative procedures and to help the average citizen to understand what his or her entitlements are. One of the aims has been to make administrative language accessible to everybody. By its nature the language of communication between administrators has to be impersonal, objective, unambiguous and unemotional, clear and precise, devoid of any sign of imagination. When the general public is being addressed, an effort is made to present information in a more imaginative way, using examples and illustrations, explaining terms and giving very precise instructions. The numerous leaflets which are available from local town halls or the relevant administrative offices use the direct form of address, sentence structure is simplified to the utmost, and sample forms are reproduced with notes giving guidance on how to complete them.

When filling in forms, rather than ticking the relevant box, the French use a cross, and this is what is expected if you are asked to **cocher la case** *(box)* **de la réponse exacte,** *but you may actually be instructed to use a cross:* **mettez une croix dans la case qui vous concerne.** *Where there is more than one option, and you are expected to strike out those which do not apply, you will be asked to* **rayer les mentions inutiles.** *Note the use of the infinitive for polite imperatives in this sort of impersonal document. For further details you will be asked for* **précisions.** *If the question does not apply, rather than leaving a blank, you should put* **néant.**

Completing official forms in the Federal Republic of Germany

In the Federal Republic of Germany there has not been an attempt to simplify administrative procedures, and the completion of official documents can be a very daunting task. You may find that you have many pages of extremely small print instructing you how to fill in a form and warning you of the penalties incurred if you are not accurate or do not comply. Examples are, however, normally given of standard responses, which may help you to understand what is required even if they do not apply directly to you.

You will probably be told to use capital letters or to type your replies: **Bitte mit Block- oder Maschinenschrift ausfüllen** *You may be instructed to fill out only certain parts of the form:* **Zutreffende weiße Felder bitte ausfüllen oder ankreuzen,** *by writing out the answers to questions or using a cross rather than a tick. Other parts of the form will be reserved for official use only, for example:* **nur vom Finanzamt auszufüllen.** *As for the date in correspondence, you will normally be expected to give your date of birth in six figures.*

Abbreviations are likely to be used, some of which should be immediately recognisable, such as: **u.** *for* **und, Nr.** *for* **Nummer, z.B.** *for* **zum Beispiel.** *Others may be less familiar, for example:* **v.H.** *for* **von Hundert,** **vgl.** *for* **vergleiche,** *and* **ggf.** *for* **gegebenenfalls.**

Completing official forms in Spain

Administrative procedures in Spain are likely to appear tedious to the British observer. It is not always easy to ensure that you have the correct form for your particular circumstances and all the supporting documentation required. For example, you may need to check that you have a form which states: **Ficha sólo utilizable en caso de matricularse por primera vez,** *if you are registering for a university course.*

You might be asked to include a number of personal documents such as your **certificado de nacimiento,** *an identity card,* **DNI** *or* **libro de familia,** *which the British do not have, and to make sure you include the* **ficha de acuse de recibo.** *Together with passport size photographs, you may also be required to enclose a photocopy of the receipt:* **fotocopia del resguardo de pago.**

When you are completing a form you will probably be instructed to print your answers in capitals: **escriba con letra de**

> imprenta los datos solicitados. *You will be asked to give your name and surnames:* nombre y apellidos. *Spaniards generally use the surnames of both their parents, giving that of their father first. If you have a middle name, this is likely to be taken for your mother's maiden name.*
>
> *You may have to commit yourself to accepting the conditions laid down on the form:* Acepto las siguientes condiciones, *by agreeing to pay fees in advance and in full,* por anticipado y libre de gastos. *The relevant authority is not likely to accept responsibility beyond that which is its immediate concern:* sin adquirir otra responsabilidad. *Finally, you may be requested to supply further information:* observaciones.

Whichever language you are working in, it is worthwhile trying to find out as much as you can about the system behind the form, so that the task becomes meaningful and purposeful.

Reports

There are many situations in which report-writing is called for. If you are in a work placement during your period of residence abroad, you may be required to write a report on the type of work you were doing or a specific problem which was of concern to the company employing you. When you graduate you may be responsible for reporting on the state of the market in a particular part of the world or you may need to report back on a visit to clients.

Although learning how to write an academic essay is an important part of the training process for preparing and drafting a report, there are major differences, not only in purpose but also in style, between the two exercises. As with administrative documents, the aim of a report is to communicate information as accurately and concisely as possible to a specific readership within a prescribed context. This involves extracting, selecting and drawing together points from a dossier of materials in as complete a form as possible. The key features of a report are its clarity, precision, concision and coherence.

In its simplest form, you may be instructed that the report should be solely informative, simply stating the facts of a case or situation. You may be told, however, that the intention is to use the information to make recommendations and that you should formulate ideas which could lead to specific actions. Another possibility is that the information is to be used to answer questions and draw out conclusions, which you are expected to initiate.

As with any task, it is essential to follow carefully instructions about purpose, readership, length, sources to consult and the date for submission. Just as you would lose marks if you did not answer the question properly in an academic essay, a report which is limited to a statement of fact when you were instructed to provide recommendations or is double the length asked for and submitted after the deadline will not satisfy employers and could put your future in jeopardy.

PLANNING AND PREPARING THE REPORT

The stages to follow in preparing a report will be similar to those for the academic essay:

1. You will need to *plan a schedule*, perhaps working backwards from the deadline so that you ensure you allow adequate time for drafting and final checking.

2. *Access to source materials* may simply involve scanning documents which are readily available, or it may require hunting in specialised libraries or contacting companies and administrative offices. Depending upon the urgency of the report—and generally deadlines are designed to be impossible—you will need to write, telephone and/or call on informants in person.

3. As with the academic essay, it is important to be able to *extract relevant information* quickly, to make notes, sift and order your materials in line with your objectives.

4. The *organisation of materials* should be relatively straightforward if you have clearly understood the terms of reference and can collect together what you need quickly. At all stages you should keep your readership and purpose in mind, for this will determine the plan of the report.

5. In *preparing to write up* the report, if the aim is solely to inform, you will probably want to order points according to their perceived importance. If you are expected to make recommendations you may want to do so at the end of each section, as well as listing them all at the end of the report. In any case, they should follow logically from your evidence, and you should aim to present a balanced and fair report without personal bias.

DRAFTING AND PRESENTING THE REPORT

Whereas the academic essay will be written in continuous prose, with few if any subheadings, the report may be presented with numbered subdivisions, using the system you may have been practising in note-taking (see 73-4). The advantage is that it makes the plan obvious to the reader. You are guaranteed that lecturers will pick their way through pages of unbroken prose in search of an argument, but the reader of a report will be looking for specific information, which can be quickly identified, and he or she may never read the whole report. The titles and subheadings must therefore be meaningful: the title should specify exactly the aspect of the field which is being examined and to what effect; subheadings will indicate the stages in the process of analysis. Headings such as 'aims' and 'recommendations' will therefore be more appropriate than 'introduction' and 'conclusions'.

In order to avoid cluttering the text with non-essential information, it is often useful to present tables, charts and other relevant documents in appendices at the end, provided they are carefully numbered, their sources are recorded and they are referred to in the body of the text. The reader may not go through the report in its chronological order: he or she may look, firstly, at the recommendations and then trace back to a section relating to any one of them which looks particularly interesting, referring to the appendices to check details. Good clear presentation will therefore help the reader to move quickly and easily around the text.

The recommendation is often made that the first paragraph should provide a crisp statement or summary of the contents of the whole report. At the very least, it should give a coherent statement of the problem, the reason for the report and its purpose. This is where skills in abstract writing (see pages 80-1) are likely to be valuable. If the summary does not convey the essence of the report, the reader may not bother to look any further.

Your style of writing should be that which is typical of administrative language: impartial, clear, concise, always to the point and impersonal. Any technical terminology used should be that of the specialism in which you are working, so that it is immediately recognisable. Neutral language is characterised by an absence of adverbs and evaluative adjectives. Even though you may have been asked to make recommendations, you should express them in the form of suggestions rather than dogmatic statements. As in the academic essay, it is the persuasiveness of the arguments, rather than the forcefulness of the language, which should convince the reader, although a judicious ordering of points can help to produce a particular effect. If the most important recommendations are put at the end of a list, then they are more likely to stay in the reader's mind.

The test of success in a task-based language exercise is whether the text you have produced provokes the action intended. It is easy to gauge in real life whether the desired effect has been achieved. As a student, you will receive feedback from your tutors, but you can also try analysing your own work objectively, for example, by using the questions suggested on pages 82-4 for text analysis.

SELF-PRESENTATION IN THE WRITTEN AND SPOKEN CHANNELS

Before you spend your period of residence abroad, particularly if you are applying for employment, or after graduation, you will need to know how to present yourself to your best advantage in a *curriculum vitae* and subsequently at an interview.

The *curriculum vitae*

A *CV* is a short, clear, legible, compact and truthful statement of your personal background, including qualifications, education, work experience, special interests and abilities which are relevant to the position you are seeking. Often you will need to submit a copy of your *CV* together with a covering letter, and you may also have to complete a job application form.

Although the information contained will be the same for most positions, the emphasis may need to be changed in order to match the requirements of a particular post. If you know how to read between the lines of an advertisement, you will be able to highlight relevant experience. An advertisement might ask explicitly for somebody with particular qualifications and work experience, but the way the firm is described (dynamic, international, looking to develop markets abroad) and the working conditions (contact with customers) will suggest that qualities such as adaptability, drive, languages, interest in travel and an extrovert personality are being sought. You should try to match your own abilities with those indicated or suggested in the advertisement, drawing out appropriate examples from your own experience. If you can put your *CV* onto a wordprocessor, it will be easy to adapt for different circumstances and you can add information as your experience increases.

The *CV* should be typed, but the covering letter can be in your own handwriting. Employers receive hundreds, if not thousands, of applications, and they will be looking for reasons to reject a large proportion of them without further ado. It is therefore in your interest to ensure that yours is well presented and will not give cause for immediate rejection.

There are no exact rules about how to present a *CV*, but conventions do differ slightly from one country to another. You should aim to cover the headings suggested below, preferably on one side of an A4 sheet of paper in plain type, although not necessarily in the order shown. If you need to use a second sheet, you should only type on one side of the paper.

Normally you would not put a title at the top of your *CV*. If you need to refer to it in German you would use the term *Lebenslauf*. Your *CV* could be presented either in tabular form or in continuous prose in the form of a letter. You can include a photograph at the top righthand side of the first page (but not a photocopy of one).

You do not need to spell out the headings used below for the sections on personal details. The main headings to include are *Education/Training, Languages, Work Experience, Other Relevant Information*. Further subdivisions have been used in the guidelines to help you organise information and identify corresponding sections on application forms. The notes again apply to the languages which will be relevant to the vast majority of language undergraduates, namely French, German and Spanish, and samples are given of a *CV* in these languages in the next chapter (pages 166-70). A few reference books are included in the bibliography giving more detailed accounts of how to prepare a *CV* and further illustrations.

DRAFTING A CURRICULUM VITAE

Nom/Name/Nombre:
In all three languages you should use capital letters for your surname, and Spaniards will normally refer to both their father's and mother's surnames.

Date et lieu de naissance/Geburtsdatum und Ort/Fecha y lugar de nacimiento:
It is helpful if you indicate your age rather than leaving the prospective employer to work it out.

Adresse/Anschrift/Dirección *or* Señas:
Use the address and telephone number where you can most easily be contacted.

Nationalité/Staatsangehörigkeit/Nacionalidad:
As a foreign applicant, it is important to give your nationality. For French and Spanish the ending of the adjective describing the nationality will agree with the person concerned.

Etat civil/Familienstand/Estado civil:
You should indicate whether you are married and have any children. *The Germans often include information about other relations* **(Eltern, Geschwister)** *and give details about their parents' professional occupations.*

Service militaire/Wehrdienst/Servicio militar:
Women can omit this heading, but male applicants in France or Germany, where there is still compulsory military service, will normally specify that they are: **Dégagé des obligations militaires** *or* **Non soumis aux obligations militaires***, or state:* **Wehrdienst abgeschlossen.** *Spanish male applicants will often be expected to quote their National Service number.*

Documento Nacional de Identidad (DNI):
All Spanish nationals are required to have a National Identity Card and to quote the number on a CV when applying for a Civil Service post. British applicants would normally give their passport number. In France and Germany this information is not needed on a CV.

Formation/Bildungsweg/Educación:
The Germans normally include information about primary and secondary schools attended **(Schulbesuch)**, *and employers will judge from the time spent whether it was necessary to repeat a year. This information is not expected in France, although it is also not unusual to repeat one or more years of schooling.*

In this section you should include details about the dates and results of qualifications obtained, with grades, or of examinations to be taken. Once you have completed higher education, you need only include your 'A' level results. It is helpful if you indicate what the equivalent qualifications would be in the other country, taking an A grade to be a **mention très bien** *and a B as a* **mention bien** *in France. In Germany the* **Arbitur** *is graded 1 to 6, where 1 is* **sehr gut, 2 gut, 3 befriedigend, 4 ausreichend, 5 mangelhaft, 6 durchgefallen.** *The Spanish do not usually include information about grades. 'A' levels would be considered as the equivalent of the* **bachillerato y COU (curso de orientación universitaria).**

You could also indicate any special option subjects which might be of particular interest, such as international marketing, computing, trade unions or accounting, and if you are following a non-literary course you could, for example, specify that it is **langues étrangères appliquées**. *There is much debate in France about whether the British degree is equivalent to the* **licence** *or the* **maîtrise**, *and it is therefore worth mentioning that yours is a four-year course. British degrees do not generally take so long to complete as do courses in France, Germany or Spain, and continental employers will welcome information about the organisation of your studies and evidence that you have had other experience.*

Autre formation/Andere Kenntnisse und Erfahrungen/Otra educación:
*Indicate any academic awards obtained, evening classes followed or vacation courses attended and their length. You could include courses and work placements (***stages/Praktikum/cursillos***) attended during the period of residence abroad, saying whether they were full- or part-time. You will need to explain any specifically British qualifications, giving their equivalent in the other country as appropriate.*

In Germany, as most qualifications are recognised nationally, it is important to mention the fact that you have a **Staatsexamen**.

Employers in France, Germany and Spain are only interested in extracurricular activities and achievements if they are directly relevant to the position being sought, even though they indicate leadership qualities and maturity.

Langues/Sprachkenntnisse/Idiomas:
Outside the UK employers are particularly interested in linguistic proficiency, and it is therefore important to stress your ability and to give a realistic assessment of your level. Where a particular context of language use is specified in an advertisement, you might find that it helps in France and Germany to add a reference to linguistic applications, for example: **Langue technique maîtrisée** *or* **Ich kann mich im technischen Deutsch schriftlich und mündlich gut ausdrücken.**

Expérience professionnelle/Berufstätigkeit/Experiencia de trabajo:
You should include any part-time or holiday jobs. As you build up longer term work experience, you can omit this information. Instead, you should give examples of any important jobs you have done. Information in these sections is probably best presented chronologically, but you should ensure that you indicate clearly what your present position is. You

may find that a reverse chronological order becomes more appropriate as you move from one full-time job to another.

Responsabilités exercées/Verantwortungsvolle Stellen/Puestos de responsabilidad:
For an application in Britain, you would normally indicate positions held while at school and in higher education, but employers outside the UK will be unfamiliar with functions such as a school prefect, for which there is no equivalent, and will not consider them relevant for most positions. As you build up work experience, much of this information will in any case become less meaningful.

Autres renseignements/Andere relevante Information/Otros:
In this section you could list the hobbies and other experience you might want to elaborate on in an interview, again only if they are relevant to the position advertised.

You may want to note, for example, your ability to drive or the fact that you are computer literate, even if you do not have a formal qualification.

Recommandations/Referenzpersönlichkeiten/Informes:
In French and German, although you may be expected to supply testimonials, you will not normally be asked for names of referees. A prospective employer may try to contact a previous employer. If requested, give names and addresses of people who know you well, including a person from your current institution, ensuring that you obtain permission to quote them. For Spain you may be asked to enclose a medical certificate. You should supply a translation of any testimonials written in English.

If you need to present the same information on an application form, it is worthwhile making a photocopy of the form so that you can do a rough draft to ensure that your responses fit into the spaces provided. It is better never to leave blanks: the terms *nul/néant* can be used in French, *nicht zutreffend* in German and *n.a.* in Spanish. You should avoid crossing out, and spelling and grammar must be carefully checked. Your responses to open questions which invite you to express your views or present yourself may be important deciding factors in choosing between a large number of candidates with similar qualifications, so it is probably worth spending some time making sure you get your message over in an appropriate tone.

You may decide to try writing speculative applications to companies which have not advertised. As many as twenty per cent of candidates interviewed in France and Germany are probably found by this means, and companies may keep files on potential employees if they are interested and cannot immediately offer a position. The reasons for approaching a particular company should be outlined in a covering letter, and you can suggest that you would be happy to go for interview. If you are writing a covering letter for an application in response to an advertisement, your letter should mention the advertisement, where it appeared and its date and reference. It should suggest briefly why you are a suitable candidate.

Job interviews

If you are applying for a job, the interview will be an important deciding factor, and you will need to ensure that you present yourself to the best of your ability. Research into the work of professional interviewers has shown that in about seventy-five per cent of cases a decision is taken about the suitability of a candidate for a job by the time the interviewer has shaken hands with the applicant. The remainder of the interview is spent confirming the first impression and the decision. This suggests that the interview may not be a very effective method of selection, but since it is likely to continue to be used for some time to come, it is important to know how to create a favourable initial impression and to confirm it in the course of the interview. There are cultural differences in the behaviour expected of candidates in interviews in different countries, and it is wise to adopt behaviour which is acceptable in the country concerned.

The advice of careers officers in Britain to candidates at interview is to pay careful attention to personal appearance and manner. Dress should be appropriate for the type of employment being sought. The Germans are less likely than the British to find a beard or long hair acceptable for employment in banking or the civil service. The French will expect women to be elegantly dressed and immaculately, but not too heavily, made up for work involving contact with customers.

Potential employers will expect you to be fairly nervous in an interview. In Britain they will probably not be well disposed to somebody who is over-talkative and too confident, whereas in France, Germany or in Southern Europe, in particular, self-confidence is more natural, and diffidence may be judged negatively. The educational system in continental Europe tends to encourage oral self-expression, argument and debate to a much greater extent than in Britain. As a language student you should have the advantage of being accustomed to expressing yourself orally, which would not be the case for many of your fellow students in the sciences. The expectation abroad is that you should be able to converse easily on a wide range of subjects, even under conditions of stress, particularly if you are seeking employment which involves direct contact with the public or with customers.

You can prepare yourself for an interview by going through your CV or job application carefully and thinking of possible questions and how you would respond to them. You are certain to be asked why you are interested in a particular job and why you think you are suited to it. As a foreigner, you will probably need to explain in more detail different points mentioned in your application. You are also likely to be asked whether you have any questions. It is always worthwhile having a few in mind, even if you already know the answers.

In an interview it is important to be able to identify oral cues and to know how to interpret para-language (see pages 104-6). Further advice about self-presentation in the oral channel, which is also relevant to the job interview, is provided in the next section.

ORAL PRESENTATION AND INTERACTIVE COMMUNICATION

The conversation class with the native language speaker is an increasingly common feature of all types of language programme, as are the multimedia classes used for the study of audio-visual materials. The function of these activities will vary according to the importance attributed to oral work. Where oral performance is a minor element (sometimes not assessed in the final degree), conversation classes will normally take the form of a small relatively unstructured group discussion on any topic which is of interest to the students or native speaker. There may be an opportunity to practise self-presentation, which can subsequently form the basis for the job interview (discussed in the previous section).

Where oral work is a major course component, spoken language classes with native speakers may be organised as seminars at which students present papers or engage in debate about topics related to the content of the course, under the general supervision of the lecturers concerned. Oral classes may also be used for role simulation exercises, such as interviewing, telephoning or business and political games.

Analysis of the use made by students of their languages in their careers demonstrates the importance of communication through the spoken language channel. During the period of residence abroad or in employment in international settings you will constantly find yourself in oral and aural interaction, either face to face or at the end of a telephone line. Unless you know something about the mechanisms of communication in these contexts and have learnt the appropriate strategies to deal with them, you may find that you cannot easily achieve the desired effect. Throughout your career as a language student, your aim should be to use spoken language classes and any other opportunities you can find to extend the range of language situations in which you can perform competently in the oral channel. For example, when you are listening to authentic broadcast discussions or interviews, it is useful to note down the discourse markers. You can also look out for cohesive devices in lectures. When you make an oral presentation yourself, you can try to introduce appropriate markers. Examiners can always identify an oral presentation which has been written and learnt by heart by a student who is not aware of the characteristics of spoken language.

In real life situations meaningful oral interaction will only be achieved if you are able to use language which is appropriate to the context. When you are abroad, you will be aiming to interact on equal terms with your foreign counterparts. If you do not know how to present your views in an interesting and convincing manner, appropriate to the oral channel, or how to interrupt and hold the floor, you may find that you rarely get a chance to speak. You should try to observe how native speakers of the foreign language hesitate without losing control of the exchange. Experienced public speakers will, for example, avert interruptions by talking more loudly, by repeating what has just been said and by using phrases like:

If you would let me finish what I was saying.
Permettez-moi de finir.
Lassen Sie mich bitte zu Ende reden.
¿Me deja usted terminar?

They may re-express a point in different words if they see from the reactions of their listeners that the message has not been understood.

In this section, two specific oral tasks are examined: conducting interviews and making telephone calls. These are both spoken language tasks which you may need to perform during the period of residence abroad or in employment after graduation, but which are not necessarily included on a language syllabus.

Interviewing

During the period of residence abroad or in employment, you could find yourself at the giving or the receiving end of an interview situation in a foreign language. The oral examination at the end of a language course is sometimes described as the 'oral interview', and the assumption is that the examiners, like the prospective employer, are interviewing you.

If you are gathering material for a project or work report during the period of residence abroad, you may need to interview officials, experts on a particular topic or fellow employees. You will want to ensure you know how to handle the situation so that you collect the maximum amount of information without wasting their valuable time.

The oral interview has advantages and disadvantages over requests for information in writing. Because the situation is spontaneous, the discussion can be guided, leads can be followed by seeking clarification and further elucidation. Information can be checked by asking questions in a different way, and the interviewer can assess responses from the tone of voice, facial expressions and gestures of the interviewee.

The disadvantage of the oral interview is that you do not have time to think through responses, as you would if you were writing. When the interviewer or interviewee belongs to a different linguistic and cultural background you might not always have the appropriate vocabulary and phraseology on the tip of your tongue. You may also have problems in recognising visual clues and maintaining an appropriate level of discourse.

In few cases will you be prepared directly for this experience, but you can learn a lot by observing others in your small group work and by analysing any interview materials available. If you have the opportunity to record yourself on video, you should be able to identify any annoying mannerisms and work at improving your style. As an undergraduate you will not be conducting interviews with the proficiency of a trained journalist or research assistant, but there are many aspects of the technique which can be picked up without a long period of training.

PREPARING FOR AN INTERVIEW

It is just as important when you are conducting an interview as when you are being interviewed to prepare yourself beforehand. If you want your potential interviewee to be co-operative and provide the information you need, you must set up the interview carefully and pay attention to details. The stages involved in preparing for an interview can be summarised as follow:

1. Firstly, you have to identify the most appropriate people to interview for your purpose from the available documentation or from informal enquiries.

2. Secondly, you need to arrange an interview, probably by writing a letter, along the lines of the model provided in the next chapter

(pages 183-5), explaining briefly what you would like to find out and suggesting that you will telephone to fix a mutually convenient time. It may not be easy to arrange an interview with a busy person, and it is useful to specify how long you think the meeting is likely to last.

3. Once you have secured an appointment, you should compile a list of points that you want to discuss.

You should ensure that you know enough about the topic and the person you are interviewing so that you do not spend time finding out factual information which can easily be obtained elsewhere. You need to decide whether the interview will be directive, semi-directive or non-directive. If you have only limited experience of interviewing, you will probably find it is best to opt for the intermediate position, where you ask questions but also allow the interviewee to develop his or her own ideas without too much prompting. You can try to formulate clusters of questions around a topic so that you can move about an interview schedule according to the direction taken by the answers. It is important to have a clear idea of what you want to cover so that essential topics are not omitted. Unlike the survey questionnaire, an interview schedule will focus on open questions and development, introduced by *why* and *how*, rather than *do you think that*, since you are more likely to be interested in explanations rather than opinions and feelings.

CONDUCTING THE INTERVIEW

In planning the interview and designing your schedule, it is worthwhile keeping in mind the different categories of questions:

- *Opening and filter questions* are intended to orient the interview. It may save time if you begin by briefly outlining the reason why you are making the study, the general field of enquiry and why you want to interview the person concerned.
- *Conceptually defining questions* provide the framework for the interview by narrowing down the area of study.
- *Factual, numerically defining and probe questions* are used to check any information or elicit additional details.
- *Opinion defining questions* are used for eliciting personal views and inviting anecdotes
- *Closing remarks* generally express gratitude and may also be used for developing other contacts.

In an interview you will need to exploit different linguistic techniques in order to phrase questions in such a way that they elicit the appropriate response, without producing a bias as a result of the way the question is expressed (generally exemplified by the question: *When did you stop beating your wife?*). You can seek further elucidation by questions such as:

> *Que voulez-vous dire?*
> *Was meinen Sie?*
> *¿Qué quiere decirme? ¿Algo más?*

You will want to know how to introduce a topic or how to change the direction of the discussion if the speaker is straying from the question or you want to move on to another topic, for example by making a logical link:

> *A ce propos, je voulais vous demander...*
> *Ich wollte dazu fragen...*
> *A propósito, en relación a lo dicho, en adición...*

Another technique is to reiterate or summarise a point which was more relevant. It is important to display interest and therefore encourage the speaker to continue by using phrases such as:

> *Je vois, oui, je comprends.*
> *Ja ja, ich verstehe.*
> *Claro, comprendo.*

You need to know how to stave off interruptions if you are having difficulty in formulating a question. Finally, you should know how to recognise clues about when to bring the interview to an end: for example, if the interviewee looks at his or her watch or falls silent.

Although you may feel linguistically at a disadvantage, if the speaker recognises that you have a reasonable knowledge of your subject and that you are genuinely interested in what he or she has to say, you should find that you are well received. It is often useful to play on the fact that you are a foreigner approaching the topic from a different cultural perspective, and you should be prepared to answer questions about the same issues in your own society.

As with all language exercises, practice and self-criticism will improve performance. It is therefore important to try out your interviewing techniques with friends or to start with informants in lower ranks, with appropriate adaptations to style and language from the less to the more formal.

Telephoning

Sometimes it is said that telephoning has produced a new register of language, since it requires different pronunciation and adaptations in sound, tone and volume, as well as special formulae and phraseology.

Surveys of the ability of large British firms to handle international telephone enquiries suggest that if business transactions were dependent upon telephone communication, the balance of trade would be in a disastrous state. Very few companies in Britain have staff who are competent to deal with queries by telephone. There is, however, evidence to suggest that the importance of the telephone has been recognised by some companies in Britain for business carried out in English, since they employ experts to teach their staff telephone skills. They have realised that it is, for example, cheaper and more efficient to be able to sort out a technical problem over the telephone rather than by sending out an engineer. This skill should be all the more important in international communication where much greater distances are involved, and the telephone provides an essential and immediate link.

Much of what has already been said about oral interaction applies to telephoning. The functions of a telephone call can be any or all of those described in the previous chapter (see pages 84-5): a telephone conversation with a colleague could combine a social function with preparation for a business transaction, requiring the mutual exchange of information and views on the subject and initiating the necessary action to get a job done. Many of the same discourse markers can be used for telephone calls, although there is often a sense of urgency and the need to move the conversation on which may not be present to the same extent in face to face contact.

The phatic function of language is particularly important in telephone interaction for establishing, maintaining and breaking off contact. In a telephone conversation you cannot resort to para-linguistic clues to judge whether you have been understood, although interjections or vocal sounds and the occasional *oui, bien sûr, ach so* or *claro, bueno, si, no* can be helpful signs. You need to be able to handle the standard forms of greetings (*allo, j'écoute, ja bitte*) and taking leave (*aufwiederhören*). In Spanish there are two key word which are used to initiate a conversation. If quick enough the caller may be able to say *escuche* or *oiga* in order to attract attention. The other party will reply *diga* and then the conversation will ensue. In French it is important to remember to insert *madame/monsieur* as in *je vous remercie, Madame*. In the absence of para-language you will need to know how to express agreement or approval and disagreement or disapproval, acceptance or refusal, interest and intention or the converse, as well as enquiring about other options.

You may find that you have a bad line and that you therefore need to spell out your name or other information, articulate more clearly, speak more slowly or repeat what you have just said in other terms. It is useful always to recap information to see whether the message has been properly understood and to check that the receiver of the message is following by intercalating questions such as *vous me suivez? verstehen Sie? ¿comprende?* It is more difficult to get past a protective secretary at the end of a telephone than when you are in face to face contact. You may have to decide whether to hang on (*patienter, wollen Sie am Apparat bleiben?*) if the line is engaged, leave a message (*recado*) or your number for the other person to return your call. You therefore need to be able to give your personal details (*coordonnées, detalles*) and show persistence in ringing again if your call is not returned. In French, German and Spanish it is now customary, when giving telephone numbers to pair figures. If you were telling somebody your telephone number, you would say *quarante-cinq trente-deux*, etc. In Spanish the first digit is usually given by itself and following digits are then paired.

Effective telephoning, like interpreting, requires quick thinking, fast reactions and a very high degree of proficiency in the spoken language. It is all too easy to misunderstand a question or misjudge the intention behind a statement, particularly when you have limited knowledge of the person you are talking to and the environment in which he or she is located. Success in making a telephone call for a prescribed purpose is therefore a good indication that you have achieved a high level of expertise in the spoken language.

TRANSLATING

Translation is a mainstay of language syllabuses in most institutions of higher education and one of the most commonly used tests in examinations, both in the earlier years of the course and in finals. It is also considered as an important learning tool, particularly for the development of logical and contrastive analysis. By forcing the learner to look up vocabulary and grammar in reference books, to handle different language registers and to search behind words for meaning, translation can extend knowledge and improve analytical skills. Under examination conditions, it can be a demanding test of ability to manipulate idiom and syntax in a number of different language registers. Translation is one of the skills graduates may be called upon to use professionally, even if they are not working as linguists, and there are several postgraduate courses which specialise in translation techniques and theory. In the professional context translation has been described as a social skill since it promotes communication and understanding between people from different speech communities. Much has been written about translation, and there are many manuals giving advice about techniques and practices. Some of the most useful for undergraduates are suggested in the bibliography.

Although most students have probably been practising translation before entering higher education, they may find they are encouraged to forget what they thought they knew and told to approach the task from a new perspective. The reason is that, in order to be a good translator, you need to have a very high level of fluency and accuracy in a foreign language and to be able to understand the thought processes of native speakers of that language by becoming completely immersed in both the language and the culture, although not to the extent of forgetting your own language. It is not enough, however, to have an excellent command of two or more languages to be able to translate. Translation is a skill which has to be learnt and practised.

Translation is generally from and into the foreign language, although the latter, sometimes referred to as prose composition, may be reserved for the last stage of a course when proficiency in the foreign language has reached a peak. You may be told that you will never be expected to translate professionally into a language other than your native tongue and that prose composition is only an academic exercise, especially if the texts you are translating are complex literary passages. It is very unlikely that even professional translators would be called upon, or accept, to translate a literary work into a language other than their own, but translators working in commercial or technical fields do translate specialised materials both from and into their mother tongue. The comments made in this section apply to translation in both directions, although translation into a foreign language does require additional linguistic skills and knowledge which are not examined here.

A distinction is often made between scientific and literary translating. Scientific texts, and the same applies to administrative documents, are expected to present information unambiguously and objectively in accordance with established norms which leave no place for idiosyncratic stylistic variations. The reader of the translation of a scientific or administrative text is looking for information and is not normally interested in the style of the original. The reader of a literary text in translation, on the other hand, does want to be able to identify the original author's style and individuality which are not constrained by rigid norms and models. The literary text is likely to be characterised by unpredictability of language and content, incongruousness and redundancy, figurative usage and frequent flights of the imagination. There are of course many intermediate stages between these two extremes: a good example of a text type which a language graduate could be called upon to translate might be publicity materials from trade journals, where there is likely to be a combination of factual information and persuasive language. Although the translation of scientific or technical and administrative texts may come close to being a mechanical process, an advertisement or journalistic text can make important demands on cultural knowledge and linguistic versatility.

Objectives of translation

The aim in translating a text from a source language into a target language (according to the standard terminology) is to act as the intermediary between the sender and the receiver of the text. The translator must analyse the form and the purpose of the source text and reformulate it in the target language so that the reader who belongs to a different linguistic and cultural community is able to grasp the meaning and the intention of the original text. Expressed in more formal terms, the process of translation involves being able to decode and encode texts at the semantic, syntactic and pragmatic levels.

Authors writing about translation theory and practice generally make a distinction between formal and functional equivalence, sometimes expressed in terms of the distinction between semantic and communicative translation:

- Achieving formal equivalence, or *semantic translation,* involves ensuring that the exact contextual meaning and structure of the original message can be grasped by the receiver in the target language. This type of translation, also referred to as transcoding, applies, for example, to medieval literature, where the aim is to understand the way in which authors wrote in another period. The translator provides a literal translation which is usually annotated in great detail. Semantic translation is recommended in contemporary texts for rendering original expression, such as in a statement by an important political figure, where the lexical and grammatical structures are likely to be important features of the utterance and where the aim is to reproduce the idiosyncratic tone of the original.

- Where functional, or what is sometimes referred to as dynamic, equivalence is the primary requirement, as in *communicative translation,* the translator aims to make it possible for the receiver to respond to the message in his or her own language and cultural context in a similar manner to the person who was the target of the message in the original language and culture. Emphasis is on the force of the message. Since the translator is more concerned with what is behind the words, the skills of interpretation come into play. The advantage of this approach for the language learner is that it stresses the value of analysing the communication process across a wide range of situations. In effect, a transposition or transfer exercise is being carried out which is inter- rather than intra-lingual, without changing the register.

An effective communicative translation will reproduce not only the meaning but also the tone of the original text. In the same way that, in the previous chapter, it was suggested that the abstract of a text should produce the same response in the reader as the original, a translation should enable the reader to identify the purpose of the author and the reactions which he or she intended. Cultural differences have to be taken into account: when translating from French and German it may, for example, be necessary to render the text in less abstract and general language if it is to be comprehensible to an English reader.

Stages in translation

The following stages are recommended in the process of translating:

1. It is important to begin a translation by *identifying the language register and the relationship between the writer and target readers*. From your experience of text analysis, you should be able to determine the purposes of a text and the characteristic linguistic features of the language register concerned. By confronting texts from the same register in the two languages, you will discover whether similar mechanisms are used to achieve the intended effect.

2. In order to derive the maximum benefit from a translation exercise, it is useful to start by *seeing how much you can translate without using dictionaries and grammar books*.

3. You can then try *compiling lists of terminology and idiomatic expressions* appropriate to the language variety you are dealing with. Your dictionary search should include hunting for alternatives, checking them in a monolingual dictionary and dictionary of synonyms, paying particular attention to examples of usage. It is worthwhile always noting down and learning any new

vocabulary items or expressions, again ensuring that you know the contexts in which they can be used.

4. It is wise to plan your work so that you can *put your translation aside for a day or two and then come back to it*, trying to ensure that it is as natural and fluent as possible. Another useful exercise is to translate back into the original text and then compare the different versions. Where official translations of texts are available, it is interesting to make comparisons and to evaluate other versions, using the criteria applied to your own work.

If you have been instructed to make a communicative translation, your final version should read like a piece of original text rather than a translation. Just as you have learnt that it would not be appropriate to open a formal letter with the same wording as in English, translated literally, this rule applies with other text-types, where you are expected to demonstrate accuracy, fluency and appropriateness in a foreign language.

Problems of translation

Considerable attention is devoted in the literature to discussion of the problems which arise in translation. A few of these are dealt with below, and some suggestions are made about how they may be resolved.

LEXICAL AND SYNTACTIC EQUIVALENCE

Translators have to accept that there may be no exact lexical or syntactic equivalent for a word or sentence between the source and the target languages on the same linguistic level. To use the terminology introduced above, a translation based on formal equivalence may be meaningless. However, it is usually possible to find acceptable functional equivalents in the target language. The advice given in the literature on translation is that the following criteria should be observed: the word, phrase or structure should be of the same level of formality, affectivity, generality or abstraction; it should have the same connotative value as measured by its ability to give pleasure, its intensity and its associations.

NAMES AND METAPHORS

Suggestions are made in the literature about when and how to translate proper names and institutional titles (Department of Education), acronyms (SPD), culturally specific names (*grande école*, public school) and metaphors (*Quai d'Orsay*, Whitehall). The main criterion for deciding what to do is to consider the target readers and the level of understanding they are expected to have. Monolingual dictionaries and encyclopedias may help you to determine whether the original term is acceptable. In many cases you can provide a gloss (in brackets or as a footnote), but if the reader is expected to be ignorant of the cultural context of the source, then you may need to find an equivalent which is meaningful in isolation from the original, thereby demonstrating your own cultural awareness. When in doubt, however, the rule is to transcribe rather than translate.

SYNTACTIC STRUCTURE

Different syntactic structures may be needed or preferred from one language to another: where the original text uses a verb, a noun may be more appropriate in the target language, or an adverbial phrase may be the best way of rendering an adjective. In German authors tend to use abstract nouns, which results in more formal language than would be the case in English. German abstract nouns are often best translated into English by concrete nouns or verbs. Sentences are generally longer in German because it favours participial and premodifying groups, often in a compound form, which is not a structure characteristic of English syntax. The result is that the English version of a German text may be at least ten per cent and as much as thirty per cent longer. Widespread compounding in German means that the language is economical in terms of the actual number of words used but not in terms of their length. Syntactic changes should not, however, be made without the justification that they represent structures which have the same frequency of use in the target language as did the equivalent structures in the source language.

CULTURAL UNTRANSLATABILITY

Cultural untranslatability occurs when the target language does not possess the same concept or relevant situational features as the source language. The words 'democracy', 'elections' or 'president', for example, have very different meanings and connotations in countries of Eastern and Western Europe, and the meaning of *Junta* in Spain and Latin America for an administrative or political council has no direct equivalent in the British context. The answer in this case is generally to use an explanatory phrase or gloss.

CULTURE-BOUNDEDNESS

The culture-boundedness of concepts may be overcome by using idioms which fulfil an equivalent function in a second language.

Proverbs, for example, may relate to very different referential systems but still serve the same functions: *have your cake and eat it* becomes *avoir le beurre et l'argent du beurre* in French and *no se puede estar en misa y repecando* in Spanish. In German there is no equivalent expression, so an explanatory phrase would have to be used.

AMBIGUITY

Ambiguity is another common problem facing the translator. You will quickly discover that the source text is often unclear. Sometimes it is possible to reproduce ambiguity in the target language, but you may have to resolve it by choosing what seems to be the most reasonable rendition. Depending upon the context of the translation, you may be able to resort to a footnote to explain other possible interpretations. This means that you are, in effect, improving on the original text, which is widely, though not universally, considered as a legitimate aim for the translator. You should not of course introduce ambiguity or destroy it where it was intentional on the part of the author.

Learning from translation

Your success as a translator will depend to a great extent on your command and level of fluency in your own and your foreign languages. It has been said that the first qualification of the translator is the ability to write naturally and skilfully in his or her own language in a variety of registers. Although you will feel under pressure to read as much as you can in your foreign language, it is important to read widely in English as well and to work at your English written style. Since each language represents a different reality, in preparing for and making a translation you will be testing out your knowledge of your own and other cultures.

Just as many authors are never satisfied with what they have written, there is no definitive translation of any text. You should be aiming to produce a translation which does not betray the meaning or the purpose of the original but does enable communication to take place. It is possible to present reasons why one version is superior to another in a particular context. An important part of the learning process is being able to evaluate and explain the effects and effectiveness of different renderings.

INTERPRETING

The place of interpreting and the type of interpreting taught (consecutive conference, simultaneous and liaison or *ad hoc*) vary considerably from one course to another, generally depending upon the emphasis given to practical oral skills. There are few language degree programmes which offer interpreting as part of the curriculum, and fewer still where it is a compulsory exercise. Even if you do not have formal classes, you may find this section of interest since most of the skills involved can be applied in other contexts.

Full-time professional openings for interpreters are also much more limited than those for translators: only very few linguists are likely to become interpreters, and of those who do most will work as simultaneous interpreters. Consecutive conference interpreting, where the interpreter makes notes and supplies his or her rendition at the end of a speech, is used less and less in international gatherings, since it increases the time required by up to seventy-five per cent. Simultaneous interpreting, where the interpreter is isolated in a booth and speaks at the same time as the orator, has now become the method most commonly used in international conferences.

Although not many linguists will work as consecutive or simultaneous conference interpreters, there are two reasons why courses in interpreting have a legitimate place on a language degree programme:

1. It is possible that, as a linguist, you may be called upon to act as an interpreter on an *ad hoc* basis in the employment context. Because you have a degree in languages, it is assumed that you can interpret. When students are spending their period of residence abroad, they are often called upon to interpret for visitors to the firm for which they are working. An embarrassing situation may arise, if they have not mastered the technique and had some practice at it.

2. Because it requires several specialised skills, interpreting is a very useful language learning exercise.

Interpreting objectives

Interpreting differs from translating in that it involves rendering an oral text from one language into an oral text in another language. As with translation, the aim is to reproduce faithfully the meaning and form of a complete text in the second language, in terms of accuracy, appropriateness and tone. The range of situations may be wider than those normally encountered by the translator, who will tend to develop a narrow specialism: the interpreter may be handling didactic, rhetorical, emotional, technical, negotiating, legal and diplomatic language. The conditions in which the task of the interpreter is performed are also very different from those of the translator, since the interpreter is expected to give an immediate rendering and does not have the opportunity to search dictionaries for the right word or polish a text before it is released. Interpreting therefore requires a very special brand of personal qualities and skills.

The qualities and skills of the interpreter

The qualities needed by interpreters are the ability to listen very attentively to what others have to say and to understand and convey a message precisely and fluently, without adding anything of their own and without being obtrusive. Understanding may not always be easy, as the interpreter will have to handle a range of accents, often from speakers who are not using their own language. He or she also needs to be able to recognise and exploit para-linguistic information. Being fluent in two languages is not enough to be able to interpret, the appropriate techniques have to be learnt for memorising material, for making notes which will be used for immediate recall and for performing the verbal gymnastics the exercise requires.

In addition to linguistic proficiency, a good memory is essential, as are a wide cultural knowledge and an interest and awareness of technical fields. Although most of the subject matter is likely to be in the scientific, technical and diplomatic areas, speakers will often make literary or cultural allusions.

Given the high degree of concentration needed, professional interpreters must be constantly on peak form. They must have physical and mental stamina and be good communicators.

Students find that interpreting is a useful learning tool in a number of ways:

- It forces them to develop their powers of concentration and to extend their memory span.
- It encourages good note-taking practices, which can be used in other contexts.
- It helps them to learn to think quickly, to acquire and use linguistic forms appropriate to the spoken language and to become more confident in presenting their own ideas in a foreign language.
- Written translation is usually also improved because of the emphasis on understanding the meaning behind the words and finding semantic equivalence, which is often easier with a spoken text than with words on a page.

There are many ways of practising for interpreting: aural comprehension and summary and dictation from one language to another are particularly useful, as is on-sight translation into a tape recorder. Specialist terminologies can be compiled and learnt, as well as idiomatic phraseology appropriate to the contexts and situations which may be introduced. It is useful to practise by listening to the radio for a few minutes in both English and the relevant foreign language and then trying to recall the main points of what has been heard before attempting to take notes. Even if you will not be working at simultaneous interpreting, you can help to speed up your thought processes by using a language laboratory with double-track facilities to record your version of a passage as you are listening to it.

Liaison interpreting

Since simultaneous and consecutive interpreting are very staff-intensive activities, and simultaneous interpreting requires special equipment, they are generally taught only on highly specialist—often postgraduate—courses to students who have demonstrated they have the necessary aptitude and plan to look for positions as conference interpreters. Liaison or *ad hoc* interpreting, while requiring the same basic skills, is less expensive to organise in terms of time and equipment and can therefore accommodate larger numbers of students. Few graduates will aspire to become conference interpreters, but many will be called upon to interpret in less formal circumstances. For this reason, the comments made here are intended primarily for liaison interpreting, although the basic techniques needed for conference interpreting are not dissimilar.

The terms liaison or *ad hoc* interpreting are used to describe the function of interpreting a discussion or exchange between two or more individuals of different languages. Whereas conference interpreting normally involves listening to a lengthy speech and then reproducing it in the target language, liaison interpreting is generally of fairly short speech acts, although they may be longer than the memory can readily retain, and some notes will probably be required.

ANALYSING SPEECH

In learning how to interpret you must be aware of the syntactic, stylistic and para-linguistic features of texts in the source and the target languages. In the same way that you probably study the characteristics of written texts from different language varieties, you need to be able to recognise the purpose of spoken language and the interactional process which is occurring between the speaker and the recipient of the message, who will both depend upon you to reproduce the tone and an equivalent form of the original. If the speaker expresses him- or herself with irony or humour, you must ensure that you understand the intention and can convey it faithfully. If the utterance is negative, argumentative, concessionary, or if the speaker introduces examples and parentheses, all these features need to be identified and communicated.

As in translation of a written text, some of the most difficult points to render are those which are culture bound. A joke may fall flat on a French or German listener; the use of an acronym may be meaningless in another society. If you cannot immediately find an equivalent in the other language, you should know why the joke or reference may not have the same effect and be prepared to add a brief explanatory gloss.

At the analysis stage, you will want to learn how to break the text down into manageable units which it is easy to remember. If you have learnt to select and summarise information and ideas, you should be well prepared for this part of the process.

NOTE-TAKING

Since it is never certain how long somebody will go on talking, you should expect to make notes. Whereas for reading and lectures, it was suggested that notes should be taken in the language you are reading or listening to (see page 77), the advice is often given that interpreting notes should be taken in the target language, as this forces the listener to register the meaning rather than the words. Research into interpreting demonstrates, however, that professional interpreters use a mixture of the two, that ideas are often retained in a non-linguistic form and that the language of the notes is irrelevant. In any case, it is useful to train your visual memory and to learn to make at least some of your notes in the form of symbols which can then apply to all languages.

In the notes you used for your reading or lectures you could afford to be selective about the information you included, you could revise and make additions as you saw fit, and the intention was to have a set of notes which you would be able to use several months or more after you originally made them. The notes you make for interpreting, on the other hand, are wanted for almost immediate recall, and you can rely on your short term memory for elaboration if you have recorded the essential points and key words.

Students generally find that it is important to use symbols or abbreviations to record details, such as the way ideas are linked together, the tense and person of verbs and variations in the tone of voice of the speaker. You cannot, however, alter the content of the message and the sequence of the ideas by reorganising them in a way which you may find more logical. Your notes serve more as an *aide-mémoire* than as a succinct account of materials, information and opinions.

You were advised in the previous chapter to develop a system of abbreviations and symbols which would be immediately recognisable, unambiguous and concise (see pages 75-7). By the time you begin practising interpreting you will probably have a well-established system of notes which you will be able to adapt, for example by adding to the range of symbols and rethinking layout. Students generally find it helpful to develop a few symbols to use specifically for interpreting such as those suggested below:

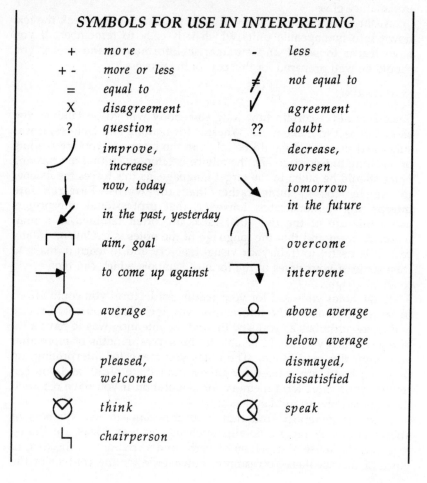

As with lecture notes or work on aural comprehension and summary, you need to be able to listen, think and write at the same time. Your notes must therefore be automatic. Clarity and legibility are essential, and a useful piece of advice is to write down narrow strips of paper (an A4 sheet folded lengthways), heavily indenting rather than using punctuation, except for question and exclamation marks or parenthesis, ruling off after each intervention, and perhaps using a different column or different coloured pen for each language, so that you can check into which language you are translating. The effect of writing down rather than across the page is that you do not waste time moving backwards and forwards across its whole width. If you start a new line for each idea, note keywords and underline any points which are stressed, you should easily be able to identify the structure of the message.

PRODUCTION IN THE TARGET LANGUAGE

Although many students clearly understand the message and are able to note it down and memorise it, they may not be good interpreters because they are unable to produce a clear and fluent rendering in the target language. If you cannot present ideas coherently and clearly, then you are unlikely to be good at interpreting. But being proficient and able to express yourself readily in more than one language does not guarantee that you will make a good interpreter. Interpreting is a technical skill, and although aptitude does help, hard work is an important ingredient for success.

As with a translation or an oral examination, there will always be vocabulary which you do not know or a syntactic structure which escapes you. It is important to learn how to get round difficulties by using a paraphrase or guessing at the meaning of words, using the clues provided by structure, content and situation. Although the original speaker hesitates or leaves sentences unfinished, the interpreter is expected to provide a fluent and syntactically complete rendering, and to some extent he or she may therefore be improving on the source text.

Interpreting can be a very satisfying activity for the language learner in that so many different skills come together to produce a good performance. There is also immediate feedback, since the interpreter can gauge the response of the listener. If the appropriate reaction is forthcoming, the interpreter can observe that the communication process is working effectively.

SUMMARY OF SUGGESTIONS

1. The range of language exercises over which you are assessed may be limited to translation, a general essay and a formal oral, but there are many tasks which you may need to perform either during the period of residence abroad or after graduation, which it is worth practising as an undergraduate.

2. You should remember that language learning is a cumulative process. The basic skills and analytical procedures you acquire serve as a foundation for task-based language exercises, which offer the opportunity to apply your knowledge in defined contexts.

3. Task-based language exercises require you to use language which is appropriate to specific situations and to know the strategies of the native speaker of the language. Through analysis you learn to identify the norms and functions of different language varieties and their cultural contexts. In the task-based exercises you apply this knowledge. Writing a formal letter, preparing a *curriculum vitae* or completing administrative procedures can only be effective if you take account of the context in which the message is to be received.

4. Writing a report involves building on analytical skills, planning and organising your work, as for an academic essay, and following instructions carefully.

5. When preparing a *CV*, it is important to read between the lines of a job advertisement, to try and predict what the reader will be looking for and to adapt the information you supply accordingly.

6. The first impression you create in a real life situation may be decisive, and it is therefore essential to ensure that you pay particular attention to the presentation of your work and to the way in which you present yourself in person.

7. It is always worthwhile trying to evaluate your own work objectively, using the criteria you have learnt for analysing texts by other writers. The main criterion to

adopt in evaluation of your own performance is whether you are likely to achieve the intended purpose.

8. It is important to know what the expectations are in face to face contact and oral interaction in different countries and to be able to adapt your own behaviour and reactions accordingly.

9. Conducting an interview requires careful preparation and attention to planning. You need to be able to guide the interview, as well as knowing how to react to the situation in an appropriate manner.

10. Telephone interaction requires a special mix of oral and aural skills in the absence of visual clues.

11. Translation from and into a foreign language is an exercise included on most language syllabuses. It can be a valuable learning tool, as well as a frequently needed skill in professional contexts. It is important to be aware of the different types of translation and to know how to produce a translation which will have the same effect on the reader as the original text was intended to have on readers in a different cultural context. Accuracy, fluency and appropriateness of language are paramount, but you must ensure that your rendering is faithful to the author of the text.

12. Conference interpreting is probably practised by very few students or graduates. Informal interpreting is, however, a good language learning tool and a useful skill, involving a number of techniques, which are worth mastering.

5 THE PERIOD OF RESIDENCE ABROAD

Most language degree courses require students to spend a prolonged period of residence abroad. In preparing for this experience, it is important to be able to choose your placement with full knowledge of the range of opportunities available. You will want to know how to handle formal procedures and what is needed to satisfy your institution's requirements. You will also be looking for ways of ensuring that you use the period of residence abroad to help further your personal development. This chapter looks at:

1. The purpose of the period of residence in a foreign country.

2. The different types of placement and how to select the placement most suitable for you.

3. The administrative procedures you will need to follow both in order to secure a placement and to complete formalities on arrival.

4. How to research and prepare a project or work report.

5. How to ensure you gain maximum benefit from living in another country.

Although you are a student of languages, it is possible that you may never have had the opportunity to spend a prolonged period in the country of the language you are studying. If you are in this situation, you should try to go abroad as often as you can during the vacations, in order to bring yourself up to the same level of fluency and confidence as your fellow students who have spent longer in the other country. Some institutions encourage students to spend their vacations abroad by making available travel funds and bursaries for which they can apply to enable them to attend a vacation course or to follow some other form of approved study. You should take advantage of whatever opportunities you can find, and these visits may help you in selecting where you go for your longer 'period of residence abroad'.

Almost all language degree courses expect students to spend anything from a term to a year, living and working or studying in the foreign country, generally after the second year of the course in the home institution. In many cases the period of residence abroad will be a course requirement to which you commit yourself when you enrol.

If you are studying more than one language, you will want to spend as much time as possible in the two countries. It may not always be feasible to split the period equally, but you will find you can normally compensate by using the vacations or by ensuring you keep up practice in the other language while abroad by listening to the radio, reading newspapers and books or attending any classes available locally.

The purpose of spending a prolonged period of residence abroad can be summarised as follows:

- To improve linguistic skills.
- To extend knowledge of the foreign society and its institutions.
- To learn how to develop personal initiative and to take advantage of opportunities for displaying independence and adaptability.

The main purpose of the period of residence abroad is to raise your level of fluency, accuracy and confidence in speaking the foreign language and to improve your ability to communicate effectively in a number of different situations, both orally and in writing. These will range from the formal, at the workplace or in your encounters with bureaucracy, to the informal or social in your non-work time.

Another of your aims will be to increase your knowledge, awareness and understanding of the society and its language by observing the behaviour of others, by interaction with them and through intelligent use of the media and other documentary sources of information.

If you are following a course in a university or in a more specialised institution, such as a business school, or working as a language assistant in a secondary school, you will be able to observe firsthand the way in which the educational system operates and gain a better understanding of different approaches to the training of the country's managers, civil servants, engineers or scientists, who may later be your colleagues or competitors. If you are in employment and you have never worked outside the educational sector in your own country, the experience of a job placement abroad will be new in more ways than one, and you will be able to learn about work practices and working conditions.

If your home institution requires you to write a dissertation, project or report, you will have the opportunity to collect information about a specialised topic—possibly a contemporary or local issue—and to plan and carry out research, using a wide range of sources. You will be able to demonstrate your ability to work independently and to take initiatives, which will be an important element in your personal development.

Whatever the type of placement or the locality, you will be representing your home institution, and the impression you create may influence attitudes towards other students. You should therefore aim to behave in such a way as to make your employers, colleagues or fellow students favourably disposed towards other British students who follow you.

TYPES OF PLACEMENT

In order to ensure that you improve your accuracy and fluency in the foreign language, you will want to find a placement which gives you maximum exposure to communicative situations involving native speakers. The experience of living and working in another society with its own cultural norms may require a period of reorientation, and you need to consider carefully which type of placement will be most suitable for you personally and the most likely to be conducive to language learning.

There are several useful publications written for foreign students on placements abroad, many produced by the relevant embassies, which you can consult for detailed information about institutional structures and procedures. Several of these are listed in the bibliography. In this section the focus is on increasing your awareness of the factors which you will need to take into account when preparing for the period of residence abroad. Many of the points made are based on comments from students, either while they were on a placement or when they have returned to complete their course. No attempt is made here to conceal the problems or the main disadvantages associated with each type of placement. The final section of the chaper offers some general advice about how to exploit whatever placement you are in, so that you fulfil your objectives.

There are three main types of placement from which you may be able to choose: the higher education course, the assistantship and the work placement. The type of placement you select or are allocated will determine, to a considerable extent, the nature of the contact that you have with other people and with the language. The work environment in an industrial or commercial company is very different from that in a school or a university.

All placements have their advantages and their drawbacks. In preparing for the period of residence abroad, you need to go through the following steps:

1. Find out as much as you can from the available literature, from the overseas placements tutor, if your institution has one, and from students who have returned from abroad. Information sessions may be arranged for you, or you may have to take the initiative of finding out for yourself.
2. Try to make a realistic assessment of your own abilities and skills, as well as your future plans, and relate them to the available opportunities, for success in any placement is due largely to your own frame of mind and to the effort you are prepared to put into making it work.

In assessing the accounts that other students give of their experience, you need to try to project yourself into the situation and to consider how you would react personally. This may also be an appropriate moment to consult your careers' office and to begin thinking very seriously about career planning, if you have not already done so. While not necessarily finding the right career by this means, as one final year undergraduate commented:

Most students discover while they are abroad what they don't want to do as a career. Although this seems rather negative, it is a start.

Every year, however, after graduation a number of students return to the country where they have spent their period of residence abroad, often to a job found through the contacts they made, so the experience may be more directly relevant to your future plans than you thought.

Higher education courses

A number of British language departments send the majority of their students on higher education courses for the period of residence abroad, mainly in universities, but also in specialised university institutes or business schools

UNIVERSITY PLACEMENTS

One of the types of placement which is relatively easy to arrange is in a university, but it is often the option which students find least attractive, both for financial reasons and because foreign universities do not normally offer the same facilities and supportive networks that you expect to find in the British higher education system.

In most West European countries access to higher education is automatic for all students who pass the school leaving examination, with the exception of subjects, such as medicine, which operate a *numerus clausus*. Since there are minimal restrictions on entry, the number of students on courses in the first year is very large. The failure rate at the end of the first year may be as high as fifty per cent. Because schooling is generally much broader than in Britain, students are less specialised when they enter higher education, and they may not narrow down the focus of their studies until after their first or second year. Possibly as a consequence, courses are also longer than in Britain.

In order to match the level of specialisation you have reached, you will probably want to enrol in the second or third year of study, if the syllabus is appropriate and you are eligible to do so. You must, in any case, ensure that your home institution approves your choice. In some instances it may be possible to select a menu of courses from different years, as one student explained:

> On the course which I followed in France, you have to construct your own selection from the lectures and seminars on offer and make it as relevant as you can.

Elsewhere, you may be expected to enrol on courses which are designed for foreign students, often in institutes connected to a university and for which the fees are generally higher. Some of the problems associated with this type of study programme have been summed up by another student:

> It was difficult to break away from other foreign students on the course in German as a foreign language. In my group it was near to 'A' level standard, although one of the other British students found his course quite interesting.

If the language you are studying is Russian, you may have no option but to follow a course with other foreigners, and you may find that you have few opportunities to mix freely with Russians. Recently, the situation has been changing dramatically, however, and it is now possible for foreign students to be much more integrated into Soviet society. If you are studying a West European or Scandinavian language, your home institution may have special arrangements for you to follow a particular course, in which case you will again have no choice. Students of Japanese may be offered intensive courses in a

Japanese institution over the summer vacation by special arrangement through government sponsored schemes.

University placements provide the opportunity to study a wide range of subjects, and a number of institutions abroad now offer applied language courses, covering practical skills and knowledge about language use in specific contexts, which you may find of particular interest. Students combining a language with accountancy or law may be able to follow a course on that subject in the foreign language. If later on they work in international finance, they have the advantage of both knowing something about the financial system in another country and being familiar with the training which their foreign counterparts have undergone. For students reading two languages it may be useful to enrol for courses in the second foreign language, for example by studying Japanese in Paris. It may be possible to follow a course in a subject of personal interest to you which you have been unable to study in your home institution.

Sometimes the course assessment will count towards your finals marks and, by sitting the examinations, you may be able to obtain a qualification and a useful addition to your *curriculum vitae* when you apply for jobs, although foreign qualifications are unlikely to give you exemption from professional examinations in Britain.

Where British institutions have exchange agreements with foreign universities, business schools or colleges, tuition fees may be waived, and assistance is generally given by the host institution with arrangements for accommodation, the selection of courses and supervision. One student on this type of placement claimed that:

> *Being an exchange student in France means that you can get to do what you want with the support and guidance of the staff.*

Although there may be no guarantee that you will be able to enrol for the course you are interested in, the possibility of receiving assistance under such an agreement is an important consideration, since it may be very difficult to find accommodation or understand course information and procedures without inside knowledge. Where such an arrangement exists you may also be able to make prior contact with foreign students from the exchange institution while they are studying at your home base.

The university environment in other European countries is generally much less structured than in the British system, where you are protected and sheltered both socially and academically. In most other countries students receive little financial support from the state, and many therefore continue to live at home. They may be working at the same time in order to finance their studies. The effect is that campus life is often virtually non-existent, and it may not be easy to meet other people or to be invited to their homes. If you already have acquaintances in the country where you are going, you would be well advised to choose a location within easy reach of them, so that you have at least one immediate source of contact with native speakers. Knowing somebody in the town where you will be living may be a vital factor in smoothing the transition period when you first arrive.

There are many university towns which seem much more attractive than others for environmental reasons: most students, given the choice, would prefer to go to Grenoble, Aix-en-Provence or Montpellier, rather than to Metz or Lille; Heidelberg, Munich and Göttingen may be more attractive than a town in Germany dominated by heavy industry; Salamanca, Málaga, Madrid, Valencia, Barcelona and Granada are more likely to be of interest to students of Spanish than Valladolid, Santiago, Murcia or Zaragoza. But you would not be the only person attracted by the pleasanter environment, and the problems created by a surfeit of foreign students are not to be underestimated. If you choose a small, less popular university town, you will probably not have to compete for accommodation and attention with a large number of other foreign students, although the smaller towns may offer only a limited range of subjects.

Whenever possible you should try to apply for courses where the number of students in seminars is relatively small. Group size is generally much larger than in British higher education, particularly in the first year. In Bordeaux, for example, approximately 2,000 students enrol to study law (a subject for which the university is highly reputed). Although only about 300 go on to complete the course, small group work as you know it in Britain is out of the question.

An advantage of spending the period abroad in a university is that you will generally have more freedom than in other types of placement, both in the way you put together your programme of study (unless it has been pre-arranged by your home institution) and in the flexibility of your schedule. Another consideration is that, unlike your fellow students who have been in employment and earning a living, you will avoid the problem at the end of the year of having to return to academic work and adapt back to student life.

Experiences can vary from one institution to another, from one course to another and from one person to another, but many students are very positive about university placements. One undergraduate commented:

The thought of going to university in Paris seemed very daunting at first, but living and studying there proved to be one of the most fantastic experiences I've ever had.

Students who have spent their time abroad in a university maintain that it is up to the individual to try to make the most of the situation by seeking out information and advice and by learning to be flexible.

As opinions diverge about the benefits and drawbacks of university placements abroad, it is useful to summarise the main advantages and disadvantages:

- *Advantages of university placements*
  They are relatively easy to arrange.
  There are opportunities to study a wide variety of subjects.
  It may be possible to obtain an additional qualification.
  Students are relatively free to organise their own programme of study and extracurricular activities.
  Because there is continuity of academic life the return to your home institution requires little readaptation.
- *Disadvantages of university placements*
  The number of students on courses is likely to be extremely large.
  Campus life is very limited.
  It may be difficult to establish contact with the host population.
  The lack of a formal structure may make personal activities difficult to organise.

BUSINESS SCHOOL PLACEMENTS

Many British institutions have exchange arrangements with business schools or business studies institutes in Austria, Belgium, France, Italy, Spain, Switzerland and the Federal Republic of Germany for students following courses in management with a language. Often they include an industrial placement. There are also a few exchange schemes with other specialised institutes for students reading subjects such as engineering, but these account for fairly small numbers and the students concerned are not usually majoring in languages.

Occasionally European business programmes are taught jointly by two or more institutions, with all the students spending a fixed period in each of two or three countries. Not all courses are completely integrated, however, and patterns of study may differ markedly (see page 6 on joint study programmes).

Comparisons which have been made between business schools and institutes in Britain, France and the Federal Republic of Germany suggest that the German and English approaches are similar. The German business courses are generally run by the higher education sector, and they therefore place emphasis on academic concepts and critical thinking. The French *écoles de commerce*, on the other hand, are not part of the university sector; they are less theoretical and do not, for example, rely on extensive and independent reading. They tend instead to use case studies as their main teaching method, with the focus on solutions rather than problems.

Whereas access to universities abroad is generally non-selective, entry to a business school or institute within the university system is generally competitive and, in France, usually requires a period of further preparation of up to two years before taking the entrance examination. Compared with the number of students in other sectors of higher education, the size of an annual cohort is very small. The motivation and expectations of the students are also different. British students who have been to French business schools tend to find the atmosphere disciplinarian, hierarchical and competitive and not unlike that in secondary school. The teaching is more practical and less academic than in a university and there are more contact hours. Most of the teaching staff in the French business schools have considerable experience of working in industry or are bought in from companies, while staff in the British and German institutions are more likely to be working full-time in the higher education sector.

Students from other countries who do not share the same background and motivation may find it difficult to adapt, although they do have the advantage of not being considered as direct competitors. They will generally be required to sit the examinations, and the marks may count towards their degree result or enable them to obtain a certificate. They are motivated to work hard, even though they will not normally be competing for a ranking in the final qualification. Some international collaborative arrangements with business schools or similar institutions in other European countries do, however, lead to a dual award.

An important point to remember is that, by spending a prolonged period in a business school, you will have been in contact with the country's future managers. The business schools, particularly in France, provide a well recognised and prestigious training for management. Students who are a product of the schools subsequently have easy access to the labour market. Although you will not be listed amongst the *alumni*, you may find that you are able to make some useful contacts for your own career. The information brochures from one of the more prestigious French business schools state that:

> *150 to 200 firms visit the campus every year in the hope of attracting the school's students.*

4,500 offers of employment are received every year for the school's 300 students.

For many British students the business schools offer the ideal combination of academic study and practical experience of living and working abroad, while also ensuring easier integration than in the universities for those who are not intimidated by the environment. As one British student commented:

> *Despite the very heavy workload, it turned out to be one of the most rewarding ways of spending the year abroad, as you can get the best of both worlds by splitting the year into two terms of study at the school followed by a placement during the third term.*
>
> *You will find that the business school students in France tend to be quite 'genned-up' on current events and history. Students, especially the first years who have come directly from the gruelling classes préparatoires, tend to be extrovert, overconfident and appear never to do any work. Your major advantage is that you speak fluent English, which is a compulsory subject in French business schools and can be used as a bargaining tool.*

Assistantships

A large proportion of language departments in British universities send the majority of their students on placements as assistants in schools. The total number of posts for foreign language assistants is, however, strictly limited and there is therefore competition for places. If you have no intention of going into teaching, are not interested in it as an activity and do not enjoy working with children, then it may be both unwise and selfish to apply for an assistantship.

The Central Bureau for Educational Visits and Exchanges in London processes application forms, considers the recommendations of tutors and makes the preliminary selection of the most suitable candidates for allocation to appropriate institutions by the relevant ministries of education. Full details are given in the Bureau's publications. The process is highly systematised and efficient, so that, by following their instructions carefully, you should have no problems in completing the formalities.

In your application you are asked to express your preferences for particular areas or types of school. Again if you already have contacts in the foreign country, you are advised to seek a post nearby. As with universities, some areas are much more in demand than others, and you may be disappointed if you limit your choice to the most popular parts of the country. Often the smaller town is more likely to provide a friendly environment, and you will have novelty value. The type of school you opt for will depend upon the age groups you are interested in teaching and, in some cases, your knowledge of more technical subjects.

The assistantship has the advantage of providing you with a regular and quite generous income for what is a relatively small teaching commitment. You may be encouraged, or expected, to attend courses if there is a university in the vicinity, but this will not always be feasible logistically and may not fit in with your classes. Generally you will find that you have ample time to travel around and to undertake individual study. Many assistants are asked to give private lessons, which supplements income and affords an opportunity to get to know families.

The Central Bureau provides a wealth of information about the work. Preliminary training courses are organised for instruction in classroom techniques. In some cases these are run by your home institution, sometimes by the relevant ministry and sometimes the region where you are placed. The school where you are posted will normally help with finding accommodation and will give assistance on your arrival. The reception does vary, however, from one place to another. The onus is always on you to announce when you will be arriving and to ask for advice.

Placements as assistants usually convince students whether or not they are suited for a career in teaching. The reaction differs considerably from one student to another, depending upon the atmosphere in the school, the attitude of staff and pupils and individual personalities. For some students the experience is rewarding and provides the means of integrating fully into another society. One student, who was given an appointment as an assistant, described how worried she was when she discovered where she had been posted but how she made a success of the placement:

> *My school was in a small country town miles from anywhere. I could not even find it on the map. The pupils were mainly weekly boarders from villages in the area, and they all went home at the weekend, so I found myself almost alone on the school premises, where I had been given free accommodation. The first month was the worst time in my life. I decided that I had to act, so I found a flat in the town and joined the only clubs there were. I had to take the first step and show that I was interested in other people, but after about four months I was completely accepted and found I got on really well with the*

teachers and pupils. My predecessor had kept herself very much to herself, and they thought I would be the same.

Work placements

There are several reasons why you may prefer a work placement during your period of residence abroad. The theoretical knowledge you gain on your course is no substitute for real work experience. You may feel that the work placement is the best way of integrating into the foreign society. There is certainly evidence to show that good students do well on good work placements, but it can be argued that because they are good students they get the best jobs or that they would do well in any sort of placement. A successful work placement may open doors for you in the future, and most employers will welcome evidence that you have been able to sustain a job. Another consideration is that many students who rely on their parents to support them feel that they would like to be financially independent while they are abroad.

Good work placements are not easy to find. Some institutions have placements tutors who arrange jobs abroad, and some jobs are passed on from year to year, but you should try to follow up any contacts you have yourself, particularly through multinational companies. Most industrial and commercial firms will select their recruits very carefully, and you will probably have to compete for a place. If you are not confident that you are well motivated for one of the few posts available and that you have a strong case to support you, it is unlikely that you will be selected. As with assistantships, the way you behave during a placement will determine whether employers will be prepared to take another student and what their expectations will be of recruits from a particular institution. You therefore have an important role to play in representing British higher education.

Most jobs for linguists will be as translators or in clerical work, often in export departments. Typing skills may give you the edge on other candidates but, even then, you should not expect automatically to find appropriate employment. If you admit to having typing skills, you may be expected to spend most of your time typing, so you need to consider carefully the way you present yourself. Students from combined subjects courses are more likely to be able to secure a work placement if they can offer what employers consider as 'usable' skills. Many jobs will be routine and will not stretch you intellectually, since you are not able to offer the qualifications and experience required for higher grade posts. Occasionally, a placement will take the form of a 'traineeship', but good ones are few and far between. It is important to remember that the work placement is a two-way process: the employer will expect to get as much out of you as you get from being employed.

A fairly typical specification for one of the better jobs might be that given to a student of business and French who was employed as an assistant to the training manager in a personnel department:

> *My duties included the organisation of training courses for personnel and all the administration involved; preparation and budgeting of the annual training plans for each company division; control and organisation of all training course details on personal computer (database, wordprocessing, spreadsheet); development, launching, promotion and control of a new auto-education system for personnel; daily telephone and personal contact with all hierarchical levels as well as with external organisations, knowledge of the company essential for the job, use of personal computer, correspondence.*
>
> *The post required somebody with a good level of fluency in spoken and written French, initiative, the ability to work with little supervision; typing was a great advantage, and slight knowledge of computers was helpful though not essential.*

A student of French and German who spent a year in a placement in the German Democratic Republic described how her work in a translation agency consisted of:

> *Translating into English, editing texts which had been translated by Germans and proof-reading English and occasionally French texts. The bulk of the material was about fashions. During the Spring Trade Fair I worked in the Press Office editing a daily bulletin, translating small articles for it and proof-reading it. One day a week I was lent out to teach English in an adult education centre.*

Many jobs are much less varied and interesting than these two. Whatever the nature of the work, the biggest shock for students who have never held a full-time job for any length of time is the sudden lack of freedom to organise their own schedule. They find that even if they have flexible hours, the length of the working day and the lack of extended holidays may be difficult to adapt to. In professional life you will have to accept these conditions, so your experience as a student could be good practice.

Another problem faced by students in work placements is their relative isolation. They find that it is not always easy to make contact socially with colleagues since they have their own family life or established circle of friends. Particularly in the larger conurbations, people may live some distance from their work and be reluctant either to stay on for social activities or to invite colleagues home.

The main advantages of the work placement, apart from the income (although this may not be much more than a full grant), are that, even if the job you do is not intellectually demanding or stimulating, you will gain firsthand experience of employment, and this should help you in your career planning.

ADMINISTRATIVE PROCEDURES

There are a number of administrative procedures you will need to go through, both in order to secure a particular type of placement and in making financial and other arrangements before and after arrival. Most of these are time-consuming, but they provide valuable practice in learning how to handle forms and in dealing with bureaucracy.

Local Education Authority grants for residence abroad

If you are in receipt of a Local Education Authority grant, the maintenance award covers the period of residence abroad if it is compulsory and you are not in employment. If the period abroad is not a course requirement, the grant is discretionary. For grant-awarding purposes countries are categorised according to their cost of living. Your LEA will normally cover between twenty-eight and forty-eight weeks of residence abroad and will pay for at least one return trip. The exact duration of the award depends upon the number of weeks required by your home institution. It is therefore important to inform your LEA of the arrangements you are making. Since LEAs can make discretionary payments over and above those laid down in the Department of Education and Science regulations, you will find that it is worth checking the situation in person before you go abroad, Practice in this respect varies from one LEA to another, as confirmed in the following advice offered by an undergraduate:

> *Each LEA is a law unto itself, so don't be surprised if friends receive more or less than you do. If you are studying for more than thirty weeks (some foreign institutions have two long terms), get a letter from your own or the foreign institution confirming this, and you should be awarded the extra amount. As far as travel is concerned, my LEA paid for three return journeys, whereas another only financed two return trips.*

Applications for placements

Whatever type of placement you are looking for, but particularly for employment in a company, if you have not already done so, you will need to be preparing a *curriculum vitae* in the foreign language, in which you present yourself realistically but to your best advantage. You will want to provide details of your educational qualifications, any work experience and special skills you have and your extracurricular interests, in order to give some indication of your personality and a basis for discussion at an interview, if one is arranged. When you are applying for a particular type of placement, you will need to demonstrate why you are interested and why you would be a good candidate.

Since the job market is very competitive, the CV often serves as a means of screening applicants. Presentation is therefore important if you are to create a favourable first impression. It is worth having a typed CV, or, even better, one which is prepared on a wordprocessor so that it can easily be updated and adapted. This may be one of the tasks you have practised in language classes. Guidelines were given in the previous chapter for preparing a CV (pages 125-30). The examples below provide models which you can follow for drafting a CV in French, German or Spanish, such as would be appropriate for a placement during a period of residence abroad.

SAMPLES OF A CURRICULUM VITAE

French example:

Barbara MILLER

Née le 3 novembre 1967, à Londres (21 ans)

112 rue Champion
75018 Paris
Tél. : Chez Monsieur et Madame Necker (1) 45 32 16 24

Nationalité britannique

Célibataire

Formation
    Juin 1985 :   'A' level (diplôme de fin d'études secondaires, équivalent du baccalauréat) en français (mention très bien), allemand (mention bien) et économie

Juin 1987 : Reçue aux examens de fin de deuxième année d'études universitaires en français et allemand (mention bien)
Juin 1989 : BA (licence en quatre ans) de français et d'allemand, en cours de préparation, Université de Londres

Autres formations
*[1983 : RLSS Award of Merit Lifesaving (diplôme de maître nageur/sauveteur)
1984 : Chief Guide Award (diplôme supérieur de scoutisme)]
1987 à 1988 : Cours de langues étrangères appliquées, Université de Paris VII (en préparation du DEUG)

Langues
Anglais - langue maternelle
Français - parlé et écrit couramment
Allemand - parlé et écrit
Espagnol - notions

Expérience professionnelle
1985 : Enquêtrice à temps partiel pour une société de marketing pendant deux mois à Londres
1986 : Stage à plein temps pendant dix semaines chez M and T, PME dans le textile, employée au Bureau de contrôle des achats

***[Responsabilités exercées**
1982 à 1987 : Chef de Patrouille (Guides)
1984 à 1985 : Senior Girl (déléguée de classe et responsable de la discipline des élèves plus jeunes)
1986 à 1988 : Membre du Comité Organisateur de la Mutuelle des Etudiants, Université de Londres]

Divers
Voyages : Séjours fréquents à l'étranger, en France, en Allemagne et aux Etats-Unis, comme touriste seule ou avec une amie et comme stagiaire

[Sports Natation, tennis, ski]

Autres renseignements:
Permis (1987)—dispose d'une voiture personnelle
Prête à voyager et à travailler à l'étranger

* This information should be omitted unless it is directly relevant to the type of work for which you are applying.

German example:

Barbara MILLER

Am 3. November 1967 in London geboren (21 Jahre alt)

Britisch

Albert-Schweitzer Straße 89
2800 Bremen 3
Tel: 0421/56 21 64

Ledig

Beruf des Vaters
   Realschullehrer

Konfession   r. kath.

Bildungsweg Grundschule von 1973 bis 1977
   Gymnasium von 1977 bis 1982

Leistungskurse
Juni 1985: 'A' level (Äquivalent des Abiturs) in Französisch (mit zwei), in Deutsch (mit zwei), in Wirtschaftskunde (mit drei)
Juni 1987: Prüfungen des zweiten Jahres der Universität von London in Französisch und Deutsch
Juni 1989: BA (vierjähriger Kurs) in Französisch und Deutsch (in Vorbereitung, Universität von London)

Andere Kenntnisse und Erfahrungen
*[1983: RLSS Award of Merit Lifesaving (Lebensrettung)
1984:   Chief Guide Award (Pfadfinderinnenauszeichnung)]

1987 bis 88:   Diplomsprachkurs/Staatsexamen
               (Universität München)

Sprachkentnisse
Englisch   - Muttersprache
Deutsch   - sehr gut
Französisch - gut
Spanisch   - Grundkenntnisse

Berufstätigkeit
1985:   Teilzeitstelle als Interviewerin für eine Marktforschungsfirma
1986:   Angestellte in einer Textilfirma (zehn Wochen)

***[Außerschulische Interessen**
Reisen: Häufige Auslandsreisen, nach Frankreich, Deutschland und Amerika
          Allein als Tourist oder mit einer Freundin
Sport: Schwimmen, Tennis und Skilaufen]

Andere relevante Information
Führerschein (1987)—für den eigenen Wagen
Bereit im Ausland zu arbeiten

* This information should be omitted unless it is directly relevant to the type of work for which you are applying.

Spanish example:

Barbara MILLER HENWOOD

Fecha de nacimiento   3 de noviembre de 1967, 21 años

Calle de los Pinos, Nº33
Son Cotoner
280038 Madrid
Tfo: (91) 522 78 64

Nacionalidad   Británica

Estado civil   Soltera

Educación
Junio 1984:   Obtuve el certificado 'A level', en 3 asignaturas, francés, español y ciencias económicas

	(Este es equivalente al bachillerato y COU)
Junio 1987	Estudié 4 años para obtener el grado de
a junio 1989:	BA en las asignaturas de francés y
	español en la universidad de Londres
	(El BA es equivalente a la licenciatura)

Idiomas
El inglés como lengua materna
El francés que lo hablo y escribo correctamente
El español en forma adecuada
También tengo conocimiento del alemán

Experiencia de trabajo
1985: Tuve un trabajo de media jornada con una compañía de estudios de mercado en Londres
1986: Trabajé de continuo con una compañía de productos textiles

Otros
Poseo permiso de conducir válido obtenido en 1987
También tengo diploma en mecanografía

Many employers will also want to see something written in your own hand, so you could practise drafting a covering letter in the relevant language, referring to the position you are applying for and your attached *CV*. You should begin by mentioning the vacancy and explain how you found out about it. You should then describe your current situation and refer to details included in your *CV* before going on to explain why you are interested in the position and why you feel you are an appropriate person for the job. Some employers like to interview candidates, so you will also need to practise oral self-presentation and think through the points made about job interviews in the previous chapter (pages 130-1).

For university places and assistantships you will need to complete the standard forms provided, but you can use your *CV* as a reference tool. Forms are supplied by the Central Bureau for assistantships and by the relevant embassy for university placements in France. Individual universities in Germany send out their own application forms. You should always check what is currently required and observe deadlines, since late applications are not accepted. You need to make sure you complete all sections and that you send the required number of copies of the form and any supporting documents asked for. It is always worthwhile keeping a photocopy of any applications you make for your own reference, in case there are points you want to check.

For many applications your tutor will be asked to supply a reference. You may be one of a large number of students needing a recommendation at the same time, so do not wait until the last minute to approach your referee. You can help speed up the process by providing a copy of your CV and a note explaining why you are interested in a particular type of placement, together with any other information of which your tutor may not be aware.

Official documents

Even though you have observed all the deadlines, it is possible that you may not have confirmation of your placement until the very last minute, but there are still many procedures you can set in motion in the weeks prior to your expected date of departure.

Although you will be able to find out much of what you need to know about procedures from official publications (see bibliography), it is always worth cross-checking any information with foreign embassies in Britain. However, you should not be dismayed if, subsequently, you find that local authorities where you are staying do not conform to the pattern you have been led to expect. As the many schemes, especially ERASMUS, for encouraging the free movement of students within Europe come into operation, it should be easier to satisfy the requirements of bureaucracy, but it will be some time before all the barriers are removed. Meanwhile, you must ensure that you know which regulations apply to you and that you observe them.

The following is a list of the documents you may be called on to produce in order to obtain a residence permit, for enrolment and other formalities. Most of them should be obtained before you go abroad:

1. A *passport* or some other form of identity. For study in another European Community country, you are not officially required to have a passport, but in most countries in Europe you are expected to carry some form of identity card with you. A passport is a useful and universally accepted document. You are also advised to take a photocopy of it, including the cover and any pages which have been stamped.

2. At least a dozen passport size *photographs*.

3. A *financial statement*. This may take the form of a letter from your Local Education Authority saying that you will be in receipt of a maintenance grant during the year, from your parents confirming they will be supporting you, from your employer

indicating that you have the means of supporting yourself financially or from your bank manager.

4. Copies of a letter in the foreign language from your own institution, confirming your *registration* as a student and indicating which parts of your course you have successfully completed.

5. The original, a copy and a translation of your *birth certificate*, as well as translations of *documents*, such as examination results for 'A' levels and undergraduate courses. You may be able to get your home institution to certify translations, otherwise you will have to go to the competent authority in the country concerned, normally the consulate, which will charge a fee for certification. Institutions may request sight of originals, but you should not send personal documents through the post, and you will want to make every effort to avoid letting them out of your hands, except if you obtain an official receipt.

6. Enough *local currency* to cover any fees and traveller's cheques to meet any initial expenditure, such as a deposit on accommodation.

7. Once you have somewhere to live you will need *proof of residence*, such as an electricity bill (a letter from a landlord or a rent receipt may not be sufficient).

8. Confirmation of your *status*. When you begin your placement you should obtain a copy of your assistant nomination papers, a letter from your employer or a certificate of enrolment from a university showing your status.

If you are going to be in France for more than three months you will have to apply for a residence permit. Procedures seem to vary from one place to another, but you are likely to need all the documents listed above, together with several stamped self-addressed envelopes. In the Paris area you have to go to a special office for EC nationals, and elsewhere to the *Commissariat de Police* or the local town hall. If you are staying for more than three months in the Federal Republic of Germany you will need to register at the local *Einwohnermeldeamt*, where you can obtain the form on which to apply for a residence permit. The address can be found at the town hall. You also need to inform the office of any change of address and when you leave the country. Similar regulations about residence permits apply in Italy and Spain, where you will also need to register with the relevant authorities. The EC's *Handbook for Students* gives advice for these and other countries in the Community. For the Soviet Union or countries outside the EC, you will need to contact the embassy or consulate in Britain and follow carefully any instructions given by your home institution.

Insurance

There are reciprocal arrangements within the EC for insurance cover, although these differ from one country to another. Your local DSS office will supply you with relevant information and the necessary forms to complete. You will probably need to send them, together with a letter explaining the reasons for your prolonged stay abroad, to the head office in Newcastle upon Tyne. For the Federal Republic of Germany, you should be eligible for cover under the family benefits scheme, if you are a student, but this has to be confirmed by the local social security office in Germany. If you are in paid employment, normal deductions will be made automatically from your salary. For Austria or Switzerland, you will need to take out private insurance, since there are no reciprocal agreements, but students in Austria are covered by a special scheme.

If you are accepted for the scheme of the country concerned, you will normally be eligible for the standard social security cover. This may mean that you will not be covered for the full cost of any treatment, and you are therefore advised to take out additional insurance. As a student in a European country, you will normally be eligible for cover by student insurance funds, which means that, for a fairly modest sum, you may receive full reimbursement of most medical expenses. You may find that you are required to pay for treatment by a doctor or for medicines and are then subsequently reimbursed when you observe the right procedures. Since most of the medicines you consume in Britain are heavily subsidised by the National Health Service, you are probably completely unaware of their cost commercially. Even a fairly minor illness may result in an unexpectedly large bill. It is therefore important to be absolutely certain that you are covered before you go abroad and to check procedures for submitting a claim. If your home institution does not have copies for you to consult, you can obtain explanatory leaflets from the local social security office in the area where you are living.

The examples below summarise the procedure for making a claim for reimbursement of expenses for medical care in France and for ensuring that you have social security cover in Spain. They should be read in conjunction with the guidelines set out in the previous chapter for completing official forms (pages 119-22).

DEALING WITH ADMINISTRATIVE PROCEDURES

Claiming medical expenses in France

In the case of a social security claim for reimbursement of medical expenses, you will be instructed to refer to your **caisse**, *which is the appropriate local office of the medical fund. You will automatically pay contributions if you are an employee, and you should take out an insurance policy if you are a student. Although central government sets the rates, each fund deals with claims at a local level. The medical fund is one of three separate* **caisses** *to which employees must contribute. Although you are unlikely to draw benefits from the other two* **caisses**, *you and your employer will be contributing for family allowances and old age and retirement benefits.*

You will be supplied with a **feuille de soins** *and with instructions about how to complete it. The term* **cotisations** *is your contribution and* **prestations** *are the payments you are eligible to receive. You are the insured person,* **l'assuré**, *and as such you have a* **numéro d'immatriculation**, *proving that you are registered, and also a* **carte d'immatriculation** *which you should take with you to any doctor.*

In order to claim reimbursement, you will be asked to **constituer un dossier**. *For reimbursement of medical expenses you will need to supply your bank account number, so that a* **virement**, *or payment, can be made into your account. For your first application for reimbursement, you will be asked to send a* **relevé d'identité bancaire**, *giving details of your bank account. If you are employed, you will need to produce a standard statement from your employer,* **une attestation annuelle d'activité salariée**, *showing that you are working. Your employer may also be asked to provide an* **attestation**, *or certificate, showing how long you have been off work, if you are eligible for sickness benefits.*

You will need to keep any duplicates of documents from your doctor, such as that for the prescription, **ordonnance**, *and also the* **vignette**, *or stamp, which is on medicines purchased from a chemist.*

Obtaining social security cover in Spain

For short visits to Spain you should follow the normal procedures for visitors within the European Community by obtaining an E111 form. For a longer stay you will need form, E109. If you enrol as a student at a Spanish university you will

> be entitled to cover under an agreement drawn up by the **Ministerios de Educación y Ciencia y de Trabajo y Seguridad Social**.
>
> Under the Spanish social security system, ninety-five per cent of the working population have five per cent of their income deducted every month, in return for which they are entitled to receive medical care and draw unemployment, industrial injury and child benefits. UK citizens working in Spain automatically join the scheme. Treatment is paid for partly by the individual, the remainder being covered by social insurance. A private medical care scheme operates along similar lines to the British one.
>
> Once you are covered by the E111 or E109 reciprocal arrangements, before you need treatment, you should go to the **Instituto Nacional de la Seguridad Social** which will supply a book of vouchers with names of local doctors practising under the **INSS** scheme and the addresses of local health centres (**ambulatorio**). If you consult an 'approved' physician, you will receive treatment free of charge in return for a voucher. Otherwise, you will be expected to pay the difference between the official rate and the actual amount charged. You will have to pay forty per cent of the cost of medicines prescribed and purchased from a **farmacia**. In order to receive reimbursement of expenses for medical treatment as a student, you will be asked to supply the following documents: **Instancia en modelo oficial; Certificado de nacimiento, DNI o Libro de familia; Recibo justificante del abono de la prima del Seguro Escolar, o resguardo de matrícula del curso correspondiente**.
>
> It is important to follow the procedures laid down, otherwise you are likely to be charged as a private patient and will have great difficulty in obtaining reimbursement of expenses.

Another form of insurance which you may need is for a motor vehicle. Should you be planning to take a car abroad, you will need to shop around to find the best deal for insurance, which is likely to be much more expensive than in Britain. If you are spending less than a year abroad you will not need to re-register your vehicle, nor will you have to pay road tax again. In most countries you are expected to carry your car registration documents and driving licence with you at all times when you are with your vehicle, otherwise you may be liable for an on-the-spot fine. Professional motoring organisations are the best people to ask for advice and assistance about the regulations in the country where you will be based.

Taxation

If you are employed abroad, except if you are working as a language assistant under one of the reciprocal schemes which operate between Britain and other countries, you will be subject to the same taxation rules as other employees in the same situation as yourself. You will therefore have to complete tax returns, showing your earnings for the year. The forms which have to be filled in can be extremely complex. A few notes for guidance are given below for students in the Federal Republic of Germany:

DEALING WITH ADMINISTRATIVE PROCEDURES

Completing an income tax return in the Federal Republic of Germany

If you are employed in the Federal Republic of Germany and are not exempt from taxation through as special agreement such as that applying to language assistants, you will need to obtain an **Einkommensteuererklärung,** *by making a declaration of annual earned income. If your job is not for a full tax year, you may be entitled to a refund. Tax is deducted at source. You will have to apply to the* **Finanzamt** *in order to make your declaration of taxable income, and the form you will be asked to complete is the* **Antrag auf Lohnsteuer-Jahresausgleich.**

Husband and wife are expected to complete one tax return and both must sign to show they are aware of each other's income.

If appropriate, you will need to provide information about any insurance policies you have, including social security, voluntary supplementary pension funds, life insurance, sickness, accidents, as well as savings bank deposits, mortgage payments and church taxes, payments for training courses, charitable works and membership of political parties. You will be asked to give your religion. Although it is not compulsory to pay dues to the Church, in Catholic areas, such as Bavaria, it is normal and expected of individuals. Church tax is also deducted at source.

Most students are single and unencumbered, but you will soon discover how much information the state requires about individuals in their tax returns.

Banking

Whatever type of placement you are going to, whether you will be receiving a grant or an income, you will need to make arrangements for banking. You are advised always to take enough money with you in traveller's cheques to cover at least two months rent and your living expenses. Grants and the first pay cheque may take this long to come through. A good alternative to traveller's cheques is to apply for a Eurocheque Book and a Eurocheque Card from you bank, which you will be able to use widely, but a charge will normally be made. Credit cards now provide a convenient means of obtaining cash and paying bills, but you may find that your particular card is not accepted everywhere, and you need to be certain that you arrange for your bills to be paid on time. You can enquire at your own bank about opening an account abroad or, alternatively, you could use a post office. In either case it is wise to arrange for your grant to be paid into your home account.

Finding accommodation

Your main worry at the start of the period of residence abroad will probably be finding accommodation. Unfortunately there are no easy solutions, and what you end up with is often a question of chance. If you have been accepted for an assistantship, in many cases you will probably be offered a room in the school, if it has a boarding section, which is not uncommon in France. The accommodation may be rather spartan, but at least you will have a base. Otherwise, you will normally be given help in finding something locally. You need to write to the head of the school as soon as you receive your posting to ask if accommodation or help in finding it can be provided. Your predecessor at the school may also be able to advise you. If you do not receive a reply after a reasonable time, it is worth ringing the school. Employers are often able to help, if you have a work placement, and, for those who are really lucky, there may be a company flat available.

When making an application for a university place, you should also apply for accommodation in the halls of residence. Rooms are usually cheap but basic. If you are not given a room, you will need to go out well before the beginning of term. Book yourself some temporary accommodation, for example in a youth hostel, and write to anybody you know to ask for advice. Although you may have been refused a room in halls of residence, it is still worth checking when you arrive whether one has become available. Student welfare offices and student unions should be approached. If you go to a commercial agent you will probably have to pay a fee of one to two months rent.

You may prefer to advertise in the local press, but you should choose your wording carefully. You can consult classified advertisements and the local advertiser, which may be distributed free of charge, but there is often no real substitute for personal contacts. You will need to check whether the price of any accommodation you are offered includes heating and electricity, whether there is a minimum length of stay, what deposit is payable and what notice must be given on leaving.

Finding accommodation may require considerable ingenuity and perseverance, and you may have to move in the course of your stay. You should try to see the experience as a test of your initiative and linguistic skills, for you will need to be able to present yourself and negotiate the details of any arrangements you make with a landlord. If, as is often the case, you have been living off campus in Britain, you may have had some practice already.

For accommodation, as for employment, you are advised to enter into a contract, even though it may not be required by law. An employment contract would normally cover the length and dates of appointment, place of work, monthly gross salary, nature of the work and holiday entitlement. An agreement for accommodation, setting out rent and terms of notice, will be legally binding. You should ensure that you have understood any contract properly before signing so that you can avoid subsequent disputes with a landlord or employer.

Coping with administrative procedures

Students have found that even when procedures are officially laid down, there is considerable room for variation. When registering at a university or applying for a residence permit in an EC country, you may discover that, even if you have taken all the documents you can think of, you are still sent from one office to another in what can be a time-consuming and frustrating process, particularly if you are not in the habit of coming into contact with bureaucracy. One student on a placement as an assistant in a school in France gave a useful summary of the procedures she had to follow:

> *SUMMARY OF ADMINISTRATIVE PROCEDURES FOR AN ASSISTANT IN FRANCE*
>
> *Before going to France I had received official notification of my post,* **extrait de l'arrêté ministériel,** *and made several copies of it. I took my original birth certificate and passport together with numerous photocopies. I ensured that I had enough money in*

traveller's cheques to keep me for about a month. I had my birth certificate translated at the university before I went. I took an E111 form to cover me for health insurance, and, once I started to receive my salary, I was covered under the French social security scheme.

On my first day at school I went to the main school office to get two other important documents I needed. These were a **procès-verbal d'installation**, *proving that I had taken up my position as an assistant. I asked to have it dated from the beginning of October, so that I would be paid for the whole month, although I had followed the assistants' course and was therefore starting a bit later. As I was being given accommodation at the school I asked for an* **attestation de logement** *which the headmaster signed.*

I was now ready to head for the **Préfecture de Police** *to get my* **carte de séjour**, *because I knew it was illegal to be working in France without one. I needed to produce the original copy of the* **extrait de l'arrêté ministériel** *together with two photocopies, my* **procès verbal d'installation** *(original and photocopies), my* **attestation de logement** *(original and photocopies), my passport and photocopies of every page, four passport photographs and two stamped self-addressed envelopes.*

I was immediately issued with a **récépissé**, *or receipt, which covered me for three months while I was waiting to be informed that I could collect my* **carte de séjour**.

Armed with all my documents I then went to the bank to open an account as a temporary resident, so that I could give the number to my school to enable them to pay my salary. I chose a bank which would give me a cheque book and a credit card. They asked to see my passport and **attestation de logement**, *and I had to make a deposit before I could open an account. I did not pay in all my traveller's cheques, since I was told that it would take about three weeks for my cheque book and credit card to arrive. I was sent a* **relevé d'identité bancaire** *which I took to the school's* **secrétariat**, *so that it could be forwarded to the* **Trésorier Général**, *in the hope that my salary could then be paid on time. The school said it might be able to give me an advance if the first pay cheque was delayed.*

As an assistant I was not taxed but I did have to pay social security contributions, and these were directly deducted from my wages.

Even though you may feel that bureaucratic procedures are cumbersome, it is worth remembering that this is all part of the learning experience. You will quickly become aware of the advantages of being a European citizen and able to speak the language. For non-Europeans the procedures are more complicated, and the attitude of officials is often unsympathetic.

RESEARCHING AND WRITING A DISSERTATION, PROJECT OR WORK REPORT

In order to satisfy the requirements of the period of residence abroad, in addition to following a course (and perhaps sitting the relevant examinations), working as an assistant or in a company for a specified number of weeks, you may be expected to complete assignments from your home institution or to write an extended piece of work. It is important that you should be absolutely clear about the requirements that your institution lays down and that you observe them carefully since the work you produce may carry considerable weight in your degree result. Missed deadlines may have serious consequences.

Since the general skills of academic essay writing were discussed in detail in a previous chapter (see pages 89-101), attention in this section is concentrated on aspects of a project or dissertation which distinguish it from an essay.

The purpose of a project

Although progress in comprehension and oral production is fairly automatic and is usually easy to detect, at least initially, proficiency in written language may need a more concerted effort. Where it is a course requirement to prepare a project, dissertation or work report, you should use the opportunity, not only as a pretext for going out and meeting people, but also as a way of disciplining yourself to commit pen to paper regularly. In this section the term 'project' is used in preference to 'dissertation' in order to emphasise the value of the planning phase and the practical nature of the exercise.

You may never have been required to write such a lengthy piece of work or to carry out personal research in preparation for assignments. When you prepare essays, you are normally given guidance about reading, and most of the materials you need are readily to hand. In the foreign country, you will probably be working under supervision, but generally from a distance, so you will have to identify suitable materials yourself, which you may not be able to borrow. The project therefore gives you a chance to launch out on your own and use your imagination and initiative, as well as your creative powers. Students who are thinking of going on to read for a higher degree will have an opportunity to taste what research is like.

Choosing a topic

If your home institution gives you a free choice of subject, the project will offer you the chance to exploit the context in which you find yourself. As an assistant you may discover that you have been sent to a small town far from the nearest university library, and it would therefore be pointless trying to write a lengthy piece of work on a topic requiring extensive library searches. Yet your local community may be hotly opposing the installation of a nuclear plant in the vicinity, and this could be an ideal subject for your project. You would want to interview local figures, study their literature and any official documents and try to weigh up the arguments being used by all parties.

The choice of topic may be limited by the supervision available or by the requirements of your home institution that you write on a subject which you are studying in combination with your foreign language. If you do have a choice, then you might find it helpful to consider the following suggestions for ways in which you can relate your area of interest to the place where you are living:

- If your studies are primarily in literature, you may be able to investigate a particular author's links with the area in which you are based, the way the town or region is depicted in literature, or how an author treats an event which is relevant to the area.
- If you are following a course which focuses on the study of institutions, you could investigate a social problem which is of particular concern in your area, or look at the way social policy is enacted, the development and functions of a local industry, the workings of a political pressure group or a local event.
- If you are studying a language and linguistics, you could consider writing a project on a regional language variety or dialect, including code switching in border areas, or you could look at the language of the classroom, of the work situation or your peer group.
- The media offer another possible area of study, with scope for looking into the role of the regional press or at a particular local radio or television channel.

Researching the topic

Most topics will require some background or secondary research. This may be historical (outlining the historical development of a political group, the background to a regional event or a social problem) or theoretical (introducing the nature of the problems involved in electoral reforms or some aspect of social change). The materials you use may be local public records, the regular newsletter produced by the town hall or accounts of visits you have made yourself and interviews and surveys you have conducted.

From the outset you should try to avoid being derivative or placing undue emphasis on secondary materials, unless that is what your institution has asked for. If you are to exploit the fact that you are living in the foreign country, then ideally you should rely much more on materials which may not be readily available elsewhere and on your own evaluation of them. In other words, you should demonstrate that you have carried out a piece of work which you could only do effectively by actually being in the country.

LOCAL ARCHIVES

In order to gain access to local materials, you can start by visiting the local public library and town hall. If anybody from the school, your workplace or the institution where you are studying can give you an introduction, you will find that you are generally well received. You should be able to explain clearly what you are trying to do and what sort of information you require.

The materials collected will provide a framework on which to base your project. From your essay writing you should be in the habit of noting down all your sources. It is particularly important to record page numbers and, if possible, to make photocopies of any material you may want to quote, as you may find it impossible to go back to the original later on for checking the accuracy of quotations.

PREPARING FOR AND CONDUCTING INTERVIEWS

As interviewing was discussed in the previous chapter (see pages 132-5), it is sufficient to develop only a few points here.

In order to secure an interview with a key informant, it is advisable always to write first explaining what you are doing and why you would like to meet the person concerned and if possible on whose recommendation. The examples below are of formal letters, such as might be used for French, German and Spanish, in a context where an interview is being sought in preparation for a project to be written during residence abroad:

FORMAL CORRESPONDENCE SEEKING AN INTERVIEW

French example:

112 rue Champion
75018 Paris
Tel. (1) 45 32 16 24

                     Monsieur G Faure
                     Commission de l'Education
                     Mairie du XVIIIe Arrondissement
                     Place J Joffrin
                     75018 Paris

                     Paris, le 5 juillet 1988

Votre réf: D/576

Monsieur le Conseiller Municipal

Votre communication du 3 juin m'est bien parvenue, en réponse à ma lettre du 30 mai, dans laquelle je sollicitais un entretien. Je voudrais vous remercier de l'intérêt que vous témoignez envers mon projet.

Parmi les dates que vous proposez, la première, le 23 juillet, me conviendrait le mieux, et je me rendrai à votre bureau à 12 heures.

Comme vous le demandez, je vous joins un résumé de mes objectifs qui pourra servir de guide à l'entretien que vous avez bien voulu m'accorder.

Je vous serais très reconnaissante, comme vous le proposez également dans votre lettre, de bien vouloir mettre à ma disposition les documents pertinents conservés dans les archives de la Mairie.

Dans l'attente de faire votre connaissance, je vous prie de croire, Monsieur le Conseiller Municipal, à l'assurance de mes salutations les plus distinguées.

Barbara Miller
Barbara Miller

P.j.

German Example:

Albert-Schweitzer Straße 89

2800 Bremen 3

Tel: 0421/56 21 64

05.07.88

Norddeutsche Zeitung
zur Hand von Herrn Klaus Hubert
Postfach 10 26 90
2000 Hamburg 38

Ihr Schreiben vom 03.06.88

Betr. Information über die Presse in der Bundesrepublik

Sehr geehrter Herr Hubert

vielen Dank für Ihren Brief vom 03.06.88, in welchem Sie mir bestätigen, daß ich Sie in Ihrem Büro am 23. Juli treffen kann, um mein Projekt über die deutsche regionale Presse mit Ihnen zu besprechen. Die vorgeschlagene Zeit ist mir angenehm.

Wie gewünscht, lege ich eine kurze Beschreibung meines Projekts bei. Ich hoffe, einige Journalisten von regionalen Zeitungen interviewen zu können, und ich wäre sehr dankbar, wenn Sie mir einige Journalisten nennen könnten, die bereit wären, ihre Arbeit mit mir zu diskutieren.

Ich freue mich, Sie bei dieser Gelegenheit kennenzulernen, und verbleibe mit den besten freundlichen Grüßen

Ihre

Barbara Miller

Barbara Miller

Anlage

Spanish example:

Madrid, 5 de julio de 1988.

Señora María Lopéz de Ruiz,
Secretaria General,
Universidad de Barcelona,
Calle Conde de Altea, Nº4.

Muy señora mía:

    Acuso recibo de su carta de fecha 3 de junio en respuesta a la mía del 30 de mayo en la que solicitaba una entrevista.

    De las dos fechas sugeridas para la citada entrevista, la del 23 de julio al mediodía me convendría más. Llevaré todas los documentos requeridos para discutir acerca del trabajo que debo presentar al final del período de mi estancia en esa universidad.

    Le saluda atentamente

Barbara Miller

Barbara Miller

Anexos

In a letter it may be worth suggesting that you will telephone to arrange an appointment, since you might not receive a reply. Once you have secured an interview, it is important to think through what you want to find out and prepare an interview schedule. You should try to identify points you want to check or discuss at greater length. Probably you will not be able to follow your schedule very closely, but it can serve as a checklist. Your informants are likely to be busy people, so you must make sure you do not waste their time by being inadequately prepared. By reading through any relevant materials you can get hold of before the interview, you will be able to avoid asking unnecessary questions.

If possible, and only after you have been given permission, you should try to record the interview. You will then be able to check back over points and also learn something about the effectiveness of the way you framed your questions. You will not be expected to act as a professional interviewer, but you should ensure that you are courteous and respectful, if you want to secure your informant's co-operation. It is always worth asking for the names of other people you should talk to and whether you can say who has recommended them. In this way you will find that the number of contacts quickly snowballs.

SURVEYS

You may have had some practice in your home institution at preparing a questionnaire. The preparatory phase of running a questionnaire survey is similar in many respects to that for an interview. Obviously lack of financial resources will mean that you have to limit yourself to something fairly simple and to a small number of respondents. If you are working in a school and you want to ask the views of pupils or of their parents on a particular topic, you should always seek permission from the head teacher. It is also important in other contexts to ensure that you have the appropriate authorisation.

There are many readily available sample questionnaires on public opinion, produced regularly by survey agencies, which you can use as models to work out your own questions. You should ensure that any materials you derive from surveys are anonymous and that you do not generalise from what will normally be a small and unrepresentative sample. You will be using the technique as one amongst many tools and should not overplay its importance. If you run the questionnaire yourself rather than sending it through the post, it will give you the opportunity to make contact with people you might not otherwise have a chance to talk to, and the experience may help you to become more receptive to other people's views.

Drafting the project

Writing a sustained piece of prose is a very demanding task, and the project will generally be longer than any essay work you have done. You will need to spend time planning and organising your draft and analysing your materials. However complete and interesting the information you collect, if you merely reproduce it without comment, you will not be writing what most institutions would consider as a piece of academic work. Academic writing is based on the principles of description, explanation, analysis, interpretation and comparison. Description is only the first stage in the process. You should aim to make a critical appraisal of the whole range of materials you have assembled.

It always takes longer than anticipated to write up a project, so begin your draft as early as possible. You may be encouraged to submit a plan and sections of the project for approval by your home institution, and you should take advantage of any advice you receive.

The procedures you have learnt through your essays about developing arguments, using source materials and presenting references should all prove valuable at this stage.

The following points should serve as a general guide when you are drafting the project:

1. The *introduction* in a project should be used to make a statement about the scope, aims and general character of the research, why the topic is of interest, what the problems are in forming judgements about it, how you intend to tackle it and what type of investigatory procedures you intend to adopt.

2. In the *body of the text* you will be following through the approach suggested in the introduction and producing the supporting evidence to develop the argument. You should try to pull together the main points of each section and lead logically into the next one.

3. In your *conclusion* you should be able to give an assessment of the state of discussion you have reached and perhaps suggest other lines of research which could be followed.

Presentation of the project

Requirements for presentation of the report will vary from one institution to another. If you are not given specific instructions, you could use the following model:

- Type on one side of A4 paper using double spacing and wide lefthand margins for binding. Make enough copies so that you are able to keep one for yourself.

- The title page should include your name, the title of the project, the name of your course and the date when the project was submitted. This will be followed by a table of contents, indicating the titles of sections and/or chapters and the relevant page numbers. If you use a large number of abbreviations, you can explain them on a separate page at the beginning after the contents page.

- Footnotes can be used in a number of instances: to explain specialist terms, for translations of quotations and foreign terms, for references to sources other than books and articles and for any points which are not central to the main argument. They should be used sparingly and presented at the end of chapters.

- The same principle should be followed in using quotations as for essay writing. Remember that quotations should never be a substitute for your own analysis. Always make sure that you give the reference at the end of a quotation, including the page number. The same applies to tables and other illustrative materials, where the source should be given at the foot of a table or diagram.
- Appendices can be used for any bulky material which cannot be easily fitted into the body of the text, such as a transcript of a section of an interview. Textual reference should be made to any material presented in an appendix
- Accuracy and careful presentation are essential, particularly if you are required to submit the project in the foreign language. Careful checking is your responsibility, and you need to allow adequate time for it.

The work report

If you are required to write a work report, many of the same guidelines apply as for the project, although it is likely that the research and preparation will be focused almost exclusively on your place of work. You may be asked simply to provide a description of the work you do and the context within which you operate, or you may be expected to investigate a particular problem or preoccupation: for example, how the company can launch a product on a new market, how it handles changes in demand patterns, the effectiveness of worker participation or the problems resulting from the introduction of new technologies. Here you will have the opportunity to show that you know how to find and process information and opinions, organise and present materials and ideas in a coherent and ordered fashion and draw conclusions from your own analysis of an issue or problem.

GAINING MAXIMUM BENEFIT FROM THE PLACEMENT

The initial problems of selecting a placement, carrying out the procedures and finding accommodation may be smoothed for you by your home institution or other organisational bodies involved, so that the start to the placement is uneventful. You may be given careful guidance about your project or academic work required during the year and receive a visit from your tutors while you are abroad. If, however, you are left more to your own devices and have to overcome the hurdles by yourself, you will have the satisfaction of knowing that you have managed to cope with the system, and this is very much to your credit.

Whatever the amount of help you have been given, and whether or not you were able to choose the type of placement, you will need to devote time and effort to ensuring that you make the most of the opportunity of living and working or studying abroad. Even if your placement is for an academic year and time seems to drag at the beginning, it is all too easy to find that you are just settling in properly as you near the end of your stay and to realise too late that you have not used the placement to full advantage.

In the second section of this chapter, some of the advantages and drawbacks of different types of placement were considered. Once arrangements have been made and you have completed all the administrative procedures, you need to think about how to overcome the drawbacks and how to make the most of the advantages and the opportunities.

You should know yourself well enough to be able to gauge how you are likely to react to different situations, but many people find that their personality changes in response to a foreign environment. You will soon realise that if you adopt the British practice of waiting patiently for your turn, you will never get a place on a bus, your purchase from a market stall or your opinion heard in a discussion. If you use the wrong form of address to an official, you may create an impression which will not induce sympathetic treatment. It is not easy to know how to interact with your colleagues and superiors, and informality away from work may not mean that it can be adopted at the workplace. If you do not know how to chat about sporting events, the latest recipes, fashions or television shows, then you may never strike a common chord with your fellow employees. If you expect the university library to provide the answer to a linguistic or legal query, you will discover that you cannot have direct access to the shelves in order to find the information you require. If you want to get the most out of the local transport system, you will need to enquire when prices are lower and how to get special concessionary rates. It is no good condemning the system for being different from the one you are used to or trying to change it, you will have to adapt your own approach and attitude and learn how to manipulate the system as it is.

Social interaction

Although you have probably lived away from home as an undergraduate, it may take you some time to settle down and to build up a circle of friends. The temptation will be to search out people in the same situation as yourself, such as other foreign students, which may not help you to meet local people or improve your knowledge of the language. If you try to think about the way you behaved towards foreign students in your home institution, you may understand better why the onus is on you to take the initiative. If you do not expect anything from other people you will not be disappointed, although you could be pleasantly surprised.

You may find that your colleagues are not interested in you or your background, but that you can show an interest in them by listening carefully and picking up any clues. If you have a placement as an assistant, you will soon discover, particularly in France, that teachers are not closely involved in extracurricular activities, as your own teachers may have been, and that there is little opportunity for social contact with them outside the classroom. The student environment may produce a similar reaction. Traditionally the French have always been reluctant to invite people outside their family circle into their homes, so they may be treating you no differently from anybody else, and you may have to resign yourself to contact outside the home environment. It is then up to you to look elsewhere. The private lesson may be your passport into a French home, or as a student you may be able to break into the baby-sitting network. Living with a family can provide the ideal solution to many problems and give you a chance to see society from the inside, although it may also restrict your freedom.

Most companies organise some social activities. In France the *comité d'entreprise* in larger firms may arrange outings and even trips abroad, and in Germany a local *Fest* can provide opportunities for social contact. You can usually find some local social or cultural organisation or sports club to join. Students placed in France and Germany have described how they succeeded in making contact with local people:

> *There are no societies, as in British universities, and organised social events are few and far between. However, there are always things happening, including many subsidised trips to the surrounding area for foreign students.*

> *I was enrolled for a course in psychology, but because of the unbelievably large number of students in classes, university life was impersonal and without direction. It is up to you to make the effort to talk to the natives. If you don't life could be a bit lonely. I joined a local football club, and a friend played rugby.*

You should get into the habit of reading the local press to find out what activities are taking place locally. The town hall and tourist information office, as well as student welfare services, will be able to supply details of local associations and their meeting times. You may not find exactly the same activities as you are used to, but there should be something which attracts your interest and can provide you with a vital link to the local community. If you have to write a project for your home institution, it can also be your pretext for going out and meeting people. If you are in a small town or a part of the country where there are not many foreigners, you may find it is easier to make contact with local people. One student who had a placement in the German Democratic Republic commented:

> *I discovered that I had great novelty value, since most people had never met an English person before. I was therefore frequently questioned in great detail about life in the West.*

The advantage of having an income, if you are in a work placement, is that you should be able to afford to pay for outings and visits. As a student you may feel more limited, particularly since the cost of living is likely to be higher than in Britain in most of the countries where you are placed. But you will be eligible for cheap rates and discounts, and food in university canteens is very reasonable.

Improving linguistic skills

You may be called upon to use your foreign language frequently in your work or in your studies, but if you are a language assistant, you will be expected to use English as much as possible, and if you are following a course for foreigners, the *lingua franca* will probably be English. In some jobs you may be employed because of your native language: for example you could spend your time sending telex messages in English. Although you will hear the foreign language spoken around you, and you may feel that your level of comprehension is improving markedly, your own spoken language and your written work will not automatically be making much progress.

Listening to radio and television and reading the press will extend your range of vocabulary and registers of language, if you note down points and learn from what you hear. But these are mostly passive activities, and you will want to find ways of working at your productive skills by talking to as many people as possible. If you are required to write a dissertation, project or work report, you can use it both as a means of talking to other people and for making notes and writing out material. Even if your final report has to be drafted in English, you can practise formulating your ideas about the topic in the foreign language by discussing what you are doing with other people.

The hints given in the third chapter about improving your reading skills (see pages 69-71) can be applied both to reading and listening. It is worth setting yourself a reading programme, covering books recommended for your courses, which you have not already read, as well as a range of literature from novels to biographies and more technical works.

If you are visited by your home tutor, you should be able to discuss the work you have done and any difficulties you are having. You may be expected to produce work assignments, so that your academic progress can be monitored. It is important to take stock of your situation while you are in the country and consider other approaches if you think you are not gaining full benefit from the experience.

Adopting a positive frame of mind

The main advice which you will probably be given by students who have completed their period of residence abroad is that you need to learn to think positively, to look for opportunities and exploit them to the full. At the time the experience may not always seem very pleasant, but it is extremely rare for students not to feel, in retrospect, that they have gained both personally and academically from living in another country.

For most students the experience of living and working abroad for a prolonged period is a positive one. They feel, in particular, that they gain in confidence and maturity, that they learn self-reliance and an appreciation of cultural differences and that they develop their interpersonal communication skills. Many students are reluctant to leave at the end of their period abroad, whereas they found it hard to adapt initially. One fairly typical student claimed that:

> *The year abroad is a unique experience, one which you will always remember fondly. It is your first step out into the real world away from the university. A challenging step which never fails to impress would-be employers. They are very curious about what you achieved whilst in Europe.*

SUMMARY OF SUGGESTIONS

1. You should take advantage of every opportunity to visit the foreign country and seek maximum exposure to the language.

2. You must check thoroughly the requirements of your course for the period of residence abroad (length of stay, type of placement, work to be produced).

3. You will want to consider carefully the aims of the period of residence abroad, so that you can approach the experience with a sense of purpose.

4. You should find out as much as you can about the placements available. If you have the choice, you should try to select a placement which suits your personality and aspirations.

5. You should learn how to present yourself in an application and give a good impression of your institution.

6. It is advisable to try to choose a location where you already know somebody or to establish contact before you arrive.

7. You should check carefully the procedures to be followed for securing a placement, ensure you have observed deadlines and have prepared all the documents required. It is worthwhile setting the process in motion before you leave or arriving early to find accommodation.

8. The project, dissertation or work report can be used as a means of exploiting your placement in a particular locality, for meeting people and using spoken and written language, but you should be prepared to take the initiative in establishing contact with other people.

9. You should aim to use all the media resources available and local information offices to find out about activities in which you can participate.

10. You can set yourself a reading programme and discipline yourself to produce oral and written work regularly.

11. You should ensure that you are aware of the personal benefits to be derived from living abroad and that you adopt a positive frame of mind.

6 LANGUAGES AND CAREERS

If you chose your course with a particular career in mind and if you have acquired appropriate skills, on graduation you will be equipped to enter professional life. It is rare for a career path to be clearly mapped out or for undergraduate training to match a particular job profile closely, so you will probably want to consider a range of career openings and to think about how you can capitalise on your individual mix of skills, interests, aspirations and abilities. In exploring the ways in which the expertise and experience acquired as an undergraduate can be applied in career planning and in the employment context, the topics covered are:

1. The attitude of the labour market towards linguists.

2. The range of careers where you can use your languages.

3. The relationship between the language skills you have learnt and the real life tasks you may be asked to perform.

4. How to plan and pursue a career with languages.

5. The relevance to professional life of the intellectual training, analytical and communication skills acquired as an undergraduate.

Amongst the reasons given for having selected their undergraduate course, students rate very highly the career outlets offered by a particular language programme. Many institutions include career profiles of former students in their undergraduate prospectuses to illustrate the value of their course as a preparation for a career. Although it is not necessarily always the case, as a language graduate you will most probably be looking for employment in which you can use your linguistic knowledge and expertise, either immediately or in the longer term. Careers advisors and prospective employers may not, however, share the same view as you about the marketability of the skills possessed by linguists. In preparing your search for suitable employment, it is important to be able to make a realistic assessment of your assets, while also trying to understand how they may match the needs and expectations of employers.

Advice to undergraduates about career planning usually stresses the importance of being self-aware, of being fully informed about the occupational fields open to them, of knowing what employers are looking for and of learning how to present themselves effectively. In addition, you will want to be familiar with the competition you are likely to face on the labour market, both in Britain and within Europe. In considering all these aspects of careers, reference will be made to the experience of other graduates to demonstrate that a clear definition of goals, effort, perseverance and initiative are rewarded.

THE LABOUR MARKET FOR LINGUISTS

Whereas in other European countries fluency in one or more foreign languages is a prerequisite for a management post and is increasingly becoming a key element in the training of engineers and scientists, the British still believe, often wrongly and to their cost, that as English is a *lingua franca* they do not need to concentrate resources on language training. In the late 1970s a Pan European Readership Survey estimated that British companies were cutting themselves off from sixty-nine per cent of major European clients, solely by not being able to trade in their languages.

In this section the ways in which the attitude of employers to language graduates is changing are discussed before going on to consider the possibilities for consolidating career prospects by further training.

The growing need for language graduates

In the early 1970s language skills were not valued very highly by industry, but by the end of the decade companies were commissioning research into their language needs. The British Overseas Trade Board, in particular, has done much to increase the level of awareness of the value of language skills for boosting export sales. Investigations of the relationship between training in international business and languages and overseas trade show considerable progress in export education over the past few years. There are many signs that proficiency in languages is being recognised as an important key to greater international and intercultural understanding.

Some companies with trading partners abroad are becoming aware that for dealings in international markets to be successful, they need to be able not only to speak the language of their clients and competitors but also to use it expertly in a number of different contexts. For these purposes a smattering of a rusty 'O' level is not enough (the Japanese may sell in English, but they will only buy in Japanese). More employers are now asking for graduate proficiency in a foreign language or for native speakers.

The prospect of the complete lifting of trade barriers within the European Community in 1992 is another incentive for recruiting graduates with European languages. In its information pack on the new single European market, the Department for Enterprise (Department of Trade and Industry) advises businessmen to maximise the opportunities afforded by recruiting personnel with language skills and an understanding of different cultures. The traffic in graduates will not, however, be one way: the suggestion is made to employers in the same document that the way of finding the new skills needed may be to look for suitably qualified recruits elsewhere in Europe. You could find yourself competing for positions, in Britain or in other countries, against the people you studied with abroad, which makes it all the more important to learn how to identify and sell your particular brand of qualifications, skills and experience.

Employers rarely specify in job descriptions that they are looking for language graduates: as many as forty per cent of jobs for graduates are advertised as being open to any discipline, whereas less than five per cent are aimed specifically at professional linguists. Where languages are mentioned, some fairly typical examples of advertisements would be:

European Surveyor: You should combine broad-ranging professional experience with genuine entrepreneurial flair. Knowledge of one or more European languages would be a distinct advantage.

European Supply Director: Competence in other European languages in addition to English would be most helpful.

European Sales Manager: Language fluency, preferably German and/or Spanish is essential.

Training Manager in Western Europe: French and/or German speaking ability is essential.

Sales Manager, Industrial Drive System: The ability to speak French and English fluently is essential and up to 40% travel should be expected in French-speaking and other territories.

If there are not already more employers eager to recruit linguists, this may be because they are not sufficiently aware of what language graduates can offer and of the extent to which language programmes in higher education have been changing over the last ten to twenty years. In the same way that, as an undergraduate, you found languages could not be learnt in a vacuum, divorced from content, you will quickly discover that employers will expect expertise in the foreign language to be grounded on technical or specialised knowledge. As a language graduate, you will know that management principles and practices, like political systems are not universal. If you have combined different subjects with your language, acquired specialist skills or followed options in international marketing or law, you should ensure you make this clear in your initial application and be prepared to expand on it in an interview.

Languages as a bonus

Proficiency in a language and the understanding of a foreign society that goes with it may give you the edge on other applicants, but it will seldom be the primary qualification sought by an employer, as the following comments show:

> *In most cases employees are recruited because of a need for a specific expertise (for example taxation, data processing, marketing). Language capability is nearly always a secondary requirement.*

> *As a recruiter for two large international concerns my remit has always been to seek out those who want to, and on their track record are likely to, make it first and foremost in a specific function. If by chance the candidate presents one or more foreign languages this is a bonus.*

> *Language skills are a valuable extra to professional skills and expertise in a particular function.*

> *Ideally linguists with technical backgrounds or knowledge of a particular country are sought.*

This means 'other things being equal a language may be an advantage', where 'other things' implies a relevant technical qualification and expertise. The evidence is, however, that very few engineers, technologists, lawyers or accountants in Britain will make an effort to reach near native proficiency in a language. Programmes such as ERASMUS, which are designed to promote the mobility of students within Europe, are certainly encouraging the development of courses in the sciences and technology where there is the possibility of a placement in a foreign institution. Small numbers of students from these disciplines are therefore being given the opportunity to acquire the necessary fluency in a language.

There are a few courses in Britain where law, accountancy, a science or engineering can be studied in combination with a language, but it is unlikely that the products from these international courses will be available in sufficiently large numbers to meet the demand within the foreseeable future. The students concerned will need to be very proficient in the language if they are to compete with scientists and engineers from elsewhere in Europe. Graduates from the French *grandes écoles*, such as *Ponts et Chaussées* or the *Ecole des Mines* have a high level of expertise in English as well as managerial skills.

Degree subjects and career prospects

In trying to put your own prospects into perspective, you may find it helpful to refer to a classification of types of graduate employment which has been derived from a study of the relationship between higher education and the labour market in Britain by Brennan and McGeevor (1988). Using data from a survey of former polytechnic students, the two authors distinguish four main types of graduates:

- The *generalist* will not have extra skills and knowledge to offer and will need to acquire them on graduation. You may belong to this category if you do not have a specialism which can be directly used in a particular job, for example if you graduate in comparative literature.

- The *generalist plus* will have both general and specialist knowledge and skills. Graduates in this category, which would include those with degrees in modern languages, may get their job because of the plus.

- The *occupational generalist* will have a degree which is the first step towards a particular job. This may apply to you if you studied European business or international marketing with a language or one of the other combined subject degrees, such as computing and a language.

- The *occupational specialist* description applies to graduates who have followed a course, such as pharmacy or production engineering which is, at least partially, a training for a specific job and where the career path is usually very clearly mapped out. This may be the case for you if you read for a modern languages degree in interpreting and translation.

Although several studies show that there are no major differences in employment rates several years after graduation, the subject mix would seem to account for quite marked differences in the ease with which employment is initially obtained, and this is a point you should bear in mind.

The institution from which you graduate and your class of degree will also affect your chances on the employment market. The more vocational nature of many of the college and polytechnic courses will to some extent balance out the advantage of the graduate from more prestigious institutions. In general, students from different institutions will not be competing for the same employment or have the same career aspirations and expectations.

Developing and consolidating skills by further training

Students who have graduated in a language and computing, business studies, or occasionally engineering, and linguists who have done options in international marketing or technical translation will be able to offer an ideal combination of subjects and usable skills. Even without this type of background, as a linguist you will have some useful skills to offer. While few degree courses in the humanities and social sciences prepare graduates directly for a career by providing them with a 'professional' qualification, many of the general skills you acquired as an undergraduate are closely related to what you may be asked to do in a professional context. In job applications you will need to emphasise that, as a graduate in languages, you possess the highly valued communication skills which are frequently mentioned in advertisements.

For most careers language degrees are likely to be considered as a plus rather than a sufficient qualification, and you should be prepared to undergo a further period of training after graduation. According to the statistics for first destinations, about forty per cent of graduates in modern languages normally go into some form of postgraduate training immediately on graduation, and many more do so later in their career. Even if you have combined language study with a vocationally oriented subject, such as management or computing, you will, nonetheless, probably need to undergo a period of further training.

Postgraduate training may be in an educational establishment if you are planning to go into teaching, bi- or trilingual secretarial work and international business or if you want to become a professional interpreter or translator. A small proportion of language graduates study for a higher degree by research, often in the institution from which they graduated. More and more firms in accountancy, banking, insurance, retailing and marketing organise their own traineeships, and there is fierce competition for places. In the absence of an adequate supply of graduates with a science or technology background who are also proficient in foreign languages, one way of answering the immediate needs of British industry in international trade is by persuading more graduate linguists to undergo training in technological subjects. This case is well illustrated by the example of a graduate in French and Spanish who was responsible for sales of aluminium plate to France, Benelux, Spain and Portugal for a British-based company only one year after graduation:

> The company recognised that, in Europe at least, it is essential for the sales representative to be able to communicate in the relevant languages. The ideal candidate for the job would probably have been someone who studied two languages and metallurgy to degree level, with an MBA thrown in for good measure. However, my company chose someone with a linguistic background, an interest in industry and some level of technical ability (nothing more than 'O' level in my case). The choice was made on the basis that it would be easier to teach a linguist a sufficient level of metallurgy and, of course, sales technique, than it would have been to teach a metallurgist two or even three languages from scratch.

It is by no means commonly agreed, but there is a case for arguing that a linguist can be more easily trained in marketing or accountancy than an export salesman or accountant in languages. It is also probably easier to master the technical vocabulary of a specialist area and to learn a new language if you are already proficient in one or more foreign languages, but you will have to be able to convince employers that this is the case and that you are still prepared to learn.

Advice to job-seekers within Europe suggests that British graduates may be at a disadvantage initially not only because their degrees are not perceived as being a qualification for a specific type of employment but also because their courses are shorter than in other European countries. By undertaking a traineeship or a postgraduate qualification and by gaining relevant work experience, you will be able to make up for these handicaps and become a strong competitor in international labour markets. The dual qualification courses described in the first chapter (page 6) or an additional qualification obtained during a period of residence abroad are other ways of offsetting the disadvantages of age and lack of practical expertise, in continental terms, which result from being a graduate from the British system.

Patterns of employment for graduates

Several attempts have been made to track the career paths of language graduates, in order to assess the relevance of degree programmes to labour market needs. A considerable body of information is available showing trends in the types of employment or training language students enter on graduation and how they move from one category of employment to another. Further details of some of these studies are included in the bibliography. In this section a general overview is given of the patterns of employment of language graduates from different institutions and at different stages in their careers.

The first two pie charts, which are derived from data from the Universities' Statistical Record, show the type of employment at first destinations for an annual cohort of British university graduates from language courses six months after they completed their courses. The data account for less than fifty per cent of all languages graduates in 1986-87 since they exclude all those who undertook further academic study and teacher or other training or who did not enter employment immediately on graduation.

Figure 1 covers 792 graduates in French, German, Hispanic studies, Russian, other European languages, Chinese and other Oriental/Asian/African languages who entered employment immediately on graduation. Figure 2 records the first employment of 874 graduates who studied a language in combination with another subject.

Figure 1   First employment by type of work for university modern languages graduates (1986-87 figures)

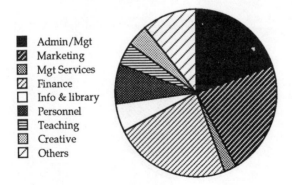

- Admin/Mgt
- Marketing
- Mgt Services
- Finance
- Info & library
- Personnel
- Teaching
- Creative
- Others

Source: Data from Universities' Statistical Record, 1987.

Figure 2 First employment by type of work for university language graduates in combined subjects (1986-87)

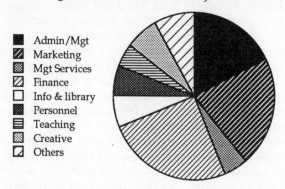

Source: Data from Universities' Statistical Record, 1987

The type of employment several years after graduation is illustrated in the other two charts. Figure 3 shows the cumulative situation for graduates who have followed a non-traditional language course in one of the technological universities, and Figure 4 is derived from data collected throughout Britain for university and polytechnic graduates in European studies. The information used in these charts is taken from questionnaire returns over a ten year period after students have completed their courses, and it therefore represents a different picture from the first destination figures.

Figure 3 Last known employment by type of work for non-traditional graduates, 1977-88 (sample size 296)

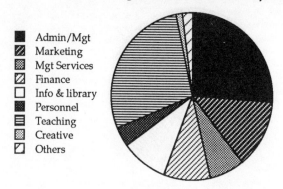

Source: Aston Modern Languages graduate data bank, 1988

*Figure 4 Current employment by type of work for 1977-87
European Studies graduates (sample size 1,282)*

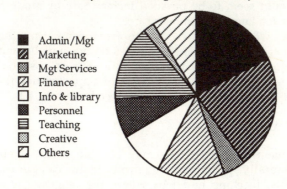

- ■ Admin/Mgt
- ▨ Marketing
- ▩ Mgt Services
- ▨ Finance
- □ Info & library
- ■ Personnel
- ☰ Teaching
- ▩ Creative
- ▨ Others

Source: UACES study conducted at Bradford University, 1988.

Since such a large proportion of languages graduates do not immediately enter long-term employment when they complete their degree, first destinations statistics present only a partial view of the situation. Comparisons with earlier years suggest, however, that more language graduates are now entering permanent employment on graduation. As illustrated by all the charts, whatever the type of degree course followed, language graduates today are going into many different fields of employment, particularly in business and commerce, international marketing, finance and administrative work. Comparisons of first destinations statistics indicate that an increasing proportion of language graduates are taking up employment in these areas, rather than entering postgraduate training courses.

If, in the past, language degrees prepared students primarily for a career in teaching, this is the option chosen nowdays by a much smaller proportion of graduates who read languages. According to the first destinations statistics for the 1986-87 cohort, less than sixteen per cent of the language only graduates and about twelve per cent of the combined subjects graduates went into teacher training or took up positions as teachers immediately on graduation. Analysis of the career paths followed by modern languages graduates from one of the non-traditional courses suggests, however, that many linguists may turn to a career in teaching later in their lives even if they did not originally intend to pursue this direction.

The category in the charts for Information Services and Library work contains a subsection for translation and interpreting. A more detailed breakdown of available figures shows that a very small proportion of graduates immediately enter employment as professional linguists: between one and three per cent. Again, this is an option which would seem to be pursued increasingly by modern languages graduates at a later stage in their career.

One conclusion which might be drawn from comparing the different charts is that, while language graduates do not initially and directly enter employment where linguistic skills are an essential requirement, later in their careers they may find opportunities for work in areas where a language is the main skill needed for the job.

CAREERS USING LANGUAGES

The careers available where graduates may be able to use their languages are generally presented in three main categories: professional linguists, teaching and jobs where the language is a secondary skill, even though a degree level language may be essential. These career paths are described in more detail and illustrated through a number of job profiles in the publications listed in the bibliography. In this section a brief overview is given of the range of possibilities, and further comments are added, describing the experience of language graduates.

Working as a professional linguist

The main forms of employment for which a very high level of proficiency in language skills is the normal prerequisite are translating and interpreting. Professional linguists are also employed in abstracting or monitoring services, for which knowledge of a number of languages is required.

If you want to work as a professional linguist, unless your course specialised in translating and/or interpreting, you will probably need to take a postgraduate qualification, either at one of the universities and polytechnics in Britain which run courses or in one of the schools elsewhere in Europe. These institutions accept only a small number of candidates every year on the basis of competitive entrance examinations, references and interviews.

PROFESSIONAL TRANSLATING

If you are intending to work as a translator, you will need to develop a specialism in a technical or scientific field, since these are the areas where you are most likely to find employment. This involves knowing not only relevant vocabulary but also the mechanics of essential processes, in the same way that you would not expect to learn the vocabulary of French politics or German economics without studying the relevant system. Literary translation is usually a sideline rather than the primary source of income.

Translators normally work only into their own language. However, in a narrow specialist area or where a company has only one translator, it is not unusual to be expected to translate into foreign languages. Translation into a foreign language may also be feasible when a polished translation is not required and the purpose is solely to convey information.

A modern languages graduate in French and Russian, who took a postgraduate interpreting and translating course, subsequently worked as a translator for a building products company exporting to Cyprus, the Federal Republic of Germany and Norway. She described what her work involved in the following terms:

> *Whenever any correpondence arrives or is sent abroad, I translate to and from French and German. I need to be able to operate the computer, and I am acquiring some useful experience in office techniques as well as knowledge of specialist vocabularies and technical products.*

Another graduate in French and biology worked in the translating unit of a pharmaceutical company. She related how her unusual combination of degree subjects enabled her to serve as a specialist translator:

> *The job is essentially that of a scientific translator, usually working into English. Most of the documents are experimental reports used for the registering of new products, which may be pharmaceutical, veterinary, agrochemical, as well as those for sale in a chemist's shop. Translations have to be very accurate, as they will be scrutinised by the relevant health authority. We also translate specialist foreign journal articles. Often the translator needs to interpret the meaning which may be unclear in the original text, so my scientific knowledge is indispensable. Frequently we have to act as go-betweens in telephone conversations with clients abroad.*

The translator generally works alone, although it is important to be able to consult technical experts, particularly when entering a new field. Translators are required to be meticulous, systematic and persevering. They are expected to work to impossible deadlines and to produce perfect copy, even if the original text was far from being unambiguous. Translating is very demanding work, and experienced technical translators may handle as much as a fifty-page text in a day. Although some translators dictate their work, it may be an advantage, if not a necessity, to invest in a wordprocessor, so that good quality copy can be produced, which is immediately usable. Some clients will want to have the translation on disk so that they can adapt the format for publication without retyping and further checking.

The large industrial and commercial companies dealing with international markets may have their own translating services, but more often they will use agencies. Translation bureaus do not normally employ many translators full-time but, if you have a good technical specialism, you may be able to get onto an agency list and build up a regular flow of assignments. One graduate recounted how, only three years after graduation, she was in charge of English translation at the headquarters of an international company, working under considerable pressure:

> *I have about 1,000 pages sitting on my desk just waiting to be translated, some 100 waiting to be edited and 350 out at an agency. Translation in a company at least has the advantage that you are working in a team and are therefore in contact with people, new developments and the vocabulary.*

A number of graduates, after gaining experience by working for a company or agency (the latter takes a percentage of the fee paid by the customer) decide to free-lance. If they have already made contacts and established a reputation for efficiency, accuracy and reliability, this may be an attractive proposition, since it gives them the freedom to establish a base wherever they want to live and the opportunity to organise their own work. One language graduate who worked free-lance as a translator in Paris described how she organised herself:

> *I get my translation work through agents, who telephone and then bring the texts to me at home. I dictate the translations which are then fetched for typing. It took me about three or four years to build up a clientèle. My work is very specialised: I translate texts on computing both from and into French.*

There are international associations of interpreters and translators which operate a selective system of membership, and whose recognition is needed in order to build up a clientèle. Free-lancing does mean that the translator will be relatively isolated from other people, and this is not to everybody's taste. In addition to linguistic skills, translators must be able to keep accounts, negotiate terms and deal with correspondence. They usually build up their own files on terminology and keep detailed records of the jobs they have done.

PROFESSIONAL INTERPRETING

Every year there will be a few full-time vacancies for professionally qualified interpreters in companies and international organisations. As there are only about 1,500 international conference interpreters in the world, less than a third of whom have English as their native language, established positions as conference interpreters are very rare, and it is more likely that the skills of an interpreter will be called for on an *ad hoc* basis. These skills were described in some detail in an earlier chapter (see pages 143-9), and it will suffice here to remind you of some of the contexts in which the interpreter will be working.

Conference interpreters mainly use simultaneous interpreting, which involves listening to speakers through headphones and reproducing the message immediately through a microphone, so that the audience or participants in a meeting can follow and respond to what is being said. The alternative method used in the conference mode is consecutive interpreting, which is now less common in international meetings since it is a slow and rather cumbersome process. The consecutive interpreter is required to make notes and reproduce what has been said when the speaker pauses.

Unless you are employed as a conference interpreter, it is more likely that you will be called upon to use interpreting skills in a less formal situation, for example, liaising between a small group of people for a business meeting or factory visit.

PROFESSIONAL ABSTRACTING AND INFORMATION SERVICES

Work in libraries and information services may involve abstracting and classifying foreign language texts. One graduate in French and German worked as a technical abstractor for a company dealing with research in metal castings production:

> *It is my job to prepare abstracts of 200 to 300 words for our bi-monthly journal from the 350 journals in the Western world on casting, metallurgy and other relevant subjects. Many are in English, but the remainder are in a variety of languages from French and German to Dutch, Hungarian and Finnish. I get some help from outside translators and abstractors for certain languages, but otherwise I have to assemble the essential information in these articles using any summaries provided, figure captions, sections headings and so on, and prepare them for publication, which brings in activities such as editing and proof-reading as well as the preparation of indexes.*
>
> *I am also involved in the maintenance and updating of the library and have to translate letters, telexes, leaflets and help*

staff with understanding foreign language material they are using in their work. All this has meant I have had to become something of a novice metallurgist and learn a lot of specialised terminology in French and German.

EMPLOYERS OF PROFESSIONAL LINGUISTS

The large international organisations, including the European Community institutions, the United Nations and its specialised agencies employ a number of British translators. For the EC it is necessary to have a professional qualification in translating or interpreting and a thorough knowledge of two of the Commission's official languages, in addition to English. Entry is selective, and only a small number of suitably qualified graduates are taken on each year. For the United Nations and other large international agencies a much wider range of languages is looked for, and entrance is very competitive.

In Britain the Joint Technical Language Service of the Civil Service recruits a small number of linguists every year, mainly for positions at the Government Communications Headquarters in Cheltenham. Although graduates in West European languages are selected, they will generally be expected to learn an East European or Asian language. The work may be translating, but more often it involves monitoring and reporting services. Again the qualities looked for are meticulousness and accuracy and the ability to concentrate for long periods of time. Discretion is an important requirement for work at the GCHQ, given the security nature of the materials being handled.

The BBC has a monitoring service which employs linguists to listen to broadcasting stations throughout the world, requiring both translating skills and a good knowledge and understanding of current affairs. The External Services of the BBC broadcast in several languages and recruit producers, scriptwriters and studio managers with a high level of linguistic proficiency.

Other government departments employ linguists for translating in conditions similar to those you would find in large companies. Such an example is the Overseas Press Services of the Central Office of Information. The material for translation is used for direct publication in the overseas press without further editing. The job description below is fairly typical of those for positions as translators, handling material which is concerned with public relations:

Translators need to have a publicity sense and be skilled in dealing with a wide variety of subjects, many of which are highly technical.

You would be responsible for translating a variety of technical and specialist texts for information or publicity purposes, for revising the work of other translators; and you would be expected to monitor developments in technology and the written language, maintain terminology files, and keep abreast of the contents of specialist magazines and publications.

The Police, the Home Office Immigration Service, HM Customs and Excise and the courts sometimes call upon interpreters for assistance. In all these situations, the appropriate technical knowledge and vocabulary are required together with an ability to think and react quickly, excellent powers of concentration, stamina and a good general education, since allusions and imagery may have to be interpreted, as well as technical details.

Occasionally posts are advertised abroad, other than in international organisations, for native English speakers, involving translating and interpreting. If you want to work abroad, any contacts you made during your period of residence in the foreign country may help you to secure a position.

Language teaching

In the 1960s it was common for language graduates in Britain to pursue a career in teaching. In the early 1970s teaching continued to be the largest field of employment. Today, in other European countries, the expectation is still that university language courses will train the language teachers of the future, and only a few institutions envisage other possible openings for their graduates. In Britain, however, teaching is now a less common career choice, as shown by the pie charts earlier in this chapter.

The normal path into teaching is via a postgraduate certificate in education, which includes both educational theory and teaching practice in schools. Justifiably, teaching continues to attract graduates who want to use their languages, and the careers information booklets in Britain present teaching as one of the few areas where a language degree is an essential requirement. Graduates from the more traditional courses may look to a qualification in teaching as the only means of entering a career where they can use their literary training, although this is becoming less relevant with the introduction of new syllabuses in schools concentrating on communicative performance.

As more undergraduate courses focus on communicative skills, and major shifts have occurred in the language teaching methods in schools, teaching also offers an appropriate means of putting these skills into practice, particularly for those who have studied more than one language. There is an abundant literature on language teaching methodology and classroom techniques. A few of the most frequently quoted titles are listed in the bibliography.

Since you have experienced the school system as a pupil, you will be well aware of the satisfactions and frustrations which the job brings, and you should know whether you have the necessary personality characteristics to make a success of a career in this field. If you were already planning to go into teaching, you might have been able to work as a foreign language assistant during your period of residence abroad, and this may have given you a taste for teaching English as a foreign language.

Many language graduates work abroad for one or two years teaching English, often to adults in private schools, before returning to take a certificate course in Teaching English as a Foreign Language. This will provide a valuable and, for some positions, essential, qualification if you want to continue to live and work abroad and enjoy teaching children or adults. Without a recognised qualification, you will find that you are easily exploited by language schools abroad. Graduates recount how they have been expected to work extremely long hours and required to do routine administrative tasks in return for very low pay and no job security. The Association of Recognised English Language Schools keeps a list of approved and reputable institutions which you might do well to consult if you are contemplating teaching English as a foreign language.

Many new opportunities for teaching English are arising in Spain and Japan. Every year about thirty graduates are offered appointments in Japan to teach English as a foreign language. Further information about this opportunity is available from the Japan Foundation in London.

Using languages as a secondary skill

The range of careers in which a language may be described as a secondary skill is very wide. A survey of graduates from one of the non-literary courses, covering career paths for several years after graduation, showed that as many as seventy per cent of those who had studied two languages were using their linguistic expertise in some way in their work. About fifty per cent of graduates who had combined a language with a subject such as business studies or computing were using their foreign language in their work, although they claimed that it was generally their training in the other subject which was the qualification looked for by employers. Expertise in the language was not always used immediately but became an important asset when, after an initial period of further training, graduates began to move around the country and abroad,

INTERNATIONAL TRADE

The types of employment where graduate proficiency in a language is likely to be of most obvious advantage are in export marketing, sales, purchasing and, to a more limited extent, in retailing, and these are common career paths for students who graduate in a language and business or follow options and postgraduate courses in international marketing. The languages most in demand are German, French and Spanish, in that order. Japanese and Arabic, and also Chinese, are important growth markets.

One graduate in French and management described how he was climbing the ladder in export sales:

> *I am employed as a sales representative in a small company manufacturing precision metal pressings for writing instruments, electronics and the leather goods industry. I am often called upon to write letters and telexes and deal with telephone calls in a foreign language. The company makes a point of visiting its overseas customers on a regular basis, and I have accompanied the export manager on several trips as well as going on my own.*

Advertising and market research may also involve working with clients or agents abroad. Languages are an important qualification for the international market consultant. One employer, himself a language graduate, maintained that:

> *Communication ability is essential to consultants. This applies both in interpersonal skills and general articulacy but also, in an international business such as ours, in the form of command of a foreign language. Language and linguistic and cultural knowledge are directly useful and are recognisable by our clients as part of the service we offer. Language ability in those otherwise qualified is also evidence of a personality with wider horizons and, probably, useful experience.*

INTERNATIONAL FINANCE

International finance is another important area with good potential for development. The clearing banks, which all have international divisions, recruit a number of language graduates for their traineeships. There may be opportunities for postings abroad during the training period as well as later in a career. Merchant banks, insurance companies and brokers often have overseas branches, where language graduates may be sent after training.

There are good career prospects in companies with international dealings for graduates who are prepared to undergo a lengthy period of training and to wait for several years before their language comes into its own, as in chartered accountancy which recruits graduates from 'any discipline'. One graduate in French and business studies recounted how her language expertise was left in cold storage while she trained as a chartered accountant:

> *While I was training I only managed to use my languages when I went on holiday or received foreign visitors socially. But as soon as I qualified, I moved to another company as Senior European Auditor, which involves travelling over fifty per cent of the time to France, Germany, Belgium etc, as well as to French-speaking parts of Africa, such as the Ivory Coast. Within a few weeks of joining the firm I had been dispatched to Germany to audit accounts.*

Chartered accountancy is an important growth area, which is becoming increasingly attractive for linguists wanting to move into management and finance through traineeships. In 1986-87 three per cent of graduate recruits to the profession had studied languages. Compared with other graduate's from 'non-relevant' subjects their performance in the professional examinations is close to the average, suggesting that they can adjust without too much difficulty.

GOVERNMENT SERVICE

Government departments, while not looking specifically for language graduates may also provide opportunities to use languages or to acquire new ones. All government departments now have European links, and language allowances are paid to staff who maintain their level of expertise, even if they are not always called upon to use it in their work.

The Diplomatic Service is a good example of work in international contexts which demands a sound knowledge of foreign languages and also an awareness and understanding of current economic, social and political events. In-service language training is provided, where employees have the opportunity to learn and use new languages, including some of the less common ones.

TOURISM

A number of language graduates are attracted by careers in tourism and the hotel and catering industries, working for tourist operators, travel agencies, airlines, tourist boards, hotel chains and large catering firms. Companies are not necessarily looking for graduates and, as there are courses for non-graduates, a high level of language knowledge and expertise is not the main requirement for the job. Valuable experience can be gained by working in this field, and graduate recruits can hope to be promoted to positions of responsibility, as suggested in the following comments:

> *I have been working for five years as a Tour Manager, which entails taking groups of many different nationalities on tours around the whole of Europe, sometimes as many as four countries in one day. This means working with people from early in the morning until after midnight, seven days of the week. It is of course very demanding work, but I have also learnt a good deal, including Italian, which I now speak fluently.*

> *I am working for a travel firm specialising in up-market villa holidays and luxury apartments in the Mediterranean area. I deal with all the correspondence in French and German and also sell the product to clients. I aim to become an assistant manager and eventually a manager.*

SECRETARIAL AND ADMINISTRATIVE WORK

The need to have a marketable skill motivates a large number of graduates every year—almost as many as the number going into teacher training—to take a postgraduate bi- or trilingual secretarial qualification. Many graduates warn against the secretarial trap, but from a good postgraduate course you can acquire a sound knowledge of administrative structures and business practice which will prepare you for work in international organisations and companies. Experience shows that secretarial and administrative skills may be the initial qualification needed for the job, but that the language graduate has other more valuable assets which can be used to climb the career ladder or to gain access to an interesting and satisfying job.

Subsidiaries of foreign companies in Britain often employ modern languages graduates with secretarial qualifications. The foreign language may be the company's official language, and employees will be involved in a wide range of tasks requiring language skills. One language graduate described her work in a French company based in Britain:

> *French is the official language. Telexes, memos and letters all have to be written in French and there are frequent telephone conversations in French. I am often called upon to translate technical information notes for our dealers. I have visited factories in France, guided foreign visitors round our centre and attended conferences and seminars. There is never a dull moment.*

The ability to type and knowledge of other office skills can be put to use in a whole range of careers, in addition to those already mentioned in this section. They may be essential for work in publishing and journalism and for those who decide to become a freelance translator.

LANGUAGE SKILLS AND REAL LIFE TASKS

In looking at specific types of employment, reference has been made to some of the language skills which graduates are called upon to use in their work. In this section an attempt is made to show how the skills acquired as a student match the real life tasks performed at the workplace.

Communicative skills

The increasing emphasis being placed on communicative competence in language learning complements the growing awareness of the value of the skills acquired from language programmes in higher education: by studying language in its many contexts, graduates are better able to respond to the varied needs of the labour market, because they understand the economic, political and socio-cultural environment within which businesses operate and international exchanges occur. Former students have found that a knowledge of different language varieties is very useful in a number of situations, as well as a thorough understanding of present-day foreign societies, their institutions, structures and culture through the medium of their language.

If language is considered in terms of communicative functions, one of the most common uses of language at the workplace is for persuasion, either in the context of sales activities or negotiations. This is often combined with the need to command in order to achieve action or to project an image of a company or product. Most graduates will be involved in collecting, processing, analysing, evaluating and presenting information as a basis for action. The ability to extract essential information by understanding the referential function of texts is therefore crucial.

Oral and aural skills

The studies made of the skills which language graduates are called upon to use regularly in their work and of the perceived needs of employers show the growing importance of oral and aural communication, particularly by telephone. Informal and social use of language also rates high. Employers have been impressed to find that their language graduates can sort out logistical problems or sustain a conversation on a range of different topics in one or more foreign languages.

INTERPRETING

If you have had the opportunity to learn the techniques of interpreting as an undergraduate, even though you are not employed as an interpreter, you will occasionally be called upon *extempore* to act as an intermediary for a foreign visitor. Many graduates working in the commercial sector have found this to be one of the most useful technical skills they acquired during their studies. A modern languages graduate employed in Britain by a German parent company described how:

> Only a few months after beginning my traineeship I was called upon to act as an interpreter between German and English when a deal was being negotiated. This was the first time I had had an opportunity to put my training to the test, and I was very nervous since so much was at stake. I am pleased to say that we won the contract.

If you have had no training, however fluent you are in the language and however familiar you are with the context, it is no mean task to perform the mental gymnastics required without some preparation and if you do not have a very high level of proficiency and accuracy in the foreign language.

SALES PRESENTATION

Many graduates are called upon to represent their company at international trade fairs, where a fluent knowledge of the foreign language is needed for answering questions about products and persuading potential clients of their qualities.

TELEPHONING

In the commercial world, the traditional business letter is doomed to become obsolete as telex or electronic mail and the telephone become the standard forms of international communication. The ability to create a favourable impression on the telephone in a foreign language, to negotiate effectively and to access information are increasingly important skills (see pages 136-7) which the language graduate should be able to offer.

These situations require much more than technical vocabulary or the ability to handle information. In telephone communication you need to be able to gauge the reactions of the receiver of the message at the other end of the line without recourse to visual cues. You should know how to use appropriate strategies to gain access to the right person, how to fend off interruptions when you are making a point and how to elicit all the information you need quickly. You should be able to use opening remarks to ensure that you hold the attention of a potential customer and arouse interest in your product before demonstrating your ability to be persuasive and convincing. You will want to be able to note down the important points while you are talking and listening, as well as any figures mentioned. You may be responsible for handling complaints, which requires different skills and would be a difficult task in your own language.

You will also need to know the best times to telephone to the country with which you are dealing: it has been estimated that contact can be made with counterparts in Western Europe for little over half the working day because of different patterns of time use.

In telephoning, listening skills are as important as the ability to convey information orally. Linguists are often called upon to take accurate notes of conversations and report on oral interaction. They are expected to grasp the meaning of a message quickly and expertly in order to avoid the need for repetition or time-consuming, and therefore costly, explanations.

Reading and writing skills

For many jobs reading and writing skills may be equally or more important. The ability to read intensively and extract information and report on it orally and in writing in English are frequent tasks for graduates who are not employed as professional linguists.

DRAFTING DOCUMENTS

Drafting contracts or reports in a foreign language is another common requirement. Few graduates, except if they are working abroad in a foreign rather than a multinational company or organisation, are called upon to write at length in the foreign language, whereas it is common for them to have to write in English using foreign language source materials, presented in the form of summaries or reports. One graduate working in export sales in French and Spanish-speaking countries in Europe recounted that:

> *I have to write a report for every customer visit as well as one general monthly report. This can be a very time-consuming task, but it is important to have a record of every stage of negotiations and to be able to present information as clearly and accurately as possible, so that other people in the company can refer to it.*

EXTRACTING INFORMATION

You may be asked to scan or skim materials, such as trade journals, in a foreign language for gist in order to see what your competitors are planning. You may need to abstract and summarise the main points in English. Speed in obtaining relevant information in all these situations may be vital. In addition, you may want to update your own knowledge of a technical field by reading widely for content.

TRANSLATING

Even if you are not employed as a translator, there are many occasions on which you could be called upon to translate texts from a wide range of language varieties. Sometimes a close translation of the technical details of a text is required; a full version of a contract or sections of a trade report may be needed. The type of text which you are required to deal with may be very different from those you studied as an undergraduate, but the general principles involved will be the same (see pages 137-43).

TELEXES AND SCREEN-BASED SEARCHES

Understanding and sending messages by telex is now becoming a frequent activity in the business environment and requires the ability to decode what may sometimes be obscure messages. Deciphering telexes and screen-based information—now a major form of international communication—may depend upon your ability to extrapolate and re-establish meaning in the absence of grammatical words.

Skills in search strategies are becoming increasingly important as more information is handled by electronic databases. You need to be able to access such databases at minimum cost, which means in the least time possible.

Relevance of undergraduate training

In all these cases, the exercises you did regularly as an undergraduate should have prepared you for real life tasks. Graduates who have described the experience of using their language at the workplace stress how important it is to possess communication skills at a high level if tasks are to be performed efficiently. Generally they have found that the technical vocabulary and knowledge of a specialist field can be acquired without much difficulty during in-service training, whereas the awareness of linguistic nuances and an understanding of the wider communicative environment of another country could not be learnt without prolonged exposure to a foreign society and in-depth study of its institutions and structures.

PLANNING AND PURSUING A CAREER WITH LANGUAGES

Surveys which attempt to follow the careers of graduates over several years show that the period immediately after graduation is one of transition. Statistics for career destinations six months after graduation do not therefore give a very clear picture of the sort of employment pursued several years later, particularly where the link between the subjects you studied and employment is not direct. You have already seen that for many jobs a period of further training is the norm.

Large numbers of graduates change jobs frequently in the first two or three years after graduation. Having tasted the experience of living abroad, language graduates often want to 'travel around' before settling into more permanent employment. Careers advisors recommend that, if you are not going into employment or further training immediately, you should be able to demonstrate on your CV that this period is 'accounted for' and 'planned' as part of your personal development and that it has been used in a positive way.

Career planning

Planning your career may have begun before you entered higher education, it may have started when you were considering how to spend the period of residence abroad, or it may be delayed until after graduation. Even if you have thought through the options, you may not have begun putting your ideas into practice before you complete your course. Many students decide that, rather than searching for employment during their final year, it is more important to use this period as an undergraduate to achieve as high a class of degree as they can. It is, nonetheless, important to begin career planning as early as possible.

Preparing and writing applications is a time-consuming task, and it is estimated that there is about a one in forty success rate for applications made. Yet, it is necessary to write a good application in order to be invited for interview. Many employers hold first and second, and sometimes even third interviews, which take up substantial amounts of time when you are under pressure to complete assignments which are going to count towards your degree result. Most undergraduates find, however, that it is worth making at least a few applications early in their final year and, hopefully, gaining the experience of being interviewed. The accountancy firms, for example, normally hold their interviews in December and January. Some students therefore secure a job at an early stage and are able to concentrate fully on their studies without having to worry about the future. The main 'milk round' takes place between January and March, when employers are invited to visit universities and colleges to interview graduates on the spot. From Easter students are expected to be concentrating on examinations and then become available again for the summer 'recruitment fairs' in late June and early July.

However you decide to organise your career plans, you will need to assemble information and ideas for a *curriculum vitae* and application forms and you will want to gain as much experience as possible of being interviewed (see pages 125-31 and 166-71). Careers officers provide a vital information service, and generally they arrange training sessions to help you assess your potential and to learn how to prepare applications and present yourself in interviews. It is very much to your advantage to use the facilities while you have easy access to them. Increasingly, departments are becoming involved in the process, and you may have opportunities to meet former students to hear about their experience and seek their advice.

At several points in this chapter, it has been stressed that in most jobs, which are not for professional linguists or are not directly concerned with overseas trade or international affairs, your language will be considered as an ancillary skill, which you may not be able to use regularly in your work, at least initially. The choice is then whether to carry on searching for work in which the language is a primary requirement or to take employment which seemingly offers little prospect of using languages. Experience shows that graduates who really want to use their languages will eventually do so. Two students, one who graduated in French and German and the other in business and French, recounted how it took several years before they eventually began using their languages in their work:

> After working for four years with a Dutch publishing company, selling advertising space, where I was never called upon to speak Dutch, and a year with a British company as a marketing manager, again requiring no foreign language skills, I came to work in the external trade department of my present company, advising exporters of motor manufacturing goods.
>
> My work includes promotion and representation overseas through exhibitions, trade missions and market research visits. My own responsibilities cover all of Europe, French-speaking Africa, Turkey and Israel. After so many years, I can say that being able to speak French and German did help me to find a job.

> After working for six years as an accountant with my company at its headquarters in the Netherlands, expanding markets and new patterns of trade created openings elsewhere in Europe. Because I had a qualification in French I have now been posted to France at one of the company's subsidiaries, a situation which has arisen as a result of my being a language graduate. Few other accountants in the company had a second language to call on.

In cases like this it is important to maintain the level of fluency by using every opportunity to meet foreign nationals, keeping up your reading of newspapers and books, listening to the radio and visiting the country as often as possible. If you are convinced that your ultimate goal is to use your language, then you may need to plan your career progression carefully, looking out for firms which have international dealings and for opportunities to work abroad once you have completed your initial training.

Factors affecting career choice and development

Subject choice and motivation are only two of the many factors affecting the speed with which you are likely to find the employment you are seeking. The class of degree and the institution from which you graduate, its links with the business world, its reputation for providing good quality graduates, the efficiency of its careers service and its geographical location will also affect your chances. The number of graduates arriving on the market with the same subject mix and the economic climate will determine the employment available and the amount of competition you have to face. Many jobs for which the entry requirement in the past was a good 'A' level now ask for a degree, although the nature of the work may not have changed commensurately. The drop forecast in the number of graduates coming onto the labour market from 1993 should, however, reduce the competition.

Some of these factors are intangible, but most surveys of graduate careers do show that gender is an important determinant in employment prospects: men generally experience less difficulty in finding work than do women. Given that between sixty and seventy per cent of all graduates reading for degrees in modern languages are women, this is likely to be a factor which is relevant to you. The proportion of women is lower for combined subjects, although it is still well over fifty per cent, and for the languages only degrees it may be as high as ninety per cent or above in some institutions.

This reflects the situation in schools and in the home which was commented on in the first chapter, whereby the sciences are considered to be suitable subjects for boys, the arts, humanities and social sciences being more appropriate for girls. Little is said in the careers literature, however, about the relevance of gender in career planning. The assumption would seem to be that female students, who have been sufficiently motivated to remain in education well after the compulsory school leaving age, will use this investment of time and money to pursue a satisfying career while also making their contribution to society in other ways.

Some recent surveys of graduate employment, which look more closely at career prospects according to gender, suggest that women graduates perform less well on the labour market: they are less likely to be recruited into the jobs which have better promotion prospects, pay, security and status, but they are also less likely than men to attach importance to these characteristics of employment. Instead, they will be looking for work which involves helping people and which provides a challenge as well as the opportunity to use their skills fully. Women are still poorly represented in many fields of graduate employment, except the caring professions where they are most often in peripheral positions.

A few women opt to forego marriage and family life in order to pursue a career on an equal footing with their male counterparts but, for the majority of women graduates, it is necessary to find a compromise between family and professional life, and this may be one of the reasons why most women underachieve in comparison with male graduates from the same courses. As one graduate in French explained:

> My son is almost two years old. I took only six months off work in editing, but it takes time to re-establish your credibility after returning to work, and in my case it has made me less keen to pursue jobs which may be better from a 'career development' point of view.

Some graduates take these personal factors into account from the early stages of planning. Teaching is the career widely considered most likely to be compatible with family commitments:

> As well as feeling I had a vocation as a teacher, I thought the hours would suit me better, since I intended to raise a family.

> I needed a career I could pursue anywhere in Britain in case my husband had to move. When my husband did move I changed to a different Local Education Authority and then returned to teaching after having children.

Secretarial jobs exist in whatever part of the country you are and offer good potential for part-time work or for home-working, as described by two language graduates:

> In view of the fact that my husband's occupation necessitates frequent moves, I have found my secretarial skills invaluable as it is relatively easy to find secretarial work anywhere.

> Before I had my first child I was planning to change direction from secretarial work to adult education. Now that I have two children I am looking at the possibility of working from home, providing secretarial or translation services.

Some banks allow women to take extended maternity leave and to return to their previous positions without loss of status after a career break of up to five years. In the Home Civil Service higher grade posts women are encouraged to make use of opportunities for job-sharing or part-time work, as one graduate in languages explained:

> I had originally planned to give up work altogether because I did not feel I would be able to cope with a demanding full-time job and a small child. However, my line manager pointed out that the Civil Service had made a commitment to accommodate members of staff who decided to work part-time and to treat them equally in terms of career progression and promotion.

Some large retailing outlets expect women employees to be completely mobile, although they are coming to realise that they may thereby lose good recruits. Obviously, companies are reluctant to invest in further training if they do not expect the employee to give several years of service in return. This applies equally to male recruits and can be a serious problem for international companies or organisations. Large sums of money may be invested in training Chinese specialists, for example, only to find that they later leave the organisation because they do not want to keep uprooting their families. The issue of mobility is particularly acute for women, since it is still rare for a husband to follow his wife on a posting abroad or to another part of the country.

In Britain, even without the problem of geographical mobility, in the absence of generous childcare facilities and nursery schooling, it is still not easy for a woman to combine a demanding career with family life, except if the level of family income enables the couple to employ full-time assistance in the home. Graduates complain that the cost of childminding is so prohibitive that, with two young children, it is hardly worth working:

> I did not want to lose touch with my career in the City, but I only wanted a part-time job while the children were small. I pay my childminder almost half my take-home pay, and I am sure a lot of people in my situation would not bother to work as it is hardly viable financially.

> I went back to teaching after my first child but will not be returning after the second one until the first is at school because of the expense of childminders when you are in part-time work.

Although it may seem unnecessary to take account of the problems of combining professional and family life at an early stage in your career, you will find that prospective employers are interested in your personal plans and will be trying to test out your degree of commitment to employment. The experience of women graduates in Britain shows that it is possible to be successful both in pursuing a career and in raising a family but that a high level of organisational ability and determination is required as well as a good income.

Changing direction

Many women graduates find, however, that after several years of commitment to employment, they must either resort to part-time work, resign themselves to what may be a damaging break in employment or try to move into a career, such as teaching, which is more compatible with family life. Women who are employed as translators often find that this is an appropriate moment at which to begin working free-lance, as one language graduate explained:

> *I had been working in a company teaching languages to their staff and doing some translating. When I had my first child I decided to set up as a free-lance translator and to work from home so that I would not have to spend so much time travelling and could spend more time with my child.*

There are many other reasons why both men and women graduates may want to change direction. You may not find your first job sufficiently stimulating intellectually, or prospects for promotion may be poor. You may decide to move from the public to the private sector or set up your own company. Having gained a professional qualification, you may want to develop a specialism. From working with documents or accounts, you may prefer to move to personnel. Most interpreters find that the demands of the job are such that, like professional footballers, they can only keep up the pace for a few years, and the same applies to work as a travel courier.

Gone are the days when, at the age of sixteen, you might have entered an office, for example in the Civil Service, and stayed there until retirement, slowly making your way up the promotional ladder. Even if you graduate at twenty-two, you will still have about forty years of professional life before you and you may prefer to taste a number of different careers before pursuing any one of them in the longer term. Or it may be that you have a long-term objective, such as setting up your own translating agency or international market consultancy company. This is something you are unlikely to be able to do without careful planning to ensure that you acquire the necessary skills and experience and also make appropriate contacts.

One study of a group of graduates several years after graduation by a careers advisor (Chamberlain, 1983) noted eleven patterns amongst the career paths of a sample of only sixty-three graduates. These ranged from graduates who identified a preferred path and then followed it purposefully, through those who hesitated or accepted a modified route or who deviated and returned to the original direction, to those who changed direction completely or who had yet to settle. There is no one model which is specially to be recommended, but there is certainly no reason to despair if the path you mapped out does not lead uncompromisingly and immediately to the goal you had set yourself. Current technological, social, economic and political developments are likely to influence career opportunities in the future, and it is therefore important to remain flexible and to ensure that you continually update your skills and knowledge.

DEPLOYING INTELLECTUAL TRAINING, ANALYTICAL AND COMMUNICATIVE SKILLS

It is likely that, in the humanities and social sciences, very few graduates will use more than a fraction of the knowledge they gain as an undergraduate in their careers and that it is the study skills or methods which are the main influence on career planning and the pursuit of a career. But it may also be fair to argue that, of all humanities graduates, linguists have some of the most practical and useful professional skills. Care has been taken in this book to ensure that precedence is not given to cognitive and technical skills at the expense of the intellect and character training and the principles underlying knowledge which are the fundamentals of all higher education. If employers were only interested in practical skills, graduates in philosophy and the classics would rarely find employment, and this is by no means the case. The combination of intellectual training and practical skills possessed by linguists can make them attractive candidates for employers.

Personal qualities and skills acquired from a language degree

It is quite likely that you chose to study languages initially because you enjoy travelling, meeting people and talking to them and wanted to find a career which would enable you to pursue these interests professionally. This motivation, combined with an extrovert and gregarious personality, may have helped you to exploit the period of residence abroad to full advantage, and it may now be an important asset when you are embarking on a career.

If you recognise that you have an extrovert personality, then you are more likely to be successful in a career involving people-oriented activity, such as marketing or personnel management. On the other hand, if you are an introvert, then employment in some areas of information processing, banking or finance might be more appropriate. It is possible to adapt and develop your style of social interaction, but this can be a strain, and it is probably better to try to find work in which the demands are in harmony with your character.

When graduates are questioned about the way in which their language degree course helped to prepare them for a career, they emphasise the intellectual character training they received as well as the practical skills, knowledge and expertise. Reference is made to the importance of learning how to be analytical, to work to deadlines, to absorb information quickly and assess situations, to be adaptable, flexible, open-minded, self-disciplined, self-sufficient, self-motivated and self-confident and able to work independently and take initiative.

It is encouraging to note that a survey of polytechnic graduates by the Council for National Academic Awards in 1985 showed that the scores of modern languages graduates were significantly higher than those of other humanities, English and interfaculty graduates for the improvement they thought their degree courses had brought in the following areas:

- Critical thinking.
- Ability to work independently.
- Organisational ability.
- Ability to apply knowledge and skills.
- Written and spoken communication.
- Self-confidence.
- Understanding other people.
- Co-operation with others.
- Sense of responsibility.
- Political awareness.

The areas where they had lower scores were logical thinking, handling numerical data and leadership. These too are now becoming important components in some undergraduate language programmes.

Personal qualities and general skills sought by employers

A number of the qualities which were fundamental for your course will be sought after and valued by employers who are looking for trained analytical minds capable of adapting to changing circumstances. Thanks to the efforts of careers officers and graduates themselves, employers are increasingly being alerted to the fact that, in addition to the skills acquired by other humanities and social science students, language graduates possess communication and information processing skills which are vital in most areas of professional life.

Although they are couched in slightly different terms, the skills looked for by employers are essentially the same as those identified by graduates. They include the ability:

- To sift and analyse documents quickly.
- To identify and classify relevant information.
- To summarise content and present it objectively, logically and clearly.
- To make decisions about the best action to take.
- To conduct a group discussion, argue points convincingly and talk knowledgeably about a range of subjects in more informal circumstances.
- To learn quickly and to demonstrate trainability and curiosity.
- To organise activities efficiently and to manage time sensibly.
- To act as a leader and inspire confidence in others.
- To display motivation towards achieving goals.
- To adapt knowledge and skills from one context to another and to be flexible.

The Civil Service describes what it is looking for in graduates in the following terms, echoing statements made by private sector employers:

> *The subject of your degree...is less important than an ability to think clearly and get to the root of a problem quickly. You should be able to express yourself concisely both on paper and face to face. You should be able to work well and productively with colleagues. You need drive and determination and the capacity to work under pressure and meet exacting deadlines. (Civil Service Commission and Central Office of Information, 1985:3)*

It is important to be able to demonstrate that you possess these skills, and that you have acquired them from a course which was not intended to prepare you for a specific career. Employers are, for example, likely to be particularly interested in graduates who have spent a prolonged period of residence abroad, since it provides the opportunity to demonstrate many of the personal qualities which will be needed at the workplace.

Adapting to the world of work

If you have had the opportunity of working during your period of residence abroad or even during the vacation, you will already have some idea of what to expect from the professional world and how it differs from academic life. In the British higher education system, as you will be well aware if you have studied abroad, your progress is carefully monitored, you receive individual attention and advice from your tutors and you are called upon to co-operate with your fellow students. There are usually sanctions if you do not attend classes or submit work, but ultimately you are the only person who will suffer. If you cannot work effectively in the team to which you have been assigned or if you do not get on with your tutor, there are generally other ways of completing a piece of work, for example by doing an individual project, and you can probably change your tutor.

In the work context you will normally be part of a team, and you will be responsible for ensuring that your contribution helps the company or organisation to attain corporate goals. If you have learnt to be punctual, to organise your time efficiently and meet deadlines and to collaborate with others, if you know how to relate to other people, handle a group situation, weigh arguments and make decisions, as well as follow instructions intelligently, you will be a valued employee as well as a good advertisement for degree courses in modern languages.

SUMMARY OF SUGGESTIONS

1. At the beginning of the career planning process, you should try to make a realistic assessment of your personal qualities, the skills and knowledge you have acquired and your personal aims and objectives.

2. It is worth remembering the importance of self-awareness, occupational awareness, employer awareness, and learning how to present yourself positively in applications and interviews.

3. Unless you are pursuing a career as a professional linguist, you can expect your qualification in languages to be seen as an ancillary skill but one which could give you the edge over other applicants.

4. You should be prepared to undergo a period of further training in order to acquire vocational skills and specialised technical knowledge.

5. If you want to use your languages in your career, you will need to convince employers that you have usable skills and that they need graduate linguists. You can

emphasise your ability to perform communicative tasks, your practical language skills, particularly oral fluency, and their appropriateness for a large number of contexts.

6. It is advisable to consider the wide range of careers which are available and the many different types of organisation in which you could work in relation to your personality, motivation and qualifications.

7. It is worthwhile using any contacts you made during your period of residence abroad if you want to work outside Britain.

8. If you do not use your languages immediately but want to do so later, you should ensure that you maintain them at the standard you achieved on graduation.

9. It is important not only to plan your career carefully, taking your personal life, motivations and aspirations into account, but also to be prepared to be flexible, ready for change and not to wait for certainty.

10. You should know what to expect of employment, as compared with the academic world, and aim to match the general skills you have acquired with those looked for by employers.

SUGGESTIONS FOR FURTHER READING

Chapter 1   AN INTRODUCTION TO STUDYING FOR A DEGREE IN LANGUAGES

Every two years updated versions are published of very useful guides containing detailed information about the content and structure of first degree courses in Britain for the main languages studied:
CAREERS RESEARCH AND ADVISORY CENTRE, *Degree Course Guides*, Cambridge, Hobsons.

Many aspects of the study of the German language in higher education are covered in:
BROWN, E. et al (1986) *German in the United Kingdom: Issues and Opportunities*, London, CILT.

Students of French language and literature are given guidance in:
SMITH, M., Cockerham, H., Barron, J. and Routledge, M. (1987) *The Right Angle: Your Degree in French*, RHBNC, Egham, Runnymede Books.

French civilisation courses in Britain and other Anglo-Saxon countries are reviewed in:
CAHM, E. (ed) (1988) *Teaching French Civilisation in Britain, the United States and Australia*, London, Association for the Study of Modern and Contemporary France.

A series of books have been published on Contemporary Language Studies, covering the French economy, politics and society and intended for advanced students of languages:
HANTRAIS, L. (1982) *Contemporary French Society*, London, Macmillan.
HOLMES, G. and Fawcett, P. (1983) *The Contemporary French Economy*, London, Macmillan.
SLATER, M. (1985) *Contemporary French Politics*, London, Macmillan.

One of the most useful reference tools for students of French society is the triennial publication:
INSTITUT NATIONAL DE LA STATISTIQUE ET DES ÉTUDES ÉCONOMIQUES, *Données sociales*, Paris, INSEE.
The same organisation also publishes annually a succinct summary of statistics on the French economy:

INSEE, *Tableaux de l'économie française*, Paris, INSEE.

For students of German guides to socio-cultural, economic and political life in the Federal Republic of Germany are provided by:
BEYER, R.A. (1986) *Deutschland Heute: Politik, Wirtschaft, Gesellschaft. Ein Studien- und Arbeitsbuch zur Deutschen Landeskunde*, Oxford, Berg.
BULKA, H.D., Michel, H.G., Wollenkord, C. (1985) *Tatsachen über Deutschland: Die Bundesrepublik Deutschland*, 5th edn, Gütersloh, Bertelsmann Lexikothek Verlag.

A comprehensive reference tool for the German Democratic Republic is provided by:
ZIMMERMANN, H., Ulrich, H. and Fehlauer, M. (1985) *DDR Handbuch*, 2 vols, Köln, Verlag Wissenschaft und Politik.

The two Germanies are compared in:
GESAMTDEUTSCHES INSTITUT BUNDESANSTALT FÜR GESAMTDEUTSCHE AUFGABEN (1985) *Facts and Figures: A Comparative Survey of the Federal Republic of Germany and the German Democratic Republic*, Bonn, Press and Information Office of the Government of the Federal Republic of Germany.

A good source for statistics about the Federal Republic of Germany is the annual publication:
STATISTISCHES BUNDESAMT, *Statistisches Jahrbuch für die Bundesrepublik Deutschland*, Mainz, Kohlhammer.

For students of Spanish a very useful comprehensive analytical bibliography, covering social, political and religious life, as well as science, technology and the press, has been compiled by:
SHIELDS, G. J. (1985) *Spain*, Oxford, Clio Press.

Although not focused solely on Spain, since the beginning of the 1980s about one hundred titles in a series of books, Colección Salvat Temas Clave, have been published by Salvat Editores in Barcelona under the general editorship of J. SALVAT. They include coverage of a wide variety of aspects of life in Spain.

A good source of statistical data on Spain, which is also available in a pocketbook edition is the annual publication:
INSTITUTO NACIONAL DE ESTADÍSTICA, Anuario Estadístico de España, Madrid, Instituto Nacional de Estadística.

Information about the Hispanic world is summarised in the regular publication:

AGENCIA EFE, *Nuestro mundo: banco de información OMNIDATA EFE*, Madrid, Espasa Calpe.

A good overview of recent developments in Spain is provided by:
ABELLA, R. (1986) *España diez años despues Franco, 1975-85*, Barcelona, Planeta.

A succinct summary of statistical information for the countries of the European Community is provided by:
EUROSTAT (1988) *Review—Revue 1977-1986*, Luxembourg, Office des Publications Officielles des Communautés Européennes.

The following is a valuable book on linguistics for foreign language learners, drawing on examples from a wide range of languages:
HARTLEY, A.F. (1982) *Linguistics for Language Learners*, London, Macmillan.

Two classics on linguistics and language study as disciplines are:
CRYSTAL, D. (1985) *What is Linguistics?* 4th edn, London, Edward Arnold.
FROMKIN, V. and Rodman, R. (1988) *An Introduction to Language*, 4th edn, New York, London, Holt, Rinehart and Winston.

A useful general book on communicative approaches, intended for language teachers is:
BRUMFIT, C.J. (1984) *Communicative Methodology in Language Teaching: The Roles of Fluency and Accuracy*, Cambridge, CUP.

Communicative approaches in language learning in higher education are examined with reference to French in:
BATE, M. and Hare, G. (eds) (1986) *Communicative Approaches in French in Higher Education*, Salford, Association for French Language Studies.

Chapter 2   STUDY METHODS AND RESOURCES

The literature on study methods is abundant. The following are a few suggestions, including some of the standard textbooks on the subject, many of which provide practical exercises and also cover the basic study skills described in Chapter 3:
ASHMAN, S. and George, A. (1982) *Study and Learn: A Self-help Guide for Students*, London, Heinemann.
DUNLEAVY, P. (1986) *Studying for a Degree in the Humanities and Social Sciences*, London Macmillan.

LAST, R.W. (1986) *Making Sense of How to Study*, Blairgowrie, Lockee Publications.
MADDOX, H. (1988) *How to Study*, rev edn, London, Sydney, Pan.
PARSONS, C. (1976) *How to Study Effectively*, London, Arrow.

Work avoidance strategies are dealt with by:
BERNSTEIN, S. (1978) 'Getting it done: notes on student fritters', in J. Lofland (ed), *Interaction in Everyday Life Social Strategies*, Beverly Hills, London, Sage, pp.17-33.

Several books will help you to find out more about using materials and resources such as video:
CRAWSHAW, R. and Renouard, M. (eds) (1983) *The Media and the Teaching of French*, Lancaster, Association for French Language Studies.
LONERGAN, J. (1984) *Video in Language Teaching*, Cambridge, CUP.
ZETTERSTEN, A. (1986), *New Technologies in Language Learning*, Oxford, Pergamon.

There is a rapidly growing literature on computers in language learning. Some of the more useful books are:
AHMAD, K., Corbett, G., Rogers, M. and Sussex, R. (1985) *Computers, Language Learning and Language Teaching*, Cambridge, CUP.
CAMERON, K.C., Dodd, W.S. and Rahtz, S.P.Q. (eds) (1986) *Computers and Modern Language Studies*, Chichester, Ellis Horwood.
DAIUTE, C. (1985) *Writing and Computers*, Reading, Mass, Addison-Wesley.
GEOFFRION, L.D. and Geoffrion, D.P. (1983) *Computers and Reading Instruction*, Reading, Mass, Addison-Wesley.
LAST, R. (1984) *Language Teaching and the Microcomputer*, Oxford, Blackwell.

Most books on study methods contain chapters on examinations. The following is devoted exclusively to the subject:
LEADER, W. G. (1984) *How to Pass Exams*, Plymouth, Macdonald and Evans.

Chapter 3   STUDY SKILLS

In addition to the general literature on study methods, already mentioned in Chapter 2, reading and note-taking skills are presented in the following book:
BUZAN, A. (1982) *Use Your Head*, rev edn, London, BBC.

Abstracting, summary writing and analysis are covered in:

ARAMBOUROU, Ch., Texier, F. and Vanoye, F. (1972) *Guide de la contraction de texte*, Paris, Hachette.
COLEMAN, J.A. (1985) *Making Sense of French Literary Commentary*, Blairgowrie, Lockee Publications.
MOREAU, J.A. (1977) *La contraction et la synthèse de textes*, Paris, Nathan.

The following books provide some very useful guidance on essay writing:
CLANCHY, J. and Ballard, B. (1983) *How to Write Essays: A Practical Guide for Students*, Melbourne, Longman Cheshire.
DESALMAND, P. and Tort, P. (1977) *Du plan à la dissertation: la dissertation française aux baccalauréats et aux concours administratifs*, Paris, Hatier.
DUNLEAVY, P. (1986) *Studying for a Degree in the Humanities and Social Sciences*, London, Macmillan.
LAST, R.W. (1985) *Making Sense of Essay Writing*, Blairgowrie, Lockee Publications.

The techniques involved in oral expression are presented by:
DOBLE, G. and Griffiths, B. (eds) (1985) *Oral Skills in the Modern Languages Degree*, London, CILT.
VANOYE, F. (1973) *Expression communication*, Paris, Armand Colin.

An interesting and lively account of the para-language used in different national contexts around the world is provided by:
MORRIS, D., Collett, P., Marsh, P. and O'Shaughnessy, M. (1981) *Gestures, their Origins and Distribution*, London, Triad/Granada.

Chapter 4 TASK-BASED LANGUAGE EXERCISES

Some useful pointers to specific task-based exercises are given in a number of publications, which mostly include worked examples. Although the following is intended for non-language students, much of the advice is applicable to foreign languages:
ELLIS, R. and Hopkins, K. (1985) *How to Succeed in Written Work and Study: A Handbook for Students in all Subjects in Universities and Colleges*, London and Glasgow, Collins.

The books written on studying for a degree in languages are intended for languages and literature students in French. Much of what was said in the following book still holds true. It is now out of print, but your library may have a copy:
KNIGHT, R.C. and George, F.W.A. (1960) *Advice to the Student of French*, 2nd edn, Oxford, Blackwell.

A much more recent publication is also aimed at students on literary courses in French:
SMITH, M., Cockerham, H., Barron, J. and Routledge, M. (1987) *The Right Angle: Your Degree in French*, RHBNC, Egham, Runnymede Books.

A number of written language skills are reviewed in:
AGER, D. (ed) (1988) *Written Skills in the Modern Languages Degree*, Birmingham and London, AMLC and CILT.

A classic book on the language of administration in France is:
GANDOUIN, J. (1980) *Correspondance et rédaction administrative*, 4th edn, Paris, Armand Colin.

A useful publication which will help you to understand administrative procedures in France is:
GILLES, M., with Pellerin, M-H. (1979) *Le guide des formalités faciles*, Paris, Editions Europa.

Correspondence is dealt with in the following books, which offer models for most conceivable situations as well as analysis of contexts:
BRAY, J. and Gómez-Sánchez (1980) *Spanish in the Office: Español para oficinas*, London, Longman.
DOURNON, J-Y. (1977) *La correspondance pratique, suivie du Dictionnaire des 1001 tournures*, Paris, Librairie Générale Française.
GANACHAUD, G. (1984) *Nouveau guide de la correspondance*, Rennes, Ouest France.
HARVARD, J. and Ariza, I.F. (1985) *Bilingual Guide to Business and Professional Correspondence (Spanish—English) Guía bilingüe (inglés—español) de correspondencia profesional y de negocios*, Oxford, Pergamon.
VIVIEN, G. (1980) *Le parfait secrétaire*, new edn, Paris, Larousse.
WYPIJESKI, W. (1984) *Erfolgreiches Korrespondieren und Texten*, Munich, Wilhelm Heyne Verlag.

Report writing is examined by the following, which also provides worked examples:
GIVADINOVITCH, J-M. (1981) *Comment rédiger des notes et rapports efficaces*, Paris, Editions de Vecchi.

In preparing for self-presentation in the written channel, there are a few books which describe and analyse the *curriculum vitae*:
COLBACHINI CONTI, E. (1986) *Le curriculum vitae efficace: Sachez vous vendre et valoriser vos compétences*, trans V. Grenier, Paris, Editions de Vecchi.

DOURNON, J-Y. (1987) *Guide de la recherche d'emploi et du curriculum vitae*, Livre de Poche, Paris, Librairie Générale Française.
MEHLER, H.A. (1986) *Die richtige und erfolgreiche Bewerbung. Anleitungen und Tips für die Stellungssuche*, Munich, Wilhelm Heyne Verlag.

Survey and interviewing techniques are examined thoroughly by:
GHIGLIONE, R. and Matalon, B. (1978) *Les enquêtes sociologiques: théories et pratique*, Paris, Armand Colin, Collection U.

Guidelines for telephoning, which can be adapted to other languages, are provided by:
NATEROP, B.J. and Revell, R. (1987) *Telephoning in English*, Cambridge, Cambridge University Press.

There are many books on the theory and practice of translation. Some of the more useful which apply to most European languages are:
BASSNETT-McGUIRE, S. (1980) *Translation Studies*, London, Methuen.
HÖNIG, H.G. and Kußmaul, P. (1982) *Strategie der Übersetzung: ein Lehr- und Arbeitsbuch*, Tübingen, Narr.
KEMBLE, I. (1988) *Translating for Pleasure: Texts and Notes. An Anthology of English Texts for Translation into German for Use on a Self-Study Basis*, Winchester, Portsmouth German Language Learning Textbooks, No. 1.
NEWMARK, P. (1981) *Approaches to Translation*, Oxford, Pergamon.
SELESKOVITCH, D. and Lederer, M. (1984) *Interpréter pour traduire*, Paris, Didier Erudition.

A useful contrastive analysis of French and English for the translator is provided by:
VINAY, J-P. and Darbelnet, J. (1977) *Stylistique comparée du français et de l'anglais: Méthode de traduction*, new edn, Paris, Didier.

An annotated bibliography of interpreting has been compiled by:
ALTMAN, H.J. (ed) (1987) *Teaching Interpreting: Study and Practice*, London, CILT.

Some books give worked examples of texts for simultaneous and consecutive translation, for example:
LEDERER, M. (1981) *La traduction simultanée: expérience et théorie*, Paris, Lettres Modernes.

Useful advice on note-taking for interpreters is provided by:
ROZAN, J-F, (1979) *La prise de notes en interprétation consécutive* reprint, Geneva, Georg.

SELESKOVITCH, D. (1975) *Langage, langues et mémoire: une étude de la prise de notes en interprétation consécutive*, Paris, Minard.

Chapter 5 THE PERIOD OF RESIDENCE ABROAD

The following publications provide useful information about preparing for study abroad, and they also include some helpful advice which is relevant for other types of placement. They are regularly revised, and you should ensure you consult the most up-to-date copy. The first two are annual publications:
CENTRE NATIONAL DES OEUVRES UNIVERSITAIRES ET SCOLAIRES, *Je vais en France (Guide à l'attention des étudiants étrangers)*, Paris, CROUS.
DEUTSCHER AKADEMISCHER AUSTAUSCHDIENST, *Academic Studies in the Federal Republic of Germany*, Bonn, DAAD.
EBEL, A. and Mohr, B. (eds) (1985) *Higher Education in the European Community: A Handbook for Students*, Brussels, Commission of the European Communities.

A guide to studying in the French *écoles de commerce* has been compiled by:
JULLIAND, V. and Sidibe, J. (1985) *Bien choisir son école de commerce*, Paris, L'Etudiant.

Information about higher education and further studies in the Federal Republic of Germany and also different types of employment is summarised in the following publications, the first of which is updated annually:
BUND—LÄNDER—KOMMISSION FÜR BILDUNGSPLANUNG UND FORSCHUNGSFÖRDERUNG UND BUNDESANSTALT FÜR ARBEIT (eds), *Studien- und Berufswahl: Entscheidungshilfen für Abiturienten und Absolventen der Fachoberschulen*, Bad Honnef, Karl Heinrich Bock.
HENNIGER, W. (ed) (1986) *Das Praktikanten Buch: Ein Wegweiser für Studenten und Abiturienten*, Frankfurt am Main, Athenäum.

Chapter 6 LANGUAGES AND CAREERS

Careers services usually have copies of the Association of Graduate Careers Advisory Services information booklets, which are regularly updated. You should find the following particularly useful:
DAY, M., Paxton, G. and Walsham, A. (1988) *Working Overseas*, Manchester, Careers Services Trust.

DIRMIKIS, S., Norman, G. and Taylor, B. (1986) *Teaching English as a Foreign Language and Teaching Abroad*, Manchester, Careers Services Trust.
FIRTH, R.A., Dane, M. and Harris, J.M. (1988) *Your Degree in..Modern Languages..What Next?* Manchester, Careers Services Trust.
RABAN, A.J. and Tobin, C. (1988) *Opportunities to Work in the European Community's Institutions*, Manchester, Careers Services Trust.

The Centre for Information on Language Teaching and Research has produced an interesting information pack on careers using languages, although it is not aimed specifically at graduates:
HEWETT, D. (1986) *Languages and Careers: An Information Pack*, London, CILT.

In association with the Aston Modern Languages Club, CILT has published a collection of papers which look at the ways in which higher education prepares graduates for work in international settings:
HANTRAIS, L. (ed) (1988) *Higher Education for International Careers*, Birmingham and London, AMLC and CILT.

The Manpower Services Commission has presented some useful profiles of careers using languages in:
CAREERS AND OCCUPATIONAL INFORMATION CENTRE (1987) *Working in Languages*, Sheffield, Manpower Services Commission.

One author has written two short books on the range of openings where languages can be used in Britain and abroad:
STEADMAN, H. (1988) *Careers Using Languages*, 3rd edn, London, Kogan Page.
STEADMAN, H. (1983) *Careers Working Abroad*, London, Kogan Page.

A useful guide for those planning to live and work abroad, although not necessarily with the intention of using languages in their work, is provided by the same publisher:
GOLZEN, G. (1988) *Working Abroad: The Daily Telegraph Guide to Working and Living Overseas*, 11th edn, London, Kogan Page.

Information on the training received in other countries and advice for job-seekers within Europe is given in:
RABAN, A.J. (1988) *Working in the European Communities: A Guide for Graduate Recruiters and Job-Seekers*, Cambridge, CRAC, Hobsons.

There is an abundant literature about the teaching profession. The following focuses on teaching as a career:
TAYLOR, F. (1988) *Careers in Teaching*, 3rd edn, London, Kogan Page.

Many more specialised publications offer guidance on classroom techniques, materials and the practicalities of language teaching and language policy. Only a few of the more useful examples can be mentioned here:
HAWKINS, E. (1987) *Modern Languages in the Curriculum*, 2nd edn, Cambridge, CUP.
PHILLIPS, D. (ed) (1988) *Languages in Schools: From Complacency to Conviction*, London, CILT.
SMALLEY, A. and Morris, D. (1985) *The MLA Modern Language Teacher's Handbook*, London, Hutchinson.

A survey of courses for interpreters, mostly in European countries, including the recommended criteria for assessing different institutions, is given in:
ASSOCIATION INTERNATIONALE DES INTERPRÈTES DE CONFÉRENCE (1984) *Guide to Establishments Offering Courses in Conference Interpreting*, AIIC, Geneva.

A presentation of the qualities looked for in an interpreter is provided in the first book ever written on the subject:
HERBERT, J. (1968) *The Interpreter's Handbook: How to Become a Conference Interpreter*, 2nd edn, Geneva, Georg.

Many public and private companies provide booklets and information sheets about what they are looking for in graduate recuits. The following is a useful source about the Civil Service:
CIVIL SERVICE COMMISSION AND CENTRAL OFFICE OF INFORMATION (1985) *Providing a Structure for Society.... Management Careers in the Civil Service*, London, HMSO.

Studies have been made of the needs of the labour market for languages and of the educational provision to meet the demand:
HAGEN, S. (ed) (1988) *Languages in British Business: An Analysis of Current Needs*, Newcastle and London, Newcastle upon Tyne Polytechnic Products Ltd and CILT.
LISTON, D. and Reeves, N. (1985) *Business Studies, Languages and Overseas Trade: A Study of Education and Training*, Plymouth and London, Macdonald and Evans and the Institute of Export.

The careers of polytechnic graduates from all subjects have been comprehensively analysed by:

BRENNAN, J. and McGeevor, P. (1988) *Graduates at Work: Degree Courses and the Labour Market*, London, Jessica Kingsley.

Every year the Association of Graduate Careers Advisory Services publishes summaries of first destinations of university graduates, polytechnic first degree and higher diploma students for all degree subjects:
AGCAS, *What Do Graduates Do?* Cambridge, Hobsons.

The following reports analyse surveys of opportunities for graduates and the careers pursued, although few are specific to language graduates. Most of the reports are not widely available, but your careers service may have a copy which you can consult, and some of the results of surveys have been published in articles:
CHAMBERLAIN, D. (1984) *Five Years On: A Study Conducted in 1983 of the 1978 Graduates from one Oxford College*, Oxford, Oxford Careers Service.
CHAPMAN, A. (1986) *Men and Women Graduates in the Labour Market: Orientations to Work and Experience of Employment one Year after Graduation*, London, CNAA Development Services Unit.
EMMANS, K., Hawkins, E. and Westoby, A. (1974) *Foreign Languages in Industry/Commerce*, York, Language Teaching Centre.
HANTRAIS, L. (1985) *Careers Using Languages: An Analysis of the Careers of Language Graduates*, Birmingham, AMLC.
MORRIS, C. (1980) 'Are modern languages of any use? A limited survey of job opportunities for modern linguists', *Modern Languages*, 61 (3), pp.109-12.
REEVES, N. (1986) 'Languages for jobs', in D. Hewett (ed), *Languages and Careers: An Information Pack*, London, CILT, pp.5-9.
SCHOLEFIELD, D.A. (1980) *Arts Graduates: Five Years On. Career Development and Personal Satisfaction*, Dublin, Higher Education Authority.

INDEX

abbreviations, in note-taking 75-6
ab initio language study 8, 10
abstracting, as a language task 79-80
  in professional contexts 207-8, 217
accommodation, finding, abroad 177-8
accuracy, checking for 58-9, 68
  in essays 97-8
  in interpreting 144
  as an objective 18
  in projects 188
  in translations 141
administrative procedures abroad 120-2, 165-80
advisors 37, 62-3
ambiguity, in translations 143
analysis, of texts 79-89
appendices, in projects 188
  in reports 124
applications, for jobs 125-30, 219
  for placements abroad 166-71
appropriateness, of language, checking for 112
  definition of 19
  in essays 97-8
  in interpreting 144
  in translations 141
Arabic, in professional contexts 211
  study of 8, 9
area studies 11, 14-6
assessment, methods and patterns of 50-61
  see also continuous assessment
assistantships 161-3
audio-visual resources 47, 112, 131
aural examinations 59-61
aural skills 25
  in professional contexts 215-6

banking, abroad 177
bibliographies, in essays 98-100
Bildschirmtext 50
business schools, placements in 159-61
business studies, in careers 199, 210
  with languages 16, 21

careers, planning of 155, 218-223
  using languages 204-14
cataloguing, in libraries 42-3

cheating, in examinations 54-5
checking
  see accuracy, appropriateness
Chinese, in professional contexts 211
  study of 8
civilisation, study of 14-6, 22
classification systems, in libraries,
  Dewey Decimal 42
  Library of Congress 43
cohesive devices, in discourse 85-7
combined honours, degrees in 5
combined subjects 13-4
commentary, on texts 81-9
communication, interactive 131-7
  interpersonal 101, 192
communicative approaches, to learning 13, 23-4, 102, 110
communicative skills, in professional contexts 210, 214-5, 225-8
communicative translation 139-41
computer-assisted language learning 47-50
computing, in careers 198, 199, 210
  with languages 13
concepts, in note-taking 72
conclusions, to essays 95-6
  to projects 187
conference interpreting 143-4, 207
content, of degree programmes 12-6
  in note-taking 71-2
contextual studies, integration of language with 22-3
continuous assessment 51-3, 56-9
correspondence, formal 111, 113-9, 182-5
culture, definition of 23
  study of 14
culture-boundedness, in translations 142-3
curriculum vitae 110, 111, 125-30, 166-71

databases, as a resource 46, 49-50
  in professional contexts 217-8
deadlines, for assignments 53, 56
degree class, importance of 17, 50, 199, 220
degree structure 3-7
departments, structure, of academic 62
dictionaries, use of 44-5, 112, 140, 142

discourse markers 85-7
dissertations
    see projects
distractions, avoidance of 38-40
double honours, degrees in 5
drafting, a *curriculum vitae* 126-9
    documents 216-7
    essays 95-8
    formal letters 114-8
    projects 186-7
    reports 124-5

écoles de commerce 160-1
economics, study of 5-6, 15, 22, 89-90
editing, of essays 97-8
employers, of linguists 17, 208-9
employment, patterns for language
    graduates 201-4
ERASMUS 6, 171, 197
essays, evaluation of 100-1
    in examinations 57
    plans 91-5
European studies 5, 15, 89
    graduates in 202-3
examinations, qualifying 51
external examiners 54, 58-9

facts, in essays 92
    in note-taking 72
feature articles, analysis of 87
Federal Republic of Germany,
    administrative procedures in 121
    social contact in 190
    taxation in 176
feedback, in interpreting 149
    from lecturers 25, 61, 91
first destinations, of language graduates
    201-4
footnotes, in assignments 100, 187
forms of address, in conversation 103-4
    in correspondence 116
France, administrative procedures in
    120, 178-9
    claiming medical expenses in 174
    social contact in 190
free-lance, translation 206, 224
French, asking questions in 135
    correspondence in 113-9, 183
    curriculum vitae in 125-30, 166-8
    discourse markers in 85-6
    ellipsis in 104

job interviews in 130-1
para-language in 104-5
in professional contexts 211
referencing in 99
study of 8, 9, 10, 89
telephoning in 136-7
text analysis in 82
fritters, for work avoidance 38-9
functional equivalence, in translations
    139-40
functions, of language 13, 23, 84-7, 136
    in professional contexts 214-5

gender, bias, in employment 221
    in language study 9
German, asking questions in 135
    correspondence in 113-9, 184
    curriculum vitae in 125-30, 168-9
    discourse markers in 85-6
    ellipsis in 104
    job interviews in 130-1
    para-language in 104-5
    in professional contexts 211
    referencing in 99
    study of 8, 9, 89
    syntax, in translations 142
    telephoning in 136-7
German Democratic Republic, working in
    164, 191
glossaries, computerised 49
    in essays 100
glosses, in interpreting 147
    in translations 142
goals, definition of 29-30
grammar, books 44-5, 112, 140
group work 101-7

hardware, computing 47-8
Harvard system, of referencing 99

institutions, knowledge of, in careers 214,
    218
    study of 11, 14-5, 19, 24, 40
insurance, abroad 173-5
integration, of language and content 22-3
interaction, social 101, 189-91
interlibrary loans 46
international marketing, in careers 9,
    198, 199, 211
    study of 16
interpreting 143-9

examinations in 60-1
 in professional contexts 207, 215
interviewing, techniques 132-5, 185-6
introductions, in essays 95
 in projects 187
Italian, study of 8

Japanese, in professional contexts 211
 study of 8, 9, 10, 156-7
job interviews 130-1
joint honours, degrees in 5-6
joint study programmes 6
journalism, analysis of 89
journals, as a library resource 45-6

labour market, for language graduates 9, 195-204
law, in careers 197, 198
 study of 5, 6, 15, 16, 22, 158
lectures, definition of 77
 notes on 77-9
 as a teaching method 12, 14, 16, 25
lexical equivalence, in translations 141
liaison interpreting 146-9
libraries, as a resource 41-7
linear notes 73-4
linguistics, study of 13-4, 21, 40, 90
linguists, labour market for 195-204
literature, study of 12-3, 21, 40, 90
Local Education Authority grants, for study abroad 165

marking patterns 53-4
materials, open access to 46-7
methodology, of language learning 25-6
Minitel 50
modular degrees 6-7
morphology, study of 13
multidisplinary courses 5, 15, 22

newspapers, as language materials 47, 89
non-verbal communication 19, 23, 104-6
norms, of language 88-9
note-taking, in interpreting 147-9
 language of 77
 on lectures 77-9

official documents, responding to 119-22, 174-6
optional subjects 7, 12, 13, 16
oral examinations 59-61, 132

oral interaction 101-7
oral presentation 131-7
oral skills, in professional contexts 215-6

para-language 23, 24, 104-6
para-linguistic strategies 19, 23
patterned notes 74-5
periodicals, as a resource 45-6
personal development, as an undergraduate 63-4, 101, 154
personal tutors 62-3
phatic language 136
phonetics, study of 13
placements abroad, benefiting from 188-92
 types of 154-65
plagiarism 54-5
political speeches, analysis of 87
politics, study of 5, 6, 15-6, 22, 89-90
pragmatics, study of 13
press
 see journalism
professional linguists 204-9
proficiency, as a goal 7, 18
projects, materials for 182-6
 presentation of 187-8
 topics for 181
proof-reading, of essays 68
prose composition 110, 138
purposefulness in interaction 19

questionnaires, in project work 186
quotations, presentation of 96, 100, 188

radio, materials for analysis 82, 89
 as a resource 47
rarity value, of languages 8-9
reading, for checking 68
 improvement of 69-71
 skills, in professional contexts 216-8
 for study 68
 techniques 67-9
real life situations, using languages in 18, 132
real life tasks 20, 110, 214-8
reference tools, in libraries 44-5
references, in essays 98-100
 in lectures 78
 in note-taking 72
registers, of language 19, 88-9, 102-3
 in translations 137, 140, 143

regulations, for examinations 51
report writing 110, 122-5
residence permits 172-3
resource centres 25, 47
Russian, study of 8, 156

scanning, as a reading technique 68
schedule, achieving a balanced 37-8
  annual 33
self-presentation 125-31
semantic translation 139
semantics, study of 13
seminars, as a teaching method 12, 16, 25, 101-2, 131
serials, as a resource 45-6
single honours, degrees in 4-5
skills, acquisition of 20
  definition of 65
  see also communicative skills
skimming, as a reading technique 67
social security, cover abroad 173-5
societal studies 11, 15
societies, knowledge of, in professional contexts 214, 218
  study of, 13, 14-6
sociolinguistics, definition of 13
sociology, study of 15, 89
software, computing 47-50
Spain, administrative procedures in 121-2
  obtaining social security in 174-5
Spanish, asking questions in 135
  correspondence in 113-9, 185
  curriculum vitae in 125-30, 169-70
  discourse markers in 85-6
  ellipsis in 104
  job interviews in 130-1
  para-language in 104-5
  in professional contexts 211
  referencing in 100
  study of 8, 9, 89
  telephoning in 136-7
spoken language
  see oral interaction
SQ3R 70-1
strategies, linguistic, in spoken language 103
structure, of texts 87
study habits, definition of 29
study methods, difficulties with 61-4
style, in essays 96-7

subsidiary subjects 4, 8, 21
summary writing 80-1
surveys 186
syllabuses 11, 110, 111
symbols, in interpreting 148
  in note-taking 75-7
syntactic equivalence, in translations 141
syntax, study of 13

taxation, while working abroad 176
teaching, of language, as a career 9, 209-10
teaching methods 12, 14, 16
telephoning 136-7
  in professional contexts 216
television, materials for analysis 82, 89
  as a resource 47
time, management of 32-40
time-budgets 35-7
timetables, for study 32, 34
tone, analysis of 83
  of speech 19, 24, 144
tool, language as a 21-2
tourism, as a career 213
training, postgraduate 199-200
translating 137-43
  in examinations 57, 58
  machine-based 50
  problems in 141-3
  in professional contexts 204-6, 217
tutorials, as a teaching method 12, 101-2
tutors 37, 62-3, 91, 101, 192

university placements, abroad 155-9

varieties of language 13, 19, 24, 25, 88-9
  in professional contexts 214
video materials 47
vocabulary, analysis of 83
  extension of 69-70, 77, 112

wordprocessing 50
wordprocessors, applications of 125, 166, 206
work placements, abroad 163-5
work reports 188
writing skills, in professional contexts 216-8